LUIGI PIRANDELLO IN THE THEATRE

Contemporary Theatre Studies

A series of books edited by Franc Chambelain, Nene College, UK

Volume 1
Playing The Market
Ten Years of the Market Theatre, Johannesburg, 1976–1986
Anne Fuchs
A volume in the Southern African Theatre section.

Volume 2
Theandric
Julian Beck's Last Notebooks
Edited by Erica Bilder
A volume in The Living Theatre Archive section.

Volume 3
Luigi Pirandello in the Theatre
A Documentary Record
Edited by Susan Bassnett and Jennifer Lorch

Additional volumes in preparation

Adolphe Appia
Richard Beacham

Israeli Playwrights in Exile
Seamus Finnegan

New York Artists Theatre
Brenda Gross

Art Into Theatre
Nick Kaye

Piscator Notes
Judith Malina

Edward Bond Letters
Ian Stuart

Three Belgian Farces
David Willinger

This book is part of a series. The publisher will accept continuation orders which may be cancelled at any time and which provide for automatic billing and shipping of each title in the series upon publication. Please write for details.

LUIGI PIRANDELLO IN THE THEATRE

A Documentary Record

Edited by

Susan Bassnett

and

Jennifer Lorch

harwood academic publishers

Switzerland • Gt. Britain • Australia • Belgium • France • Germany • India • Japan • Malaysia • Netherlands • Russia • Singapore • USA

Harwood Academic Publishers

Poststrasse 22
7000 Chur
Switzerland

5301 Tacony Street, Drawer 330
Philadelphia, Pennsylvania 19137
United States of America

3-14-9, Okubo
Shinjuku-ku, Tokyo 169
Japan

Post Office Box 90
Reading, Berkshire RG1 8JL
United Kingdom

58, rue Lhomond
75005 Paris
France

Glinkastrasse 13–15
0-1086 Berlin
Germany

Emmaplein 5
1075 AW Amsterdam
Nethelands

Private Bag 8
Camberwell, Victoria 3124
Australia

Library of Congress Cataloging-in-Publication Data

Luigi Pirandello in the theatre : a documentary record / edited by
    Susan Bassnett and Jennifer Lorch.
        p.   cm. — (Contemporary theatre studies : v. 3)
    Includes bibliographical references (p.   ) and index.
    ISBN 3-7186-5375-3 (hard). — ISBN 3-7186-5376-1 (soft)
    1. Pirandello, Luigi, 1867–1936—Knowledge—Theater.
    2. Theater Philosophy.   3. Compagnia del teatro d'arte di Roma.
    I. Pirandello, Luigi. 1867–1936.   II. Bassnett, Susan.
    III. Lorch, Jennifer.   IV. Series.
    PQ4835.I7Z6653   1993   92-41548
    852'.912—dc20   CIP

For Clive

CONTENTS

Introduction to the Series

Contemporary Theatre Studies is a book series of special interest to everyone involved in theatre. It consists of monographs on influential figures, studies of movements and ideas in theatre, as well as primary material consisting of theatre-related documents, performing editions of plays in English, and English translations of plays from various vital theatre traditions worldwide.

FRANC CHAMBERLAIN

ACKNOWLEDGEMENTS

A book of this kind is much indebted to those both past and present who have written about Luigi Pirandello. Some of the material has been taken from already published books and articles and we wish here to acknowledge and thank the relevant publishers:

Abete, Rome for extract from Corrado Alvaro (1976) *Cronache e scritti teatrali* edited by Alfredo Barbina (see Document No. 29);

Aufbau-Verlag, Berlin for extract from H. Jhering (1961) *Von Reinhardt bis Brecht, III, 1930-32* (see Document No. 56);

Bulzoni, Rome for extract from Livia Pasquazi Ferro Luzzi (1983) *Un manoscritto autografo inedito dell "Enrico IV" di Luigi Pirandello* (see Document No. 19); for extracts from A.C. Alberti (1974) *Il teatro nel fascismo* (see Documents Nos. 25, 26, 47); and for extract from *Teatro archivio* 4 (see Documents Nos. 15 and 28);

Feltrinelli, Milan for extract from Giorgio Strehler (1961) *Per un nuovo teatro* (see Document No. 57);

L'Age d'Homme, Lausanne for extract from Jacqueline Jomaron (1979) *Georges Pitoëff, metteur en scene* (see Document No. 23);

Le Monnier, Perugia for extract from AA.VV. (1967) *Atti del congresso internazionale di studi pirandelliani* (see Document No. 18);

Mondadori, Milan for extracts from Luigi Pirandello (1973) *Saggi, poesie e scritti varii* edited by M. Lo Vecchio Musti (see Documents Nos. 1, 2, 3, 6, 8, 10, 51 and 58);

Pan, Milan for extracts from Sarah Zappulla (1980) *Pirandello-Martoglio, carteggio inedito* (see Documents 4 and 5);

Sellerio, Palermo for extracts from Alessandro d'Amico and Alessandro Tinterri (1987) *Pirandello capocomico* (see Documents 31, 48, 49 and 50);

Teatro di stabile di Genova, Genoa for extract from Adriano Tilgher (1973) *Il problema centrale*, edited by Alessandro d'Amico (see Document No. 12).

Every effort has been made to trace the copyright holders of extracts in this publication. If copyright has been infringed, we will be pleased, on being satisfied as to the owner's title, to make proper acknowledgement in future editions.

We also wish to thank warmly:

the staff of the following libraries for their help and cooperation in the preparation of this volume: University of Birmingham; the Biblioteca Teatrale Burcardo, Rome; the Museo dell'Attore, Genoa; and the University of Warwick;

the Frederick May estate for access to the Frederick May Pirandello collection;

Sacha Pitoëff for allowing us to consult his father's stage copy of *Six personnages en quête d'auteur*;

the Pirandello estate for permission to translate and publish essays from Luigi Pirandello (1973) *Saggi, poesie, scritti varii*, edited by M. Lo Vecchio Musti, Milan: Mondadori;

the Biblioteca Teatrale Burcardo, Rome for permission to translate and publish the letters in Documents Nos. 24, 27, 36, 37, 38, 40, 41 and 42;

the Museo dell'Attore for permission to translate and publish the material in Documents Nos. 43, 44, 45, 46, 52, 53, 54 and 55.

In addition we have been both encouraged and helped by a number of people to whom we are most grateful for their time and trouble: Peter Thomson, for advice on the organization of the material; Renate Becker and Richard Lorch for advice on translations from German; Sandro d'Amico, Enzo Lauretta and Alessandro Tinterri for sharing their specialised knowledge of Pirandello and the Italian theatre; to Tony Howard for constructive suggestions, to members, past and present, of the editorial committee of the Society for Pirandello Studies, especially David Hirst, Felicity Firth and Laura Lepschy; and to the Society's past chairperson, Clive Barker to whom this book is dedicated, for his constant and unstinting advice and support.

We are grateful to Irene Renshaw and Ann Lakey who typed the manuscript in its early days and to Pauline Wilson for her skills and dedication in making camera ready copy of the final version of the text.

Our warmest thanks go to those women in our lives who have given of their help and support; to Meg Stacey who has listened with unabated sollecitude to Jennifer's joys and sorrows as the volume progressed; and to all those who enabled Susan to have the physical time to write: her daughters, Lucy and Vanessa, her mother, Eileen, and the staff of the University of Warwick creche.

Susan Bassnett
Jennifer Lorch

ILLUSTRATIONS

1. The Teatro d'Arte stage and auditorium.

2. *The Festival of Our Lord of the Ship* at the Teatro d'Arte, 1925.

3. The striped flats of Pitoëff's production of *Six Characters in Search of an Author*, 1923.

4. The cast of Salvini's production of *Tonight We Improvise*, 1930.

5. Egisto Olivieri, Marta Abba and Lamberto Picasso in Pirandello's production of *Six Characters in Search of an Author*, 1925.

6. Egisto Olivieri, Marta Abba, Lamberto Picasso and Gino Cervi in Pirandello's production of *Six Characters in Search of an Author*, 1925.

7. Ruggero Ruggeri in *Henry IV*, 1922.

8. The end of Pitoëff's production of *Henry IV*, 1925.

9. Virgilio Marchi's set design for Dunsany's *The Gods of the Mountain*, 1925.

10. Enrico Job's set for Missiroli's production of *The Mountain Giants*, 1979.

11. Puppets in Missiroli's production of *The Mountain Giants*, 1979.

12. The funeral of Ilse (Valentina Cortese) in Strehler's production of *The Mountain Giants*, 1967.

(Photographs by courtesy of the Museo d'Attore, Genoa)

THE DOCUMENTS AND THEIR SOURCES

Document 1: Spoken Action, 1899 ("L'azione parlata" in Luigi Pirandello (1973) *Saggi, poesi e scritti vari*, edited by M. Lo Vecchio Musti, pp. 1015-1018. Milan, Mondadori).

Document 2: Illustrators, Actors and Translators ("Illustratori, attori e traduttori" in Luigi Pirandello (1973) pp.207-224).

Document 3: Sicilian Theatre? ("Teatro siciliano?" in Luigi Pirandello (1973) pp. 1205-1208.)

Document 4: Letter to Martoglio 29.1.1919 (in Sarah Zappulla (1980) *Pirandello-Martoglio*, pp. 69-72. Milan, Pan).

Document 5: Letter to Martoglio 4.2.1919 (in Sarah Zappulla (1980), pp.73-75).

Document 6: On dialect ("Dialettalità" in Luigi Pirandello (1973) pp.1209-1211).

Document 7: Virgilio Talli's *Right You Are! (If You Think So)* from Sabatino Lopez (1931) *Dal carteggio di Virgilio Talli* pp. 138-43, 82-3. Milan, Treves).

Document 8: Theatre and Literature ("Teatro e Letteratura", in Luigi Pirandello (1973) pp. 1018-1024).

Document 9: Letter to Stefano Pirandello (from *Almanacco Bompiani 1938* (1937) p.43. Milan, Bompiani; see also *Almanacco Bompiani 1987* (1986). Milan, Bompiani, 1986).

Document 10:   Narrative fragment of *Six Characters in Search of an Author* ("Foglietti" in Luigi Pirandello (1973) pp. 1256-1258).

Document 11:   Pirandello at rehearsals of *Six Characters in Search of an Author* (in Dario Niccodemi (1920) *Tempo passato,* pp. 82-88. Milan, Treves).

Document 12:   Adriano Tilgher's review of *Six Characters in Search of an Author* (in Adriano Tilgher (1973) *Il problema centrale*, edited by A. d'Amico, pp. 125-32. Genoa, Edizioni del Teatro Stabile di Genova).

Document 13:   Desmond MacCarthy's review of the Stage Society's production of *Six Characters in Search of an Author* (in D. MacCarthy (1948) *Drama* pp. 161-5. London and New York, Putnam).

Document 14:   George Pitoëff's version of the Director's speech to set the garden scene in *Six Characters in Search of an Author* (from privately owned ms.).

Document 15:   Virgilio Marchi at the Teatro Odescalchi (from Virgilio Marchi (1981) "Ricordi sul Teatro d'Arte". *Teatro Archivio*, 4, 14-54).

Document 16:   Rudolph Pechel's review of Reinhardt's production of *Six Characters in Search of an Author* (in *Deutsche Rundschau* (1925) January to March, 239-240).

Document 17:   Letter to Ruggero Ruggeri (in *Il Dramma* (1955) 31, Nos. 227-228, 67-68).

Document 18:   The first reading of *Henry IV* (from Carlo Tamberlani "La riforma dell'interpretazione nella drammaturgia pirandelliana" in AA.VV. (1967), *Atti del congresso internazionale di studi pirandelliani*, pp. 483-99. Perugia, Le Monnier).

Document 19:   An earlier version of *Henry IV* (from Livia Pasquazi Ferro Luzzi (ed.) (1983) *Un manoscritto autografo inedito dell' "Enrico IV" di Luigi Pirandello*, Rome, Bulzoni, pp. 166; 175).

Document 20:   Letter from Silvio d'Amico to Virgilio Talli.

Document 21:   Review of Henry IV (in *Comoedia* (1922) IV, 5, 240-241).

Document 22: Stark Young's review of the American premiere of *The Living Mask* [*Henry IV*] (in Stark Young (1948) *Immortal Shadows*, pp. 48-51. London and New York, Scribners).

Document 23: Pitoëff's production of *Henry IV* (from Jacqueline Jomoran (1979) *Georges Pitoëff, metteur en scene*, pp.147-8. Lausanne, L'Age d'homme).

Document 24: Letter from Stefano Pirandello (ms. Biblioteca Teatrale Burcardo, Rome).

Document 25: The Constitution of the Teatro d'Arte (in A.C. Alberti (1974) *Il teatro nel fascismo*, pp. 123-6.   Rome, Bulzoni).

Document 26: Lamberto Picasso's proposal for a small theatre (in A.C. Alberti (1974) pp. 126-130).

Document 27: Letter from Pirandello to Mussolini (ms. Biblioteca Teatrale Burcardo, Rome).

Document 28: Virgilio Marchi's memories of the early days of the Teatro d'Arte (from Virgilio Marchi (1981) "Ricordi sul Teatro d'Arte". *Teatro Archivio*, 4, 14-54).

Document 29: Corrado Alvaro's review of the opening night of the Teatro d'arte (Corrado Alvaro (1976) *Cronache e scritti teatrali*, edited by Alfredo Barbina, pp. 76-86. Rome, Abete).

Document 30: Marta Abba (in Marco Prago (1925) *Cronache teatrali, 1925*, pp. 102-4. Milan, Treves).

Document 31: Marta Abba's Repertoire (reconstructed from Alessandro D'Amico and Alessandro Tinterri (1987) *Pirandello capocomico*. Palermo, Sellerio).

Document 32: The review in *The Times* of *Six Characters in Search of an Author* (in *The Times* 16.6.1925).

Document 33: The review in *The Times* of *Henry IV* (in *The Times* 19.6.1925).

Document 34: The review in *The Times* of *Clothe the Naked* (in *The Times* 25.6.1925).

Document 35: Pirandello at the New Oxford (Francis Birrell (1925) "Pirandello at the New Oxford". *The Nation and the Athenaeum*, 37, no. 13, 399-400).

PREFACE

This collection of documents is the first attempt in English to bring together a body of material on Luigi Pirandello as multi-faceted man of the theatre. Because relatively few of his works have been easily available to English language readers, he is thought of most frequently as a playwright, the author of *Six Characters in Search of an Author* and *Henry IV* in particular, and his contribution to theatre, both in theory and in practice, has tended to be overlooked.

As this collection of documents reveals, Pirandello was far more than just a dramatist. Coming quite late in life to the theatre, after years of prose writing that had earned him a literary reputation of considerable merit, Pirandello became fascinated by the process of creating plays, from written text through to scenic representation, and took his inspiration from a range of European masters, from Copeau, Rouché, Pitoëff, Reinhardt, Fuchs, Stanislavsky and Evreinov among others. He began to work in the theatre after the First World War, inheriting problems that afflicted the Italian theatre of the day and which he set out to try to solve - the tradition of individualism, which meant that actors had little or no concept of working as an ensemble; the tradition of the prompter, whose task it was to read the text aloud during the performance, so that at times the actors' voices were all but obliterated, leading them to develop an over-elaborate gestural style of playing to compensate; the lack of repertory theatres with stable companies and of course, the absence of a serious, middle-class audience.

Pirandello tried to tackle some of these problems by creating his own company and by founding an Art Theatre in the tradition of other Art Theatres elsewhere in Europe. In 1924 he set up the Teatro d'arte, and attempted to bring a greater rigour to both the training of actors and the choice of repertoire. Contemporary accounts of his rehearsal techniques stress the importance that he attributed to discipline on the part of the actors and his insistence on the idea of a company working together. He resolutely opposed the tradition of the prompter and has sometimes been credited with the responsibility for ending the power of the prompter in Italian theatre. Having begun as a writer, he began later to incorporate some of the practical theatre techniques he acquired into the writing of plays, and some of his most ambitious and structurally most innovative works were written in the late Twenties and early Thirties when he had begun to work closely with actors and to manage and direct his own company.

The international acclaim that Pirandello gained with the success of *Six Characters in Search of an Author* directed by Pitoëff in 1923 and with the early tours of the Teatro d'arte company died down towards the end of the Twenties, and Pirandello's letters show a growing sense of disillusionment. He went for a time into voluntary exile in Germany, returning to Italy with some reluctance. Perhaps because of this sense of not being appreciated by his own nation, Pirandello's tendency to destroy notes and records seems to have increased, and in assembling this collection of documents we have noted with regret the lack of much material that would have been of value to scholars today. Pirandello cannot be blamed entirely for the gaps in our knowledge - the years of Fascist rule in Italy and the devastation caused by the Second World War contributed to the loss of documents and the absence of a tradition of Theatre Studies as a discipline in Italy has caused many more documents to be discarded or overlooked. In his book *Luigi Pirandello, Director*, Richard Sogliuzzo suggests that prompt books, diaries, letters and unpublished manuscripts often remain in the possession of actor families and their descendants and are therefore very difficult to trace. It is likely that there are many documents by and relating to Pirandello that are at present in private collections, unknown to anyone but their owners.

Coordinating the material, we have arranged the book into four sections: I - *Theoretical Beginnings and Early Practice*; II - *International Dramatist*; III - *The Teatro d'Arte*; IV - *The Later Years and After*. In Section I we have provided documentation that covers Pirandello's gradual involvement with the theatre. Section II refers to *Six Characters in Search of an Author* and *Henry IV*. Section III contains a selection that recounts Pirandello's growing involvement in the practical processes of theatre-making. The material in this section covers the founding of the Teatro d'Arte, details of the company's repertoire and the eventual demise of the company and collapse of Pirandello's great hopes for a new future for Italian theatre. In the fourth section the documentation focuses on two of Pirandello's later more radically experimental works that are not so well-known to English language readers - *Tonight We Improvise* and *The Mountain Giants*.

In addition to the documentation on productions, etc., the sections contain Pirandello's own theoretical essays on theatre, many of which have hitherto been unavailable in English. From the early "Spoken Action" of 1899 [Document No. 1] through to his 1934 Address to the Volta Congress [Document No. 55], Pirandello continually tried to formulate his ideas about theatre, and we have provided a selection of those statements that reveal not only the changes in Pirandello's views across a thirty six year period, but also the constancy with which he held onto his very strongly expressed views on the theatre and its possibilities.

This collection of documents aims to place Pirandello less in the familiar tradition of twentieth century dramatists, than in twentieth century theatre history. His achievements as a director did not result in the establishment of a Pirandellian school of acting, which might perhaps explain why his directorial skills have been largely ignored, but nevertheless in setting up an Italian Art Theatre firmly in the tradition of other similar European ventures and in laying down a disciplined approach to ensemble acting work, Pirandello was a radical force in the Italian theatre and deserves to be remembered as such.

INTRODUCTION

The Early Years

Luigi Pirandello was born on 28th June, 1867, in a house overlooking the sea just outside Agrigento on the island of Sicily, named appropriately, Caos. The symbolic significance of the place of his birth remained with him throughout his life, and when he died nearly seventy years later he left instructions for his body to be burned and for his ashes to be either scattered to the winds or placed "in some rough stone" near Agrigento. From birth in Caos to final resting place, Pirandello's ties with the land that he was compelled to leave were indissoluble.

Because he spent most of his life in Rome teaching, writing and eventually working in the theatre, it is easy to regard Pirandello's Sicilianness as being of secondary importance. In fact, the opposite is true, and it is possible to trace certain key motifs throughout his works that derive explicitly from his regional origins, motifs such as the driving need to sustain a sense of honour in the eyes of the world, the traumas caused to individuals, particularly husbands, by marital infidelity, the cleaving to a piece of land as a sign of identity, the gap between private pain and the maintaining of a public facade. These motifs recur through all Pirandello's works, prose and drama, regardless of whether the settings are specifically Sicilian.

Pirandello's deeply rooted sense of Sicilian identity led him to experiment with dialect writing, and the doctoral thesis that he wrote when he finally moved to study in Bonn, after studying first in Palermo and then in Rome, was on the phonetic development of the Agrigento dialect. Gaspare Giudice, his biographer, emphasizes the enormous importance of Sicilian social convention and regional tradition in Pirandello's life and works[1], and, like many Sicilian patriots, Pirandello shared the belief that Western culture owes its greatest philosophical tradition to Sicily, to the Graeco-Sicilian period.

Pride in his native land, however, contrasted sharply with the economic decline of Sicily and Southern Italy in the nineteenth century. Pirandello's father owned a sulphur mine, one of the few flourishing industries on the island; consequently Pirandello grew up in a bourgeois household and did not suffer the same deprivation as many of those around him. But the appalling poverty of the peasants is frequently portrayed in his writings, and obviously impressed him deeply. Sicily in 1867 was in especially miserable straits. The natural barrenness of the land intensified agricultural destitution, the lack of industries drove millions of islanders to emigrate, in much the same way as the Irish peasantry of the same period were also forced to emigrate. Cholera epidemics frequently devastated the population, and in the few months from October 1866 to the summer of 1867 some 53,000 Sicilians died of cholera.

Poverty in Sicily was in no way helped by the unification of the Kingdom of the Two Sicilies with the rest of Italy, following the legendary landing of Garibaldi and his Redshirts at Palermo in 1860. Hopes for a new future were quickly lost in the mesh of bureaucratic confusion that followed unification, as different administrative systems were brought together. Through the latter years of the nineteenth century the destruction of the idealism of the Risorgimento became a source of considerable bitterness and provided a breeding ground later for the national socialist ideas of Mussolini. Italy's belated attempt to carve out an African empire, with the campaigns in Libya and Abyssinia, did little to shore up the sense of crumbling pride, and corrupt, incompetent government both at regional and national levels increased the general disillusionment.

Against this background, the young Pirandello went to university, first to read law and then to specialize in phonetics and finally returned to take up a teaching post at the Magistero in Rome. In 1894 he married the daughter of his father's business partner, Antonietta Portulano, and had three children, Stefano born in 1895, Lietta born in 1897 and Fausto, born in 1899. He had begun to write stories from an early age, and in 1904 the publication of his novel, *The Late Mathias Pascal (Il fu Mattia Pascal)*, gave him his first international success. He followed this with a series of novels and short stories, establishing a prestigious literary reputation for himself. In 1908 his essay *On Humour (L'umorismo)* appeared, in which he set out the philosophical basis of his concept of existence - that life is a fluid process which can never be halted or controlled, so that in order to give themselves an illusion of control, human beings create a series of masks for themselves, a set of fictitious structures that disguise the fear they feel at confronting perpetual change. Out of this paradox - that life is movement and people are forever trying to pretend that this movement does not exist - comes Pirandello's concept of humour. Pirandello looks at the absurdity of the human condition and finds a simultaneous blend of the funny and the pitiable, a combination that we also find in the work of many of the best silent film comedians such as Charlie Chaplin or Buster Keaton.

The pitiful and the comic together could clearly be seen in Pirandello's own life in 1903, when flooding in the sulphur mines led to the loss of Pirandello's father's capital, together with the loss of his wife's dowry. The shock of this loss, according to Pirandello's biographers, led to an onset of psychotic disturbance which took the form of obsessive jealousy in Antonietta's mind. Her persecution mania increased so dramatically in the following years that finally in 1918 Pirandello had her committed to a nursing home where she remained for the next thirty years until her death. The onset of Pirandello's international literary reputation therefore coincided ironically with the loss of his wife's sanity. By the time he was forty years old he had learned that the gap between public acclaim and private well-being can be very wide indeed.

Dialect Theatre

Pirandello had experimented with playwriting in his youth, but did not seriously start to write for the theatre until around the time of the First World War, writing twenty-eight plays between 1916 and 1924. The number of plays he wrote, the speed with which he wrote them, his age (he was fifty in 1917), seem to indicate an unleashing of previously repressed skills, and perhaps significantly, he often used his own stories as plots, rewriting and reshaping to suit the new form. Giudice, however, stresses the importance to Pirandello of his work in dialect theatre, suggesting that "Sicilian theatre...served him as a launching pad from which to leap onto the great prose stage."[2]

On December 9th, 1910, Nino Martoglio (1870-1921), director, dramatist, writer and collaborator of Pirandello's, staged two one-act plays by Pirandello, *The Vice (La Morsa)* and *Sicilian Limes (Lumíe di Sicilia)* at the Teatro Metastasio in Rome. Five years later, in 1915, *Sicilian Limes* was presented in Sicilian at the Teatro Pacini in Catania by Angelo Musco (1872-1937) and his company, and years later in his autobiography, Musco was to attribute to himself the honour of having first presented a Pirandello play to the public and thus enabled "this most famous playwright...to win his first theatrical laurels".[3]

In spite of Musco's grandiose claims, he did certainly have some impact on the early development of Pirandello's writing for the theatre. Musco specialised in Sicilian dialect performances, having started his own career as a "voice" in the famous Sicilian puppet plays, and by 1915 he had his own company. Widely praised for his exuberent energy - Bragaglia gives no sources but claims that Edward Gordon Craig described him as "the greatest actor in the world" and André Antoine claimed never to have seen such a powerhouse of energy on a stage - Musco exemplified the old tradition of Italian acting.[4] He was a master improviser, rarely bothered to follow a text and indeed saw the text simply as the starting point from which he could begin to work. He was very much an individualist, refusing to discipline himself to the demands made on him by colleagues or by the author, an attitude which contrasted sharply with Pirandello's belief in the importance of the written text. In the letters to Nino Martoglio of 1917 (Documents Nos. 4 - 5) the ambiguity of the relationship between Musco and Pirandello is apparent. Pirandello is clearly angered by what he perceives as Musco's cavalier attitude to his plays, but at the same time acknowledges Musco's abilities as an actor, comparing him favourably with his rival, Giovanni Grasso (1873-1930).

In spite of the temperamental differences between Pirandello and Musco, it was nevertheless in order to provide a role for Musco that Pirandello wrote his play, *Think it Over, Giacomino! (Pensaci, Giacomino!)* first performed in 1916 at the Teatro Nazionale in Rome, and he followed this with several other plays, the most notable of which was *Liolà*, also performed in 1916 at the Teatro Argentina, in Rome. Writing in *Avanti*! on 29 March, 1918, Antonio Gramsci declared that:

Musco has the theatre he deserves only because he does deserve it, he understands it, he relives it. And he does not always deserve the same praise; sometimes he forces impossible interpretations, but only because the play is totally devoid of meaningfulness. But he becomes great when an author offers him an artistic starting point, which he can develop and elaborate. You only have to remember Pirandello's *Liolà*, one of the finest of modern plays...[5]

The collaboration between Musco and Pirandello was therefore a fruitful one for both: it gave Pirandello the chance to write plays tailored for a particular actor and it gave Musco material worthy of his talents. For both of them, the collaboration was based on their shared belief in the value of dialect theatre as a living force.

In 1909 Pirandello wrote his essay on "Sicilian Theatre?" (Document No. 3) and posed two fundamental questions: can a Sicilian writer be truly said to "own" the material he chooses to write about, or do the demands of the public necessarily force him to conform to other requirements, and can a truly Sicilian theatre exist outside the confines of Sicily itself? Attacking what he calls the "exportable" Sicilian theatre of character actors like Grasso, Pirandello came reluctantly to the conclusion that dialect theatres can only be meaningful to those who have some understanding of the social context of the plays. To Italian mainland audiences in middle class theatres, the Sicilian dialect theatre could be nothing more than a curiosity, enabling them to sample the quaintness of an alien culture.

What Pirandello failed to perceive completely was the logical conclusion to be drawn from his sense of dissatisfaction at the way in which mainland audiences responded to Sicilian theatre. He attacks the audiences for their ignorance, but never questions the fundamental composition of the theatre-going public. A similar sense of dissatisfaction was later to lead Russian, French and German writers and directors to question the audiences more profoundly and to devise a type of theatre that could be taken out to new, predominantly working class audiences, thus changing the pattern of theatre-going altogether. For Pirandello, the concept of working class theatre, of mass theatre, was totally alien, since although he could plainly perceive the inadequacies of the kind of bourgeois public that frequented the theatres, he was a firm believer in the innate value of the written text, the work of art, and that text was not to be compromised.

Dialect theatre was a particularly contentious issue in Italy during the late nineteenth and early twentieth centuries. With political unification established it was felt necessary to impose one official language on the whole nation. The choice, not unexpectedly, was literary Florentine, the language of the three major writers of the fourteenth century, Dante, Petrarch and Boccacio and, from the sixteenth century, of all literary writers in the accepted canon. This stress on one viable language for a country where regional dialect tended to be the dominant language in an individual's life led to an undervaluing of dialect drama and theatre. The new establishment feared that dialect writing and performance would inhibit the social cohesion which, it was hoped, would be a consequence of political unification. In other words, it led to a reluctance to value a large part of Italy's theatrical inheritance and to a search for new plays in Italian with which to represent the nation. As a Sicilian Italian Pirandello felt the dialect/language tension deeply. He had a strong allegiance to his own native land and less sympathy during the early part of his theatrical career with a wider Italian nationalism. In the essay we have called "On Dialect" (Document No. 6) (in Italian Pirandello chose to call it "Dialettalità" to contrast it with the word "italianità" - "Italianness") Pirandello sought to justify the continuation of dialect traditions in Italy and Sicily by arguing that from Dante and Petrarch onwards, no one region had been able to lay claim to representing the Italian nation. He claimed that the continuity of dialect forms served to enrich Italian culture rather to fragment it.

The essay on dialect was Pirandello's last statement on dialect theatre. After *Liolà* he had already begun to turn his attention away from dialect theatre. The limitations of such a theatre were all too apparent and he had too much respect for his own place of origin to want to turn out folksy pieces for actors who traded on their reputation as typical regional characters. Significantly, Pirandello saw *Liolà* as a milestone in his career, and in a letter of 1916 to his son Stefano, he claimed that he wrote the play in two weeks during the summer, adding that "the protagonist is a poet-peasant, drunk on sunlight, and the whole play is full of songs and sunshine and is so light-hearted that it doesn't seem like one of my works at all."[6]

The Italian Theatre Context

Throughout his life Pirandello held strong views about the theatre and in his letters and essays he expounded some of his chief concerns together with his views on ways forward for the Italian theatre in the twentieth century.

The Italian theatre of the early twentieth century had inherited a number of problems from the previous century. Chief among these was a star system that enhanced the status of a few actors and offered little incentive to others to improve their techniques. From the photographs of actors like Eleonora Duse, the Grammatica sisters, Lamberto Picasso and Ruggero Ruggeri, some impression of their physical stage presence emerges, with the stage space as a kind of vortex in which they struggle for dominance. Duse reputedly held silences for as long as ten minutes, compelling audiences to relate to her physically rather than through the verbal medium. Such an acting tradition did not encourage the concept of ensemble work, and companies were all too often simply the supporting players behind the star attraction.

The star, or *mattatore*, as this actor was called, came into being in the second half of the nineteenth century in response to the economic difficulties imposed upon theatre as a result of political unification. Before 1861 nearly all Italian theatrical companies were privately run and peripatetic. A few, the envy of other companies, were subsidised by the royal houses of Turin, Milan, Parma and Naples, and enjoyed what was known as "il privilegio" which gave them the right to present their plays in the theatres of the respective royal houses. On the disappearance of the royal houses after 1861, with the exception of the house of Savoy which became Italy's monarchy, this monopoly ceased. At the same time the national state did not assume the responsibility for theatre that the royal houses had done. Theatre was

considered a local, municipal responsibility.   A number of the newly
established municipalities built their own theatres at this time, which accounts
for the enormous increase in theatrical buildings in the second half of the
nineteenth century, but did not see it as their responsibility to support the
theatrical companies.   With the disappearance of the monopoly these too
increased, from a handful in the 1840s to about 940 in 1873.   There was not a
commensurate increase in the size of the theatre going public, however, which
meant that more companies were competing for only a slightly enlarged
number of spectators.   A viable response to this situation was the star actor
supported by a small, often mediocre cast.   The star drew in the audience; and
the box office returns, the company's sole support, continued the life of the
company for a little longer.   An extension of this response was the foreign
tour.   Tommaso Salvini, Ernesto Rossi, and Eleanora Duse, to name but three
of the famous Italian stars of the late nineteenth century, toured extensively
and were accused by Italians of being more abroad than in their own country.
Again the eager response of the foreign audiences contributed to the retention
of a theatrical system that stultified rather enlivened theatrical practice.   The
star system reached its zenith in 1880 when Tommaso Salvini accepted what
he considered at first a very strange invitation from an American impresario:
to play Othello in Italian with a supporting cast who were to play their roles in
English.   The experiment proved popular and was repeated with other plays in
other countries.

Dual language performances also give some indication of the status of the
text for an Italian company in the late nineteenth and early twentieth centuries.
A dramatic text was not considered as a piece of writing of artistic merit
whose worth was to be validated through the interpretation of actors: it was
seen rather as a vehicle for the actors and was liable to amendment and cuts as
suited the particular actor or company.   Sergio Tofano recalls how the famous
Ermete Novelli rewrote *The Merchant of Venice* and renamed it *Shylock*.
Other apocryphal stories show how close the text was at times to a cross
between a commedia dell'arte scenario and a variety performance: famous
actors would interrupt their performance of one role, if requested by the
audience, and slip immediately into another stock role in their repertoire,
returning to the play in hand when the digression was over.

The commedia dell'arte was, in fact, a major legacy inherited by the
Italian theatre of Pirandello's time.   Not only does the actor based concept of
theatre go back to this form of theatre, the rigid construction of theatre
companies owes much to these first professional theatrical companies.
Commedia dell'arte companies of the sixteenth, seventeenth and eighteenth
centures were made up of about ten to twelve actors, with each actor
performing the same role in every performance; that is, for example, an actor
would be employed by contract to play Arlecchino for a year and would
probably go on playing that role for the rest of his professional life.   With the
predominance of text based theatre in the mid eighteenth century the role,
rather than the character, became the status within the company.   Companies
"di prima categoria" would expect to comprise a *capocomico, primo attore*
(leading man) and *prima attrice* (leading lady); *brillante* (comic actor) and
caratterista (character actor); *madre* (mother); *primo attore giovane* (juvenile
lead) and *prima attrice giovane* (young female lead) *seconda donna* (second
actress); *promiscuo* (an actor able to take on various minor roles); and several

generici (that is, bit part players who had not yet established themselves in roles). That this system survived well into the twentieth century is attested by the work of Claudia Palombi who interviewed a number of retired actors in 1985. With the exception of one, all of them had belonged to companies run on the role system.[7]

Further legacies of the commedia dell'arte companies were the peripatetic nature of the work of theatrical companies and the very tight programme within which they rehearsed and performed. Because they were travelling players, all except the very affluent, had to keep their equipment to a minimum. (In earlier days this would have been horse-drawn - in fact the earliest extant contract (1545) gives due space to the horse; later the players used the railways.) This meant that there was little opportunity to elaborate scenery above the bare minimum. The performance and rehearsal schedule made in-depth interpretation and detailed rehearsals rare. The following extracts from Palombi's book give some indication of the working life of a travelling player in the early twentieth century.

> (a)   At eight in the morning we were already at work rehearsing the farce; because at that time the evening performance used to end with a comedy - a farse it was, that is, a very funny one-acter. So in the morning we began rehearsing with the comic actor at eight. Then at nine, half-past or about ten the capocomico or director would turn up and then the rehearsal proper would begin. Then you had a bite to eat in a great hurry, then back to the theatre, then there was the performance. After that you went back to sleep and then in the morning started all over again.

> (b)   There was only time for theatre. Every blessed day my mother would wake me early in the morning, give me a cup of coffee, and I'd go to the theatre. We rehearsed every day from ten until four in the afternoon with a half-hour break around midday for something to eat. At half-past eight you had to be in the theatre again. The performance started at nine or half-past and you didn't finish until late at night because in those days the performances lasted a lot longer than they do today, in the intervals there were orchestral interludes which made everything longer.[8]

Plays were divided into four kinds: classical tragedy, romantic tragedy, comedy and drama. An actor who was hoping to reach the top, that is to become *primo attore*, or even *primo attore assoluto* would be expected to be able to play all in all four genres, in addition to specialising in one.

It was probably the sheer volume of words that an actor was expected to know that led to the significant position held by the prompter. That the prompter had been an important part of a company is made clear by his role in Goldoni's *The Comic Theatre* (*Il teatro comico*) a play in which the eighteenth century dramatist announced his reform of the commedia dell'arte by staging a company's rehearsal. In the early twentieth century the prompter still spoke the whole play in a tone audible to both actor and audience. This ensured that there were no embarassing silences while players who dried floundered their way back to the part unaided by a sleepy prompter; but this particular system of prompting probably also contributed to the rather frequent references in reviews to badly learnt parts.

With good actors this was not a problem. Both Ernesto Rossi and Tommaso Salvini testify in their memoirs to the importance they gave to learning their parts. In fact, what is remarkable is just how many parts made up an actor's repertoire. The repertoire sent by Ernesto Rossi to Cesare Dondini of the Teatro de' Fiorentini in Naples numbered over sixty plays. The following anecdote drawn from Tommaso Salvini's memoirs indicates how important it was for an actor to be able to play these parts at short notice. As *primo attore assoluto* of the Compagnia dei Fiorentini, it was his privilege to choose the opening play of the season. He chose Voltaire's *Zaire*, only to learn that the company had no suitable set for this play. So he chose a play called *The Harpist*; the leading lady did not yet know her part. Undeterred he changed to *Orestes*; he learnt that the actor playing Pilades was ill. In the end he took the company's advice and, best known as a tragic actor, found himself playing the part of Lord Bonfil in Goldini's comedy *Pamela*.[9]

The problems created by trying to adapt a theatrical practice insufficiently attuned to a modern age were felt acutely by Pirandello. This is particularly clear in his attitude to the commedia dell'arte. A number of Italians of the early twentieth century, particularly those who saw themselves as part of a cultural elite, despised the commedia dell'arte as an outmoded theatrical practice. During Pirandello's lifetime, however, there was a resurgence of interest in this theatrical form outside Italy. Duchartre published his influential volumes, *La comédie italienne* in 1924 and 1925, and in 1927 Constantin Mic brought out *La commedia dell'arte ou le théâtre des comédiens italiens des XVI, XVII et XVIII siècles*. In Italy, Gordon Craig published several articles on the subject in his periodical *The Mask* from 1911. In 1922, Vachtangoff staged Gozzi's *Turandot* at the Moscow Arts Theatre in a style thought to be a revival of the commedia dell'arte. This interest in the Italian improvised comedy exhibited a particular attitude: commedia dell'arte was seen less as the first professional theatre of Europe than as "pure" and "original" theatre, a form of national folk art: "pure" because improvisation meant that there was no intervening text, folk art because of the masked characters and use of dialect. This attitude was in marked contrast to the attitude of the Italian literary establishment who denigrated the commedia dell'arte precisely because it was actor and not text based. Matilde Serao, novelist and essayist, sums up the Italian attitude in the following statement from one of her lectures:

> Commedia dell'arte is the wayward improvisation by bright actors who have no desire to follow the thoughts of another, that is, the thoughts of the author; it is the whim of those who appear on stage and seek to cover over an old and jaded plot with the illusory colours of natural acting; it is the substitution of the personal consciousness of the actor for the certainly higher and nobler consciousness of the author. Not just one step backwards along the path of art, but most assuredly, a thousand steps backwards.[10]

As an Italian man of letters, Pirandello shared this view; as a European man of the theatre he thought that the commedia dell'arte was the form of theatre closest to life and was in that sense the purest theatre. The tension that these conflicting views presented for him is visible both in his early essays, (see, in particular "Illustrators, Actors and Translators" (Document No. 2) and his late plays, *Tonight We Improvise (Questa sera si recita a soggetto)* and *The Mountain Giants (I giganti della montagna)*.

It was as an Italian man of letters that Pirandello initially approached theatre. His major concern was the presentation of the dramatic text. From his earliest writings on theatre, Pirandello stressed the importance of discipline, of a carefully balanced relationship between playwright, director and actors. Although he so often wrote with specific actors in mind - Musco as Liolà, Ruggeri as Henry IV, Duse as the tragic old lady Donna Anna in *The Life I Gave You (La vita che ti diedi)* and Marta Abba in so many of his later plays - Pirandello nevertheless saw the role of the actor as that of giving life to the character in the stage translation of the writer's creation. The task of the actor, in his view, was therefore that of faithful translator of the text before him, and the actor's responsibility to that text was as great as the responsibility of the writer in originally creating it. It is not hard to see a relationship between Pirandello's idea of the role of the actor and Stanislavsky's ideas, and in fact Pirandello began work at the Teatro d'Arte by giving lessons on Stanislavsky and the Russian theatre.

Opposed as he was to the tradition of the *mattatore*, Pirandello was equally critical of other dominant trends in the Italian theatre. He attacked naturalistic theatre in his theoretical writings, arguing that a theatre of situation almost inevitably leads to bad writing and to inadequate performances, since the situation in which the characters are placed precludes any bringing to life of the individual role. His most obvious exposé of naturalistic theatre comes in *Six Characters in Search of an Author*. Later he was to question what became known as "director's theatre", most notably in *Tonight We Improvise*.

Pirandello saw the solution to the problem of what he termed bad writing and self-indulgent acting as lying in the creation of the state subsidised theatre, where stable companies could have both the time and the security to rehearse adequately a well-conceived programme of plays. He complains about the absurdly short rehearsal times, the excessive touring, the ever-changing repertoire that was felt to be necessary in order to bring audiences into the theatres. And with regard to those audiences, Pirandello aligns himself with arch proponents of the Art Theatre movement in Europe, men such as George Fuchs, founder of the Munich Kunstlertheater and author of *Die Schaubühne der Zukunft* (1905) and Jacques Rouché, founder of the Théâtre des Arts and author of *L'Art Théâtrale Moderne* (1924). What all had in common was a belief in the need for a cultural renaissance in the theatre, for a revaluation of the place of theatre in society. Pirandello wanted a rigorously disciplined theatre that would attract intelligent audiences and raise the level of Italian culture, and when he founded his own art theatre in 1924 it was with the hope of filling precisely those needs.

It is easy to understand why, in spite of the shared sense of dissatisfaction with the existing state of affairs in the Italian theatre, Pirandello should have had so little in common with Marinetti and the whole Futurist movement.

What was absent in Pirandello's vision of theatre was the political dimension, and although he publicly joined the Fascist Party and declared his support on frequent occasions for Mussolini, he seems to have genuinely believed that art could exist outside politics. Consequently, he remained aloof from many of the alternative theatre movements of his time, from Marinetti's futurist vision that saw theatre as representative of the chaos and anarchy of the new technological age, from attempts to create workers' theatre or people's theatre on a massive scale. Pirandello saw the theatre as an art, and had little patience with what he considered to be cheap tricks to divert an audience's attention.

In the years that Pirandello was writing for the theatre, the old Italian system was in decline. The star actor who improvised his or her roles became part of a company, the all-powerful prompter began to disappear, even though his presence was still so striking that during the 1925 London tour of the Teatro d'arte critics complained about the noise which drowned out the voices of the actors. The tradition of the *capocomico* or principal actor who was also the director declined, and by 1931 Silvio d'Amico notes that the term *regista* (director) was in use.

By stressing concepts of realism as a basis for acting and establishing a style of actor training based on close textual study, on the creation of an actor's subject, on the need for close co-operation between all the stages of creating theatre, Pirandello established a new method of theatre work. He remained convinced of the superiority of the text and wrote nothing that might suggest he had any views on scenography, though Guido Salvini claims that the age of modern scenography in Italy began with the Teatro d'Arte and Sogliuzzo points out that Pirandello's copious stage directions indicate that he had some physical concept of the staging and some sense of how he wanted certain scenes to be lit.[11] Pirandello's major contribution was the creation of a different acting style. Guido Salvini described it thus:

> Pirandello established a faster and more compact rhythm of line delivery for his actors than the precipitous and empty style we were usually accustomed to, since we had worked primarily in the conventional acting companies of that period. But Pirandello strove to concentrate the meaning of the lines in seconds, to embellish a thought in a fraction of a second with the admirable result that he achieved a style of line delivery that was faster than the usual rhythm of spoken Italian.[12]

Following Pirandello's career from his early work in dialect theatre through to the founding of the Teatro d'Arte shows a man eager, almost desperate to learn about theatre. Alongside the great rush of playwriting that carried him through a dark period in his life, there was obviously a frantic search for practical knowledge. Pirandello was well over fifty when he started to direct, and he must have acquired his rehearsal technique from long hours of watching other people and deciding what did and what did not work. Ironically, he seems to have taken less from the Italian theatre, from the experimental staging of the Futurists, the skills of the virtuoso actors of the old school, whether performing in naturalist pieces or in poetic dramas and to have derived more from the work of European practitioners working in other traditions.

The Years of Success

Giudice suggests that Pirandello threw himself so totally into writing for the theatre as compensation for the traumas in his personal life. The outbreak of the First World War and the period of social unrest, with strikes and violent demonstrations in the major cities was a source of concern to Pirandello, as was the health of his wife who was finally committed in 1918. During the war he suffered agonies of worries about his son, Stefano, away in the army and in a letter to Stefano of 24th October 1915 he stated despairingly:

> It seems to me that my whole life has been drained of meaning, and I can no longer understand the reason for the actions I perform, nor for the words I speak, and I am almost amazed that other people can move about outside this nightmare of mine and speak and do things...[13]

In spite or because of his feelings of alienation, Pirandello wrote plays in rapid succession, and on May 10, 1921 *Six Characters in Search of An Author* was performed for the first time at the Teatro Valle in Rome, a production directed by Dario Niccodemi, with Luigi Almirante, Vera Vergani, Luigi Cimara and Jone Frigerio in the leading roles. On 30 September the play moved to Milan and on 30 December it opened in Turin.

Today this play has its assured place in the twentieth century canon and its theme shocks no one. But after the first night an uproar broke out in the theatre as this contemporary review shows:

> Pirandello seemed quite calm. He thanked the actress who had stood up well to the protests and who, one month later, was to take the play in triumph to Milan, to Spain and to America. He did not go out through the main door; it was advisable to go out through the side door into the alley, a filthy alley full of dead cats. From there he could get to the tram stop by Sant'Andrea delle Valle. To try and hail a taxi - which were still very rare in those days - would have aroused suspicion and warned the public who were waiting by the main door to jeer at him.
>
> He walked out with his daughter on his arm. He was recognised as soon as he stepped under the streetlight. People gathered round him to protect him. Beautiful women were there with painted lips, laughing and repeating "Madhouse". Elegant young men in white ties were grinning and shouting insults. His daughter, clinging to her father's arm could hardly move a step. Other people ran up, jeering and laughing. Even the local police did not know whether they ought to intervene on behalf on "that crazy Pirandello". A taxi approached. Under the lights of the little square, Pirandello met the insults head on, a tiny ironic smile hovering round his mouth. We had to stop a fight starting until the car left. He let his daughter get in. Then he got in after her, and you could still see his face

framed in the car window while he gave the address of that distant lonely house in which he would start work again next day. The elegant young men threw coins at him. And the ladies did too, hurriedly opening their precious handbags. I can still hear the sound of copper on the pavement, the laughter and the insults.[14]

The initial hostility to *Six Characters* made the play a *succès de scandale* overnight, and it has remained one of the most frequently performed of all Pirandello's plays. In London, in 1922, the play was deemed to be obscene and banned from public performance by the Lord Chamberlain, but it was staged by the private Stage Society in 1922, in a translation by Mrs. W.A. Green, directed by Theodore Komisarjewsky.

In 1923 Georges Pitoëff directed *Six Characters* at the Comédie des Champs Elysées in Paris, and in May 1924 Reinhardt directed the play at the Komödie in Berlin. Both these productions were significant, not only because they testify to the international impact of the play itself, but because of the method of staging. Pitoëff's production had the *Six Characters* arrive on stage in an elevator, lowered from above, an innovation which was strongly opposed by Pirandello at first, but which later he came to appreciate.

When Pirandello rewrote the play for the 1925 Teatro d'Arte version, he seems to have been influenced by the Pitoëff production. The redevised ending of the play, where he has the Stepdaughter leave the stage and exit through the auditorium, is, however, entirely his own. There are consequently two different endings to the play, the 1921 and the 1925 ending, and the English version by E. Storer, published in 1922, is a translation of the earlier text. Later English translations follow the 1925 version. Reinhardt's production, in contrast, stressed the magical, ghostlike quality of the characters. In his version, the Characters did not appear either through the auditorium or by any mechanical means, but were present on stage from the beginning, in darkness, and were then picked out by a white spotlight. Whether directly influenced by Reinhardt, in the 1925 version of the play Pirandello includes detailed stage directions of lighting changes in the final moments of the play. The director shouts "Lights!", and all the lights come on both on stage and in the auditorium; he calls to the lighting technician to turn the lights off, there is a split-second blackout, he calls for a bit of light so he can see where to go and immediately a green spotlight, projected from the back of the stage casts giant shadows of the four Characters left alive at the end of their scene. The director leaves the stage in terror "at the same time the back projector is turned off, the stage is lit with the bluish evening light of the previous scene". As this setting is created, the Characters appear on stage, the Son first, followed by the Mother with her arms outstretched imploringly, then the Father stage left, and with the three of them fixed in tableau, the Stepdaughter runs out, across the stage, down the small flight of steps and out through the auditorium, laughing wildly and the curtain falls. This use of shadow play, the deliberately anti-realist lighting and instructions to the actors show that Pirandello had learned something from European techniques, and some of the stage directions in his later plays reveal this interest even more fully, particularly in plays such as *Tonight We Improvise* (1930), *When One is*

Somebody (Quando si è qualcuno) (1933), *Finding Oneself (Trovarsi)* (1932) and *The Mountain Giants* (1936).

The success of *Six Characters* and *Henry IV* in particular made Pirandello a figure of immense popular acclaim, and in 1923 he went to the United States for a Pirandello Season at the Fulton Theatre, New York. He completed his last novel, *One, No-one and A Hundred Thousand (Uno, nessuno e centomila)* in 1924, and in addition to travelling and writing, he was finally able to bring to fruition his dream of an Arts Theatre in October 1924. The principal aims of the new theatre are set down in the documents reproduced in this book (Nos. 25 and 26) and can be summarized briefly as (1) to set up a permanent company, working out of a theatre especially created for that company's needs; (2) to create a solid repertory of plays, both ancient and modern that could be put on with adequate rehearsal time and with adequate funding; (3) to encourage new audiences and so to raise the general level of taste of the theatre-going public, in other words, to establish the claims of the middle class to their own theatre; (4) to act as a centre for information, with library facilities and a regular newsletter, and to maintain contacts with similar Art Theatres abroad.

Ostensibly, the aims of the Teatro d'Arte were similar to the aims of the French and German Art Theatres, and in this respect Pirandello can be placed in the context of the tendency in Europe and America towards the establishment of permanent repertory theatre companies. What distinguishes Pirandello's theatre, however, is the fact that in order to obtain state subsidy, Pirandello had to work closely with Mussolini and become, in effect, an apologist for the Fascist regime both at home and abroad. Pirandello joined the Fascist party in 1924, shortly after the murder of the Socialist Deputy Matteotti by right-wing extremists, and in the wave of anti-fascist feeling that swept across Italy as a result of the revulsion felt by the murder. Pirandello joined the party, therefore, in a way calculated to gain maximum publicity. He sent a copy of his letter to Mussolini, in which he declared that he would "consider it the greatest honour" to become one of Il Duce's "humblest and most obedient followers", to the Fascist newspaper *L'Impero (The Empire)* and in a letter written to Mussolini in 1925 (Document No. 27) he announced his intentions of "carrying out active propaganda work for Italy" during the tours of the company.

Pirandello's commitment to Fascism was, and still is, an enormous problem for future directors, critics and readers. The obvious implication to be drawn from his public commitment to the party is that he was desperate to ensure the success of the funding of the Teatro d'Arte and was therefore willing to stoop to even the most squalid of gestures in order to ensure that success. At the same time, Pirandello was a man of some principle, a patriot whose bitterness at what he perceived as the end of the hopes of the Risorgimento and the humiliation of Italy after the First World War may well have led him to embrace the ideals of Fascism, the belief in law and order and national pride that was a keynote of Mussolini's impassioned speeches. Moreover, the ideology of some of the later plays would certainly seem to show that Fascism for Pirandello was more than skin deep; he was committed to ideals of the regime at the point when he decided to join the party, and if he later became disillusioned - *The Mountain Giants*, his last work, is a very troubled, disturbing play - then it still does not alter the strength of his feelings expressed in 1924 when he genuinely supported the Fascist cause.

The fundamental problem for Pirandello, as has already been suggested, is that he tried to divorce art from politics in a society where even the pretence at such a division could not be minimally maintained. In order to fund his theatre, Pirandello had to collaborate with the government in power and, as Klaus Mann has shown so skilfully in *Mephisto*, his novel *à clef*, based on the life and career of the German actor-director-manager in Nazi Germany, Gustav Grundgens, funding from government sources inevitably involves government in the decision-making process of repertoire, the hiring of actors, technicians and designers and in the choice of venues.

For the opening of the Teatro d'Arte on 2 April, 1925, a date which marks Pirandello's debut as artistic director, he chose two plays: Alfred Lord Dunsany's *The Gods of the Mountain* (the play which was to later inspire him to write *The Mountain Giants*) and his own *Festival of Our Lord of the Ship (Sagra del Signore della Nave)*, a one-act play that was to have premiered in Milan the previous year but which had been banned by the police. The decision to open with such a play was therefore particularly curious: the play had been banned once, it required a cast of more than 130 people, reminiscent of the mass theatre spectacles of directors like Evreinov, following the ideas outlined by Romain Rolland in *Le théâtre du peuple* (1903), and the subject matter was described by Pirandello himself as "the tragedy of human bestiality". The staging was highly stylized, with the set designed by the painter Cipriano Oppo, who also painted a huge figure of Christ saving a ship on the curtain. The setting was simple - a box set with drop cloths, but as contemporary photographs show, painted on a house at stage right was a *trompe l'oeil* window, with a colourfully dressed couple leaning out to look at the crowds. Pirandello's strong visual sense was also evidenced by the lighting changes - red for the dance that leads to orgy, purple at the end of the play when the procession of the Crucifixion appears. In this production, as in the later *Six Characters* production, Pirandello used the auditorium, having the procession enter through the auditorium and move up onto the stage (Document No. 15). The critics were generally enthusiastic about Pirandello's skills as a director, but the play was not popular and it was not performed again for twenty-five years.[15]

The first foreign tour of the Teatro d'Arte company was to London, to the New Oxford Theatre in 1925, and this was followed by tours in France and Germany. Details of a month of the 1926 tour are given below (Document No. 49) and the strenuous gruelling programme cannot have been easy for a man approaching sixty, though Giudice gives accounts of how Pirandello seemed to have a new lease of life once the theatre project had become a reality.

Another source of energy for him must also have been his relationship with Marta Abba (Document No. 30). Marta Abba joined the company in 1925 as a young, unknown actress, but rapidly became the centre of attention. In 1926 Pirandello wrote *Diana and Tuda (Diana e la Tuda)* especially for her, and thus established the pattern for the future. Marta Abba became his leading lady and the woman who inspired him to write, and was later to hold the copyright of many of his most experimental plays.

The Years of Disillusionment

In 1926 the Teatro d'Arte company toured Eastern Europe and in 1927 went to South America, where they enjoyed a huge success. But despite the artistic acclaim, the company lost money steadily and in the Summer of 1928 the government withdrew its support. Pirandello's dream of an Italian art theatre collapsed. Lucio D'Ambra describes Pirandello during the final days of the company's life, at Viareggio:

> He is sad. Maybe the rest of the world has treated him well, but Italy hasn't...A refugee from the theatres of the world...these last performances are sad and badly done. And one evening, after struggling for four years, Pirandello's dream of being a director collapses in a final performance in front of a row of benches, of Ibsen's *Lady from the Sea*... And so ended the company that had been life, suffering and passion for him for four years, there among friends, and Pirandello was stunned...Stunned, saddened, tired out, Pirandello let himself be dragged around anywhere, by anyone. The Mayor of Viareggio wants to offer the great writer a banquet and a gold medal? Pirandello goes to the banquet. Society ladies want to meet him and and invite him to their homes? Pirandello goes to see them...and pays no attention. Where has his energy gone?...[16]

Faced with the ruin of his hopes, Pirandello decided to leave Italy and for the next five years he lived in voluntary exile, in Germany and in France. He went to Germany in order to turn his attention to the cinema, under contract to write screenplays for three films based on his own plays. He worked at first with Adolf Lantz on a film version of *Six Characters*, but the film ran into financial difficulties and was never completed. In 1929, at the invitation of British International Pictures he went to London to try to arrange for an English language version of the film, but the fear of censorship made this out of the question. Whilst in London Pirandello saw his first talkie, which he described in a letter to his son Stefano as "monstrous", an opinion that can be seen in his essay 'Will The Talkie Do Away With Theatre?' (Document No. 51) His attempts to work in cinema were largely unsuccessful, and the only major success for any of his plays was the 1932 film version of *As You Desire Me (Come tu mi vuoi)* with Greta Garbo and Erich von Stroheim.

During the years of exile Pirandello continued to write, though few of his plays premiered in Italy. Although these plays were later performed in Italy, largely due to Marta Abba who by now had her own company, they were not generally well received. *The Changeling (La favola del figlio cambiato)* was banned in Germany and failed dismally when it opened in Rome. Pirandello returned reluctantly to Italy in 1933. In 1934 he was awarded the Nobel Prize for Literature, an honour which did not enable him to overcome his sense of bitterness and feelings of grievance. His letters, especially to Marta Abba, show a man who feels badly treated by a world that has failed to recognise genius. Every bad review of a new play was further evidence to him of the

obtuseness and lack of feeling of the society in which he lived. He died on 10
December, 1936, leaving detailed instructions for the disposal of his ashes and
asking for there to be no funeral ceremony. Denied what he saw as the fruits
of success in life, he requested that his death should be as unobtrusive as
possible.

In 1961, years later, Lamberto Picasso who had been one of his star
actors, paid tribute to Pirandello's work. He pointed out that Pirandello had
"worked assiduously to rid the actors of all the false tricks of the trade they
had assimilated", demanding that actors should bring a new rigour and a new
depth to their work.

> This was a new reality for actors: attentive, profound, subtle,
> and therefore demanding. He required a rigid discipline of the
> actors; they were to think before speaking, because words began
> in thought and were not to be nullified or falsified by an actor's
> whims or idiosyncrasies.

Picasso attributes a great deal to Pirandello's skills as a director, and
although the occasion of the speech invited laudatory statements, Picasso does
genuinely seem to feel that the impact of Pirandello on Italian theatre was
considerable. Pirandello is chiefly remembered today as a writer, above all as
a playwright, but his contribution to theatre history has not been adequately
stressed. Picasso sums up the sense of magic, the devastating impact of his
ideas in his tribute to his former director when he tells us that:

> Pirandello exploded like a bomb amidst all the false traditions
> of the Italian theatre, traditions that had pervaded the theatre for
> years and had suffocated any spark of originality; traditions that
> had become a second life for the actors who seemed incapable
> of freeing themselves of these artificialities.[17]

Notes

(1) Gaspare Guidice, *Luigi Pirandello*, Turin, U.T.E.T. 1963, Tr. as *Pirandello, A Biography*, London, O.U.P. 1975 (N.B. abridged version).

(2) Gaspare Guidice, *Luigi Pirandello*, 1963, p.316.

(3) Angelo Musco, *Cerca che trovi*, Bologna, 1930 quoted in Guidice, *Luigi pirandello*, 1963, p.309.

(4) Leonardo Bragaglia, *Interpreti pirandelliani*, Rome, Trevi, 1969, p.14.

(5) Antonio Gramsci, *Letteratura e vita nazionale*, Turin, Einaudi, 1954, p.322.

(6) Leonardo Sciascia (ed.) *Omaggio a Pirandello*, Milan, Bompiani, 1986 which also carried a reprint of the *Almanacco Bompiani 1938*. The text of Pirandello's letter of 24 October 1916 to his son Stefano is on p.39 of this reprint.

(7) Claudia Palombi, *Il gergo del teatro: l'attore italiano di tradizione*, Rome, Bulzoni, 1986.

(8) Palombi, *Il gergo del teatro*, p.34.

(9) Tommaso Salvini, *Ricordi, aneddoti ed impressioni*, Milan, Fratelli Dumolard, 1895, pp. 159-60.

(10) Matilde Serao, "Carlo Gozzi e la fiaba" in A.A.V.V. *La vita italiana nel Settecento, conferenze tenute a Firenze nel 1895,* Milan, Treves, 1896, p.256.

(11) A. Richard Sogliuzzo, *Luigi Pirandello, Director: The Playwright in the Theatre*, Metuchen, N.J. & London, The Scarecrow Press, Inc., 1982, pp.76-105.

(12) Guido Salvini, quoted in Sogliuzzo, *Luigi Pirandello, Director*, p.65.

(13) See note 6. This letter is on p.32.

(14) Orio Vergani "L'ora dei Sei Personaggi", *Corriere della sera*, 15 December 1936, quoted in Guidice, *Luigi Pirandello* (1963) pp.335-6.

(15) When the play was revived, it was directed by Tatiana Pavlova, a Russian emigrée who taught directing at the National Academy of Dramatic Art when it was founded in 1926. She has sometimes been credited with being the first director in Italy to eliminate the prompter altogether during a performance.

(16) Lucio d'Ambra, quoted in Guidice, *Luigi Pirandello* (1963) p.491.

(17) Lamberto Picasso, quoted in Sogliuzzo, *Luigi Pirandello, Director*, p.56.

SECTION I: THEORETICAL BEGINNINGS AND EARLY PRACTICE 1899-1918

Introduction

As we have indicated in the Introduction, Pirandello's involvement in theatre came relatively late in his life. His first international success, *Six Characters in Search of an Author*, belongs to his fifty-fifth year. Until then he had gradually established a reputation in his own country as a writer of short stories and novels, and later of plays. He had begun writing plays when very young, but had then destroyed all the texts by the time he was twenty. There is also some evidence that he had taken part in amateur theatricals as a young man. From the age of 20 to 32 he had intermittently turned to drama; some of these texts remain: *The Vice (La morsa)*, *The Kite (Il nibbio)* and *Scamander (Scamandro)* but none of these plays were performed at the time they were written. As a man of letters and essayist, however, Pirandello interested himself in a number of topics and theatre was one of these. Indeed, much of his thinking about theatre at this early stage remains unchanged much later in his life. The play that brought him to the attention of the European theatrical scene, *Six Characters in Search of an Author*, deploys a number of the ideas, and at times the very same phrases, of these early essays.

"Spoken Action" (1899) is the first of Pirandello's essays on the theatre, in which he establishes his unshakeable belief in the superiority of the written text, which he describes as "the work of art". This belief remained constant throughout his life, regardless of his later experiences as writer and as director and company manager. For Pirandello, the role of the writer was fundamental, and he refers to playwrights as "artists", at times as "poets", as if to emphasise the literary and artistic significance of their work. The actor at this stage was for him an essential though unfortunate part of the process of creating theatre, since the actor inevitably changes the original composition of the writer and alters it in performance.

"Illustrators, Actors and Translators" dates from 1908, the same year in which he published his *Essay on Humour*, and much of the earlier "Spoken Action" essay is repeated in this longer work. He develops his ideas on the role of the actor, drawing parallels with what he perceives as the equally flawed task of the illustrator, whose job it is to interpret the written text and produce a pictorial version, and the translator, whose task involves re-writing an author's original text in another, alien language.

The flowery, often opaque philosophical language of "Illustrators, Actors and Translators" conceals one interestingly modern point. In his attempts to distinguish between the concept and the sound of a word, Pirandello prefigures what Saussure was to describe as the "signifier/signified" distinction that lies at the heart of contemporary semiotics. Moreover, in his recognition of the impossibility of a single reading or single interpretation of a text, he anticipates later twentieth century debates on the plurality of reading.

Pirandello's essays place him in the context of Italian and European theatre history as a man with roots firmly in the century of his birth. He was a product of the latter part of the nineteenth century and his values reflect that position, just as they also reflect the fundamental problem for an Italian - and more so for a Sicilian - intellectual in the period of turmoil following unification. After centuries of fragmentation, the impulse was towards the creation of a national culture, and at first the enthusiasm with which Italian writers adopted naturalism, creating their own school of *verismo*, suggested that this might be the way forward. But the painful psychological and social realism of *verismo* that could so easily be turned to bathos was not an adequate base on which to construct a newly emergent national tradition, and Pirandello's rejection of naturalism was understandable. A man of the middle class, Pirandello's hopes for Italy were coincidental with his strivings for upward social mobility, in keeping with millions of others of his time, and he therefore rejected both the over-emphasis on the miseries of the poor and the aristocratic excesses of the protagonists of the poetic school of writers, exemplified most obviously by D'Annunzio, perceiving these two lines of development as extreme. Faced with no models in Italy, it was only to be expected that he would turn to models from other traditions, and the essays show clearly that he was receptive to a wide variety of ideas and influences from elsewhere.

Document No. 1: Spoken Action 1899 (L'azione parlata)

What I mean by this is: dramatic dialogue. It would seem to me to be a suitable occasion to draw the reader's attention to this splendid definition which, alas, is not mine, since almost all contemporary dramatic output has its roots in narrative and derives its plot material from novels or short stories, rather than from drama, which is, inevitably, bad. Firstly, because a story in the narrative mode, generally speaking, cannot be adequately reduced and adapted to the needs of the stage, and secondly, because of the tyranny and, in my view, misunderstood rigorousness of modern techniques, a veritable Procrustean bed, which both restricts and diminishes that accumulation of material. It is of course true that even Shakespeare took the plots for some of his plays from Italian short stories, but which playwright ever transformed a story into action from start to finish better than he did, without ever sacrificing anything to the foolish demands of techniques that are only superficially disciplined?

Every descriptive or narrative prop should be abolished on stage. Can you recall Heinrich Heine's marvellous fantasy on Geoffrey Rudel and

Melisande? "Every night in the castle of Blaye one could hear a rustling, a scraping, a whispering: suddenly the figures in the tapestry began to move. The troubadour and his lady stirred their ghostly limbs from sleep, came down from the wall, moved round the room below."[1] Well, the dramatic poet must use the same miracle as that performed by the ray of moonlight in the ancient, uninhabited castle. For did not the greatest ancient Greek tragedians create that miracle once, Aeschylus in particular, breathing a powerful lyric soul into the grandiose figures in the magnificent tapestry of the Homeric epic? And those figures began to move and speak. Through the miracle of art, characters should step out from the written pages of the play, alive in their own right, just as the Lord of Blaye and the Countess of Tripoli stepped down from that ancient tapestry.

Now this miracle can only happen on one condition: that a language can be found which is in itself spoken action, the living word that moves, the expression of immediacy at one with action, the single phrase that must belong uniquely to a given character in a given situation: words, expressions, phrases that are not invented but are born when the author is fully at one with his creation so as to feel what it feels and to desire what it desires.

In discussing dramatic dialogue, I am not concerned therefore with the outer form, although in the work of our own dramatists it is badly flawed, due to a fundamental defect in their work. What they do is to focus on a given *fact* (when they see one) or a given situation. They have, or believe they have, a perspective on a given feeling or situation in life that they believe is original and which they think they can turn into a play, rather like a conclusion to be drawn from a process of reasoning. To this, they add external elements, carefully studying patterns of relationship, which they graft together and combine. Having thought of the *fact,* they set about devising the characters most suited to reinforce that fact. There may be three, five or even ten of them, and they spread the parts around, giving some more to do and some less, occasionally even thinking about the actor who will have to act that part, leaving him wretchedly to find inspiration through his skill according to the roles.

That is how it is done. And no one thinks or wants to think that it ought to be done the other way round: that art is life and not a process of reasoning, and that if one starts with an abstract idea, or with an idea suggested by a fact or by a more or less philosophical consideration and devises symbolic images through a process of cold reasoning and studious thought, what results is the death of art itself. The play does not make people: people make the play. And therefore one must have people before anything else, living, free and active. In them and through them comes the idea of the play, the first seed in which their destinies and their form is contained, for inside every seed the living being is already stirring, and within the acorn there is already an oak tree with all its great branches.

When we talk about *dramatic style*, a sharp, incisive, fast moving, passionate style is in our minds. But in talking about theatre we need to extend the meaning of that word *style* or even to reinterpret the word altogether. For style, the intimate personality of the dramatist, should not emerge in the dialogue, in the language of the characters of the play, but should instead be revealed through the spirit of the story line, in the way this is shaped and drawn out and in the means used to develop it. If a dramatist has truly created characters, if he has put human beings on stage and not puppets, then each person will have a particular mode of expression, so that in reading it, the play will seem to have been written by several people and not by a single author, and to be made up of individual characters within the action and not by a single author either.

Now I must admit that it is this point which seems to me to mar the plays written so far by Gabriele D'Annunzio.[2] His plays appear too obviously devised by their author and rarely, if ever, spring from the characters themselves. His plays are essentially *written*, they are not *alive*. I do not know how far my colleagues on the *Marzocco*[3] will share my views, but I feel that the author has not been able to relinquish his own personal style, his own special mode of expression and has not been able to give any of his characters a separate individuality independent of his own.

A word of warning, however: I certainly do not agree at all with those few men who might be termed *theatre professionals* who have greeted D'Annunzio's work with a sort of respectful pity, treating it as the whim of an author whose reputation was established in another field and who is therefore out of place in the theatre because "he lacks experience in the tools of the trade". His work is judged to be literary and not theatrical, but bear in mind that this judgement is based not on any stage contrivance but on the way in which the plays are written.

Theatre for these people is not an art at all, it is virtually a trade. Nor do they consider a play to be a literary work. The slovenliness of so-called French conversational style - this is the stuff with which their dialogues are padded.   At times one can hear the shallow ring of a silly remark overheard in a drawing room or in the street, at other times the crumpled trace of a lawyerish tirade. And even here the characters all talk in the same wretched way without any individual speech patterns. So even though up to now D'Annunzio has written *elaborately* instead of just writing good plays, these others have written *coarsely* and therefore badly.

And this situation is unlikely to change unless it is fully understood that every action and every idea contained in that action needs *free* human individuality before appearing in the flesh, living and breathing. And in that free human individuality, to use a Hegelian phrase, *pathos* must be the motivation, the need for characters. Of course a character will be that much more determined and superior the less he is, or seems to be, subject to the intentions and devices of the writer, to the need to develop the imaginary fact. And the less he shows himself to be the passive instrument of a given action, the more he will reveal his own being together with a concrete particularity in every gesture. Since the various complex elements in a character must be blended in with a given plot, located solidly in a given situation, they must find expression in an essential physiognomy that serves all purposes and results in specific actions.

All of our being is always in all our actions. What can be seen is merely in relation to another immediate action or to one which appears to be immediate, but at the same time the totality of being is evoked. It is like the face of a polyhedron, touching the respective face of another the same, but nevertheless without excluding the other faces looking out on every side. The greatest difficulty for an artist to overcome is simply this:

to merge the subjective individuality of a given character with his place in the play itself, to find the word that fits the immediate action taking place on stage and at the same time expresses the totality of the character who utters it.

And how many writers today are capable of overcoming that?

Document No. 2: Illustrators, Actors and Translators, 1908 (Illustratori, attori e traduttori)

Some time ago in France it became fashionable to use photographs to illustrate certain novels and short stories, examples of so-called realism that seeks to restrict art to pure and simple imitation of nature. Now for that kind of work, which has no other ambition than to appear as a photograph of contemporary life, we can agree that this new kind of machine-produced illustration is indeed suitable.

I recall the novelist in Maupassant's *Notre Coeur* who "was armed with a vision that took in images, attitudes and gestures with the precision of a camera".

Behind the character of Lamarthe in that novel, Maupassant himself was concealed, and it is well known that Flaubert had advised him: "Look carefully!" - since in his view the strength of art lay in doing just that - "go for a walk and then tell me in a hundred lines everything you saw".

But neither Flaubert nor Maupassant, great artists as they were, succeeded in being two photographers, in spite of their theories. Moreover, the former did not even succeed in being a true naturalist. This difference between art and nature, constituted precisely in the changes that art makes on nature, is quite obvious in Flaubert's ironic disdain for the mediocre realities he chose systematically to describe and which he instinctively hated. It is also obvious in Maupassant's proposals continually to contrast secure, firm instinct with uncertain, indecisive reason, thus showing the basis of our existence to be bestiality itself, and showing how that solid basis can sustain itself against the vagaries of the imagination and the errors of the intellect.

So they were painters, if anything, not photographers. Nor were they painters in the manner understood by Blaise Pascal. He took up Aristotle's concept in the *Poetics* (and subsequently repeated many times by others), but failed to take into account the refraction of objects in the artist's mind, when he expressed the belief that there can be no other aim in painting than to arouse admiration "for the resemblance to things we do not admire in the original" and exclaimed, "Painting is mere vanity!".

Let us return to illustrations.

They are immensely popular at the moment, not only in books, magazines and newspapers, but everywhere: and - it must be said in passing - in music.

When a musician takes a play, or a bad play, but one which is complete in every detail (such as *Tosca*, for example, or *Fedora*) and frames it and fills it out with musical orchestral comment, bringing in little pieces of melody here and there, is he not also an illustrator, even though working in another field?

We know that the libretto for an opera ought to be virtually unintelligible to the reader, and seem stunted or cut off as a work of art; in other words, it ought to leave the reader suspended, dissatisfied, desperately wanting the rest of it, not as an addition but as part of it - that is, the music which has to be joined and integrated with the text to form the complete work of art: the opera. Anyone who sets *Tosca* or *Fedora* to music shows that he has not understood or will not understand what an opera is or ought to be, for the simple reason that in such plays, however well written, music only represents a lazy, superficial trimming, and, in the classic sense of the word, is also an unworthy contamination.

Just as, in my view, is equally the case with the photograph or sketch in a book of poems.

For if music offends because it introduces vague feeling, true to its own forms and modes, into precise ideas and representations in a realist drama, then the illustration offends because it determines too much and almost fixes in too precise an expression the images of the poet, when it does not actually falsify them.

This same aesthetic problem has been discussed for centuries, and was resolved by Lessing against the ideas of Spencer on the close links between poetry and painting in the ancient world, and the ideas of Count Caylus who rated a poem more or less highly according to whether or not a painter could depict it. It is the aesthetic problem that Croce[4] wrongly declared does not exist, believing as he did that the relationship between the aesthetic, that is the artistic vision, and the physical, that is the instrument which serves as aid to the reproduction, is purely intrinsic.

Now for me, in art, what Croce terms theoretical activity is less than nothing unless the artistic is integrated in the practical activity that has become one with it. Neither the communicative means of aesthetic representation (words, music, colours, etc.) nor technical skills have any extrinsic relationship with the internal aesthetic. On the contrary, in art they actually *are* the aesthetic, not a single aesthetic but several aesthetics. For me, in short, technical skill is that very spiritual activity that slowly frees itself in movements that translate it into a language of appearances: technique is the free, spontaneous, immediate movement of form. The painting emerges from the soul of the painter and descends to his fingers, moving them, and does not cease until it can see itself reflected on the canvas.

Execution is therefore conception itself, alive in action. From the artist's inspiration what must follow is the craftsman's cold skill. It is a question of creating a reality that is both material and spiritual at the same time, as the actual image of what lives within the artist's mind. It is appearance that may also be image, but become tangible. Now this could not happen unless the image itself had a spontaneous tendency to transform itself into the movement that will bring it into being. Practice, technique, work has to be spontaneous, almost unconscious. Any skills acquired cannot be used after reflecting on them: technique in the artist has to become virtually an instinct; and create precisely in itself that mobile, certain instinct, that species of fatality which, acting on desire, makes the image respond to the movement that expresses it. Being able to appropriate the technical language of art to the point of being able to speak it naturally is the prime condition of being a true artist.

In this sense, it must be understood that art comprises all practical activities, techniques, communicative methods of representation, the physical in relation to the aesthetic whose unity cannot be safeguarded but must be compromised, seeing two where there can only be a single one. And it will therefore be easy to see that this aesthetic factor cannot be merely one alone, the same for all the arts; since the external difference of the various arts implies that the internal factors are also different. An artist does not become a painter, musician or poet by chance or practice, as Croce thinks. Some people gain a vague impression from a landscape rather than an image; some see vague forms rather than precise visions, but always have their souls stirred by deep feelings and find their natural language in music. The painter thinks in visions; the logic of the painter, one might say, is the expressive play of light that can gleam or darken at will, and his feelings have colour and form, or rather, colour and form are feelings for him.

And the poet is truly less limited than the painter and less free than the musician. Of course it sometimes happens - and we have many examples of this - that a visually imaginative writer sees rather more than he thinks, and that a philosophical painter thinks rather than sees. The writer sketches in ten pages that which should be seen at a glance; the painter overlaps his own successive ideas in an image that divides them in the same way as the action of the mind that conceived them. In both cases the painting will need a commentary: the painter will need one in order to be understood, the writer in order to be seen.

Cesareo[5] writes that: "When Lessing, in the *Laocoon*, delineates the boundaries between painting and poetry he treats it as a question of technique and we cannot say that he is wrong to do so. The technique of painting which is the instantaneous representation of space, nevertheless excludes the progress of time: through the laws of physics we cannot see two different aspects of the same thing at one and the same time. And so the technique of poetry, which is the representation of several consecutive moments of time, excludes the excessive lingering over details of every moment; through the laws of the psyche we cannot take in the single whole image of things thought of at different moments in time. The more immediate the sensitive perception of a thing, the more it will be forbidden to the poet to break it down into parts; the work of art is not perception, but it is ruled by the experimental results of that perception and a single, synthetic perception cannot break up into delayed, analytical, unsuitable sensations. This would be to decompose the concrete unity of perception in a system of feelings: the individual would not be expressed psychologically, but logically. It is permissible for the poet to represent successive perceptions of time; it is not permissible for him to describe the details of an instantaneous vision of space. For this purpose we have the connotative paintings of men and women, the prolix descriptions of living nature or still life that Zola liked, the reshaping in verse of the contents of famous paintings and similar time-wasting activities that are absolutely not poetry. But, we might say, how can a poet represent his intuition of beauty, a woman, a garden, a stormy sea, the starry firmament and so forth? We cannot say how; there are norms for the criticism of expression but not for its production. All that is necessary is for the poet not to oppose himself to the techniques of his own art." And suffice it to think of Dante and how he represented Beatrice's beauty, or to quote the old but ever important example of Homer who does not so much describe Helen's beauty as the astonishment of the old Trojan men who see the fatal woman go by.

From all this it can be seen that painting is more restricted than poetry; and that an illustrator, no matter how well he interprets the poet's feelings, will never succeed in rendering that which is variable in the poetic expression simply because of the very nature of his art. Feeling made visible and reproduced in all the outlines of the drawing becomes sensation instead. The poet's images, once fixed, diminish.

This I repeat, happens when the illustrator does not falsify, that is, does not interpret the poet's images wrongly. And faithful interpretation is so difficult, it is well-nigh impossible. The better the artist, the more he will see and express in his own inimitable way. Three painters given the same conditions of light and space, if they had to paint someone in front of them, alive and breathing, will paint three different portraits. Imagine what they would do with an idealised figure, with the fictitious scene from a book. Anyone can see what happens when they have had the misfortune to see their own novel or story published in some magazine or other, with illustrations.

And in another field, in another medium, there is the impossibility or very near, of a faithful interpretation of anything written for the theatre. Because, in dramatic art, what is staging if not a huge, living illustration in action? What are the actors if not illustrators in their own right?

But necessary illustrators in this case, alas.

*   *   *   *

When we read a novel or a story, we amuse ourselves in depicting the characters and the scenes as they are described and represented to us by the author. Now let us suppose for an instant that these characters suddenly, miraculously leap out of the book alive before our eyes, in our own room and begin to speak in their own voices and to move and act without any narrative or descriptive assistance from the book.

Nothing to be surprised at. This miracle is precisely what the art of theatre performs.

Do you recall the beautiful fantasy novel by Heinrich Heine about Geoffrey Rudel and Melisande?

> Every night in the castle of Blaye one could hear a rustling, a scraping, a whispering: suddenly the figures in the tapestry began to move. The troubadour and his lady stirred their ghostly limbs from sleep, came down from the wall, moved round the room below.

Here the miracle is effected by the ray of moonlight in the old uninhabited castle. The greatest Greek tragedians had created it, breathing a powerful lyric soul into the grandiose figures of the magnificent tapestry of the epic poem and the ancient Hellenic legends. Shakespeare put it into effect later, taking the most tragic, most complex figures out of English and Roman history, besides a few others out of the clever plotting of Italian stories.

But in order that the characters can leap out of the written pages alive and animated, the dramatist must find a language that is at the same time spoken action, the living word that moves, the expression of immediacy that is one and the same as action, that unique expression that can be nothing else and belongs to one given character in one given situation; words and expressions that are not invented but which are born when the author is so involved with the character that he can feel as it feels, desire as it desires.

The most simple phenomenon that lies at the basis of the creation of every work of art is this: an image (that is, the one kind of immaterial yet living species that the artist conceives and develops with the creative activity of the spirit) an image that tends to become, as has already been said, the movement that brings it into being and makes it real externally, outside the artist. The creating process must emerge alive from the conception and through that conception alone, not through any contrived stages but freely, that is urged on by imagination itself which wants to liberate itself, that is to translate itself into reality and live. It is a question of creating a reality, as I have said, which will be both material and spiritual just like the image, an appearance that will be the image become tangible. Together with the network of images structured within the artistic conception there must also be a network of structured movements, put together through the same set of relationships, and tending to create an appearance which will not change the basic characteristics of the image, nor disturb in the slightest degree that spiritual harmony it lays claim to, but will bring it into the real world. All the features of the conception must therefore be found likewise in the execution.

Can this happen in dramatic art?

Unfortunately, there always has to be a third, unavoidable element that intrudes between the dramatic author and his creation in the material being of the performance: the actor.

As is well known, this is an unavoidable limitation for dramatic art. Just as the author has to merge with his character in order to make it live, to the point of feeling as it feels, desiring as it desires itself, so also to no lesser degree, if that can be accomplished, must the actor.

But even when one finds a great actor who can strip himself completely of his own individuality and enter into that of the character that he is playing, a total, full incarnation is often hindered by unavoidable facts: for example, by the actor's own appearance. This inconvenience can be improved slightly by the use of make-up. But we still have what is more an adaptation, a mask, than a true incarnation.

And that same distasteful surprise that we feel when we read an illustrated book, and see in the illustrator's portrayal a picture quite different from the one we had imagined of a person or a scene, is felt by a dramatic author when he sees his own play acted out by actors in a theatre. No matter how much an actor tries to enter into the author's intentions, it will be hard for him to succeed in seeing as the author saw, in feeling as the author felt and in transferring the character onto a stage as the author would have wished.

If the miracle referred to above could ever happen, that is, if we could ever read a novel and see the characters come alive before us out of the pages of that book and see them not as we ourselves had imagined them but as they had been conceived by the illustrator in the sketch that had affected us so distastefully, then we should surely feel a sense of outrage, like a nightmare, and we would rebel and shout: "No, not like that, not like that at all!"

And yet how many times does some poor dramatic writer not shout: "No, not like that" in the same way, when he is attending rehearsals and writhing in agony, contempt, rage and pain because the translation into material reality (which is necessarily someone else's) does not correspond to the ideal conception and execution that had begun with him and belongs to him alone.

And yet, reminded by the author, the actor suffers too, in his own way, because the actor thinks and feels differently and perceives the author's vision and will as an outrage, and a nightmare. Because unless the actor wants the written words of the play to come from his mouth artificially, through a mouthpiece (and he cannot possibly want that to happen), then he has to reconstruct the character, that is, construct it in his own way himself. The image that has already been expressed must be taken back and restructured inside him so that it can become the movement which will carry it out and make it real on stage. For the actor too, the process of making has to come straight out of the process of conception, alive, and only because of that can it have being, through movements suggested by the image itself as it lives and is active not only within him but becoming one with him, body and soul.

Now since it was never spontaneously born in the actor but aroused in his mind by the writer's expression of it, can the image ever be the same? Can it ever not change and be modified as it moves from one consciousness to another?

It will not be the same. It will be an approximate image that is more or less similar, but never the same. That given character on stage will repeat the same words of the written play, but the character will never belong to the writer, because the actor has recreated it in himself, the character's expression belongs to him even though the words might not, the voice, body and gestures are all his.

And the same is true of the translator.

*   *   *   *

Illustrators, actors and translators, if we consider the matter, all find themselves in the same position regarding aesthetic values.

All three are faced with a work of art that has already been set down, that is, has already been conceived of and effected by someone else, and the first must translate it into another art form, the second must translate the material into action, the third into another language.

How can these *translations* be possible?

Benedetto Croce rightly notes in his *Estetica* (*Aesthetics*) that it is impossible to reduce something that already has its own aesthetic form into another form, albeit aesthetic, and that every translation inevitably diminishes or spoils. The expression remains the unique property of the original, since the other is more or less defective and therefore not a proper expression; in short, it is impossible to have a reproduction of the same original expression, at best one can have a similar expression, something that is more or less close to the original.

Croce says this about actual translations proper, that is, in the case of someone translating from one language to another, but it is also true in the case of illustrators and actors, just as it is true that in all three cases what happens is a diminishing and a spoiling.

Let us first consider the case of the actor.

Now then. Material reality, the daily reality of life limits all things, both men and their actions, impedes and distorts them. In reality the actions which bring a character into focus stand out against a background of unimportant details and small everyday trivia. A thousand unforeseen unexpected obstacles change actions, disfigure characters; vulgar minutiae often diminish them. But art on the other hand frees things, frees men and their actions from these valueless details, these vulgar obstacles and trivial miseries; in a certain sense, art abstracts them, that is, art rejects everything that gets in the way of the artist's conception without thinking twice, and instead brings together everything that is in harmony with it and gives it greater strength and richness. So a work is created that is not without order, as Nature is (at least overtly) and spiked with contradictions, but is rather a tiny world in which all the elements are linked and cooperate with one another. Precisely in this sense does art idealise. Not simply because it represents types or depicts ideas; it simplifies and concentrates. The idea that one has of one's characters, the feelings that they inspire, evoke expressive images that are united and combined. Useless details disappear, everything that is imposed by the living logic of the character is brought together and concentrated in the unity of a being who is both less real and at the same time more true.

Now, what does an actor do? He does exactly the opposite of what the writer does. That is, he makes more real and yet less true that character created by the writer, he takes away from him just so much ideal, superior truth as he gives back in ordinary, material reality, and so makes him less true because he is translating him into the fictitious, conventional reality of the stage. In other words, the actor gives an artificial consistency, in an illusory, artificial environment, to persons and actions that have already received an expression of life far superior to material contingencies and which are already alive in the essentially ideal characteristics of poetry, that is, in a superior kind of reality.

The same thing happens in the case of translations (of literary works only) from one language to another. We are reminded of Dante writing in the *Convivio*:   "And therefore let each man know that nothing which is harmoniously inspired can be transposed from its own language to any other, without breaking all its sweetness and harmony".

It is like transplanting a tree that has sprung from one soil and flowered in one kind of climate into a soil that is not its own; its foliage and flowers will be lost in the new climate, and by foliage and leaves I mean native language, and by flowers I mean those particular graceful features of the language, its essential harmony, all of which are inimitable. The words of a given language have a value that goes beyond their material meaning for the people who speak it, and which is created by many things that cannot be analysed even by the most careful study, since they are, like the soul itself, intangible.   Every language arouses its own specific feeling and even the graphic form of the words has value.   If we translate the German word *liebe* with the Italian *amore*, we are merely translating the concept of the word and nothing more - what happens to the sound?   That particular sound with that particular echo that it arouses in the mind and on which perhaps the writer had wanted to focus at that precise moment?   And what about the grace that derives from the special placing of words, constructs and specific attitudes belonging to a given idiom?   We will therefore certainly be able to transplant the tree, but we shall compel it to grow other kinds of leaves and to flower with other kinds of blossom: leaves and blossoms that will gleam and rustle in other ways because they will be stirred by another ideal breeze, and in the best of cases, the tree will no longer be the same, while in the worst of cases, that is, the more we try to force it to retain its former luxuriant growth, it will appear bare and wretched.   In his *Pensieri e discorsi* (*Thoughts and addresses*) ,[6] Giovanni Pascoli talks about art and the ways of translating art, specifically works by ancient classical authors, and says:

> ...What is translating? - this was the question put a short while ago by that most gifted of German philologists, who then replied: - The external must become new; the internal must remain as it is. Or, more precisely, the soul must remain the same while the body is changed: true translation is metempsychosis. I could not put it any better, but that astute definition does not diminish the doubts we all share.   To change clothing (*travestire*) in Italian can be '*travestimento*' and '*travestire*' has an unfortunate ring in Italian. *
> So let us be clear: we have to give the ancient writer new clothing but we do not have to misrepresent him.   In the past we have misrepresented   too   many,   both   on   purpose   and   at   times unknowingly.   Perhaps the special fates of language and literature are to blame, but the fact remains that the problem of translating is not a simple matter for us.   We do not always or even often have the right clothing to offer to the ancient writer of prose or poetry, or rather we do not often have it ready unless we know how to choose it there and then.   And as for metempsychosis (at least with regard to translation) is it right to distinguish between body

---

*Translator's note: *Travestire* can signify "change, dress up", but also "travesty, misrepresent".

and soul? It is not right. If we change the body, we change the
soul as well. It is therefore not a question of preserving in ancient
form the soul in a new body, but of deforming it as little as
possible; it is a question of choosing new clothing for what is
ancient in order not to make it appear as different and as absurd
and clumsy as possible. In brief, we must endeavour while
translating to keep the same proportions as the original text in the
relationship of thought with form, body with soul, internal with
external.

Pascoli notes quite rightly that it is wrong to distinguish between body
and soul. If the body changes, the soul changes too. But what does he
mean by body and soul? By body, he means the form, by soul he means
the idea, and alas, he falls into a trap, as if De Sanctis[7] and all those other
worthy gentlemen who discussed aesthetic criticism had spoken to us in
vain, the old error of classical and Romantic criticism, that of perceiving
form as something *exterior*. If artistic content could really be separated
from its form, thought would be body and form would be soul. The
thought of an ancient or modern writer, what he wanted to express, the
concept of things, can, in fact, be rendered adequately, be translated into
another language and be understood, but we cannot render the soul, that
form which in art means everything. If the body, that is the idea, is
changed, the soul, that is the form, changes too, that much is obvious. But
if we recreate the body, the idea, can it be given a new soul, a new
expression? This is what translation tries to do. And it tries to do the
impossible: as if a corpse could be revived by breathing into it another
soul.

*   *   *   *

What the Count of Caylus wanted was for the greater or lesser worth
of a poem to be judged according to whether it could be depicted by a
painter or not. Similarly, the greater or lesser worth of a play is judged by
the evidence of performance, and it is even said that a *written* play as
expressed by the writer cannot be evaluated. Now I have shown that what
takes place in the theatre is not the true, proper representation of the
genuine, original expression, but is a translation, that is something which
resembles the original more or less closely, but which is never the same,
and I have given reasons why it is also a diminished and more or less
destructive expression.

To a much lesser extent, we can also say this of the translation that
everyone makes of someone else's work, not so much during the actual
reading of it, when the mind is disposed to accept and consider the ideas
that the writer is expressing or the impressions aroused by the work, but
when we describe those ideas and impressions of the reading to others or to
ourselves, that is when we think over the written text. When the transfer is
made from one mind to another, changes are inevitable. How many
writers are unhappily surprised to see what happens to their own work
when it goes through the mind of some reader or other, who perhaps

congratulates a writer for having created certain effects he never even dreamed of creating.

- How you made me laugh!

And the writer never even intended to cause the slightest smile. And how rarely does it happen that a writer feels that his own work has remained the same, or nearly the same for a critic or a reader as he tried to express, and does not become something else that is badly thought out and arbitrarily reproduced.

In this lies the greatest difficulty for the critic. First, we must never assume that other people, outside ourselves, are only as we perceive them to be. If we do assume that, it means we have a unilateral consciousness, that we have no consciousness of others, that we do not realise the others in ourselves, to use Josiah Royce's expression, with a living expression both for others and for ourselves. The world is not restricted to the ideas we may have of it; outside us the world exists in its own right, alongside us, and therefore in our representation we have to try to realise it as best we can, creating a consciousness in which it can live as itself in us, and see it as it sees itself, feel it as it feels itself.

Now this process of realisation is extremely difficult. It can happen, in fact it happens quite often, that while we read we think over what the writer has thought rather better, and express for ourselves rather better what the author expressed badly or did not express at all, and so find in a book something that is not there, something that we are able to realise which the author was not able to do.

It is the same for the actor who, in performance, improves instead of diminishing, enhances instead of reducing the play that has been entrusted to him. But in such a case (which in truth is not infrequent) then it is due to the merit of the actor and the play is bad. So a translation can be better than the original, but in that case the original becomes the translation, in so far as the translator has taken the original as rough material and recreated it with his own imagination, just as the actor has taken the play as a rough draft and breathed life into it on stage. The same can be said of those illustrators who take as inadequately expressed material the work of secondary, descriptive or decorative writers, those who have a pictorial imagination and are not able to render their paintings visible with the inadequate means of communication of words.

Now a while ago a Rome newspaper organised a referendum among contemporary theatre writers to find out whether actors had the right to evaluate plays, both tragic and comic, offered to them for staging, or, to put it another way, whether actors should be regarded as the best instruments of communication between a writer and the public, as the most legitimate judges.

Among those who replied to the questions posed by the referendum, no one was able to tackle the most important question, the one which any penetrating, understanding mind would have seen as running through the questions. It is usual to say that the writer is not the best judge of his own work and that an actor cannot recognise the artistic merits of a play because he is only looking for *a good part* in it, and if he finds one, then the play is good, and if he doesn't, then it is bad.

Now it is a fact that reflection for a writer is almost a form of feeling: as the work comes into being, that process of reflection criticises it, not coldly as a dispassionate adjudicator would do, analysing it, but gradually, thanks to the impression the work gives. In short, the work for the writer is a feeling analogous to that which it inspires in the spectator: it is *experienced* rather than *judged*.

The same thing happens with the actor, who cannot possibly be considered as the mechanical instrument who passively communicates. If he were to examine the work he is to play coldly, as a dispassionate judge would do, analysing it, and were to move on to playing his role from this cold process of examination, then he would never be able to bring a character to life on a stage. Precisely in the same way as a writer could never create a living work if he were not first inspired by a vision of the whole and composed all the different elements separately up to the point of bringing them together in a thought-out composition, in a carefully reasoned-through conclusion. The actor, in other words, *experiences* and does not *judge*. Just as the writer suddenly senses the subject he wants, through a feeling, a sudden surge of sympathy for an episode in life that is ordinary and unmeaningful for others, or in the telling of a story, so the actor has to feel an emotion, an unexpected sympathy for the part that he wants, he has to *experience* in himself the character that he will bring to life on stage.

Of course, it can happen that the actor who lives in the theatre and by the theatre, that is, by everything most conventional and trivial on a stage, is inclined to see all that is most theatrical in the work of art, just as happens to an illustrator, when given a book to illustrate, who can only see that which is most suited to be drawn. So the actor sees not so much the ideal reasons of art but the material reasons of staging and rather than seeing the superior truth of artistic expression, he sees the fictitious reality of his stage action.

Now is it not the case that those theatre writers who compose plays for specific actors are abandoning that specific truth which is essential and characteristic of art in favour of the artificial sham reality of the stage? Can they not be compared, in one sense, in terms of aesthetic judgement, to those writers who write the blurbs under cartoons in illustrated magazines? At all events, both groups show that they do not understand the level of idealism and the duties proper to their art. But nevertheless the theatre writers are undoubtedly the most deserving of excuse, because when they do this, all they are doing is being loyal to the sorry necessity of their art. They are paying attention not so much to the creatures of their imagination, but to a given actor or actress in a scene, and allowing themselves unhappily to be inspired or affected by their skill as performers. If they start with such more or less practical considerations and produce a work by a process of cold reasoning with images that have already been previously determined, incarnated in some actor, what kind of work can result? Slavish works, above all, for those same actors, for their means and attitudes, slavish works that do not belong to art, because art has an unalterable need for its own freedom.

The play does not make people, people make the play, and first of all there must be free people. The drama will emerge from them and in them.

Every idea, every action needs *free* human individuality in order to materialise before us and live, and that individuality will be an effective motive: in other words, what is required are characters. Now a character will be just so much more determined, superior, the less he is or appears to be subject to the intentions and mannerisms of the author and the requirements of the development of the imaginary factor. And the less he appears to be the passive instrument of a given action, the more he will reveal in his every action almost a whole being together with a concrete individuality.

The characters created by Shakespeare are like this. And here it is hard for the theatre illustrators to win. For why are there so few great interpreters of Shakespeare? Because his tragic figures are so great and have their own characteristics so strongly delineated that very few can manage to fulfil them, and as soon as someone tries to create his own sketch in the design of the scene, he shows up his own tiny stature, his absurd insignificance.

The play, the work of art already expressed and alive in its own essential characteristic ideal qualities is one thing; its representation on stage, the translation or interpretation of it is quite another: this is a copy that more or less resembles the original and which lives in material reality that is nevertheless fictitious and illusory. If we wish to draw the ultimate conclusions from this aesthetic enquiry, if we do not want a translation that is roughly faithful, but want the original actually in the theatre, then we have the commedia dell'arte - embryonic blueprint, and the free creativity of the actor. Yet, this would always be, as it was, trivial, because it is an improvisation, in which it would not be possible to discard those obvious, common details and there could not therefore be that ideal simplification and concentration characteristic of the superior work of art.

Dialect Theatre

At the age of forty-three, motivated primarily by economic concerns, Pirandello turned again to theatre and wrote the play *Limes of Sicily (Lumie di Sicilia)* which was presented in 1910 at the Metastasio Theatre in Rome by the Sicilian actor manager Angelo Musco along with the early *The Vice (La morsa)*.

The essay on "Sicilian Theatre?" shows the predicament in which Pirandello found himself in attempting to create a regional theatre. His passionate involvement with the creation of a Sicilian culture caused various problems, chief of which was his realization that a regional culture cannot be exported and therefore only exists within the region itself. The poverty and widespread illiteracy in Sicily, together with the depopulation caused by high mortality rates and emigration meant that Sicily was not the ideal place for the emergence of the educated, middle class public that Pirandello felt was essential to good theatre. As a result the kind of theatre that could flourish was the artificially Sicilian theatre of comic stereotypes and situations and for that Pirandello had nothing but contempt. His essay on Sicilian theatre shows the limits of his idealism, and points the way forward to the time when he would abandon all pretence of creating a regional theatre, concentrating instead on the establishment of an Italian Art Theatre.

Document No. 3: Sicilian Theatre?, 1909 (Teatro siciliano?)

Let me say from the outset that I am not opposed to dramatic art, only to that trivial, conventional world of the stage in which the dramatic work is, regrettably, inevitably doomed to lose some of its ideal, superior truth even while it gains material and at the same time fictitious reality.

For me, the work of art, be it tragedy, drama or comedy, is complete when the author has appositely expressed it. What we hear in the theatre is a translation of that work, a translation which, as I have already shown elsewhere, inevitably spoils and diminishes the original. Art does not represent types, nor does it depict ideas, but by its very nature it idealises, that is, it simplifies and concentrates, freeing things, and people and actions from the obvious, commonplace constraints, from worthless minutiae, from vulgar daily obstacles. In a certain way it abstracts them, that is, it rejects out of hand everything that stands in the way of the artistic creation and pulls together everything which gives it greater strength and richness of expression in accordance with it. The idea that the writer has of his characters, the feelings that they produce, arouses the most apposite images, while useless details disappear. Everything that the living logic of the character imposes is brought together and concentrated in the unity of a being who is less real, perhaps, but at the same time is more true.

The actor does the exact opposite of the writer. He makes the character, created by the poet, both less true and more real. He gives a contrived consistency in an artificial illusory environment to people and to actions who have already received an expression of life superior to the dictates of material being and who are already alive in their essential idealism characteristic of poetry.

If at times this kind of translation into material reality which we see on stage does not spoil or diminish the play, it means that the writer was not able to express himself adequately in his work, he has not created a true, authentic work of art that can express itself and live freely and completely by itself, but has created instead a kind of sketch (like a scenario of the commedia dell'arte, rather more fully drawn but a sketch nevertheless) which has to be created by a given actor or actress on stage.

The thing created can only exist once and be original, and it must belong either to the poet or to the actor. If it belongs to the poet, then the actor is merely producing a more or less faithful translation, one which is more or less effective, but remains for all that a translation, and so inevitably diminished and slightly spoiled. If it belongs to the actor, then all the poet does is provide the material that has to be developed and shaped on stage.

Having stated this, I cannot turn my mind to considering translators', or rather actors', explanations. I was asked the following question about the newly emerging Sicilian dialect theatre which those two renowned actors, Grasso and Aguglia,[8] are now taking on tour round the world, causing audiences to be enthusiastic and appalled at the same time: can a Sicilian author claim to own his own subject matter in view of the tastes and tendencies of the public and the expressive qualities of the performers?

We must reply that if art wants to be art, it needs its freedom above all else. To try and force a playwright to take into account the actors' performance abilities when he is busy creating is rather like trying to force a poet to write a sonnet in rigid rhyme. The writer does not have to adjust to the performers' abilities, the performer has to adjust to the writer, or rather to the work that he must bring to life on stage. If the actor does not know how to do this or cannot do it, then that means he is a bad actor or a limited actor. And if Sicilian dialect theatre does not have actors today, then this signifies that it still does not have the life and strength in itself to make more actors, and that Sicilian dialect theatre does not exist and that given the present conditions we cannot make one. At best we can have sketches and commedia dell'arte scenarii for the brilliant talents of Mr. Grasso and Madame Aguglia.

And as for the tastes and tendencies of the public...what public? This is another even more complex problem.

What are the reasons why a writer might be persuaded to write in dialect rather than in the standard language?

The act of creating, the activity of fantasizing which the writer has to use, is the same, regardless of whether he is using standard language or dialect. What is different is the means of communication, the patterns of speech. Now what are words taken like that in the abstract? They are symbols of things in ourselves, they are the larvae that our feelings must bring to life and that our willpower must move. And before feelings and will can intervene, the word is pure objectivity and knowledge. Now these words, this means of communication, this awareness are universal, not universal in the abstract sense since there are no logical abstractions, but general representations. They are, for example, *house, road, horse, hill,* etc., in general, not that certain house, that certain road, that certain horse, that certain hill, with a determined way of existing and a determined and particular quality. Historical and ethnographical reasons, conditions of life, habits, customs, etc. either enlarge or limit the boundaries of our awareness of these objectivizations of things within us.

Now certainly a large number of words in a given dialect are more or less (give or take the phonetic changes) the same as those in standard language, but as concepts of things, not as a particular expression of them. As an abstraction made from that particular feeling, even the concept of things will not be intelligible wherever there is no knowledge of the words as such. But there are a great many other words that can only be understood within the boundaries of a certain region, once the particular feeling and the special echoes that their sound arouses in us is taken into account.

Now why should a writer choose to employ such a restricted means of communication when the creative activity that he must make use of will be the same? For a variety of reasons, which limit dialect production as knowledge because they are indeed reasons of knowledge, of words, or of things represented. Either the poet does not have the knowledge of the widest means of communication, that is, standard language, or else he does, but feels that he cannot use it with the same liveliness, with that precisely appropriate spontaneity that is a principal, indispensable condition of art; or else the nature of his feelings and images is so deeply rooted in the earth whose voice he seeks to be, that any other means of communication except dialect would seem unsuitable or incoherent; or else what he wants to represent is so local that it could not be expressed beyond the limits of a knowledge of the thing itself.

A dialect literature, in other words, is made to remain within the boundaries of dialect. If it goes beyond them, it can only be enjoyed by those who have some knowledge of that particular dialect and of its particular uses and customs, and in a word of the particular life expressed by that dialect.

Now outside the island, what does anyone know about Sicily? People have a very limited knowledge of a few characteristics, violent ones that have by now become mannered.

The dramatic character of Sicily is fixed by now, typified in the terrible, marvellous bestiality of Giovanni Grasso.

Lacking any other awareness of Sicilian life in all its variety and diversity, clearly every other expression of Sicilianness becomes almost meaningless. Let us not talk therefore about the tastes and tendencies of the public, here we are talking only about knowledge.

A dialect theatre that represented the varied, diverse life of Sicily could only be enjoyed and greeted with enthusiasm in Sicily. Outside Sicily the only success it could have would be through those manifestations that are well known, that have now become typical. That is, Mr. Grasso and Madame Aguglia can be successful because they don't even have to speak to be applauded; all that's needed is mime.

To sum up: do we want to create a truly Sicilian dialect theatre or do we want to manufacture a Sicily for export via Mr. Grasso and Madame Aguglia?

That splendid poet and dramatist Nino Martoglio tried the former quite seriously and neither could, nor did have any success outside Sicily, not on account of the tastes and tendencies of the public, I repeat, but because of the ignorance in which the public still remains regarding Sicily, regarding that basic first stage of any artistic creation, the cognitive material. Art is creation, it is not learning, but art is not created *ex nihilo*, it needs knowledge. It needs, that is, to be known first in the abstract and in the word which is its symbol and general representation, in order to be understood and to be enjoyed in all its individuality for the subjectivizing of the objectivity in which art consists.

Martoglio's attempt failed. Mr. Grasso and Madame Arguglia in contrast are successful, but I do not believe that Sicily has very much cause to rejoice.

Letters to Martoglio (1917)

The following letters to Nino Martoglio[9] show both the extent to which Pirandello was committed to dialect theatre and the growing frustration that he felt at the inability of the public and the performers to understand the seriousness of his work. In the letter of 29 January 1917 which is largely a personal complaint about the way in which *Liolà* has been set aside in favour of a play that he calls a common farce, Pirandello expresses the sense of injury he feels and hints strongly that he is reaching the end of his patience. In the letter dated 4 November 1917 the dilemma he was facing becomes clearer; he did not feel able to accept the kind of character acting popularized by the popular Sicilian actor, Giovanni Grasso and sees himself compelled to work with Angelo Musco despite the latter's failure to understand the value of Pirandello's writing.

From these letters it is clear that Pirandello was unhappy with the status quo. He complains about money, about the way in which the audiences in Milan respond to dialect theatre, about Musco's choice of repertoire, and shortly after these letters were written he had begun to move away from the ideas he had cherished for a regional theatre. In the essay *On Dialect*, written in 1921, his change of position can be clearly seen. Arguing that it is not only not a defect but is actually a great advantage, Pirandello claims that Italian writers "create their regions" themselves and are therefore dialect writers only in this sense.

With the decline of *verismo*, the Italian version of naturalism, the problem of the cultural autonomy of the various regions with their own distinctive dialects and traditions was once more brought into focus. The contribution by *veristi* writers in Sicily, Naples and the south of Italy had created a link between naturalism and these economically deprived areas, but although he made use of *veristi* techniques in his prose works and in some of the plot outlines for his plays, Pirandello was more concerned with the establishment of a national theatre tradition, one in which the regions would have a role to play but would not dominate at the expense of others. In this respect his class position is the key to understanding why he withdrew from working in Sicilian theatre; he belonged to that group of some of the new property owning class that had become wealthy during the industrialization of the nineteenth century and he believed firmly in a concept of art that was both educative and based on moral integrity. Since the mainland audiences could never experience Sicily as anything other than a theatrical fabrication and since even actors like Musco seemed prepared to humour them in this, then Pirandello could not continue to write for what he perceived as a bankrupt endeavour. His way forward lay in the establishment of a serious Art Theatre into which the wealth of regional cultural traditions could, hopefully, be poured.

Document No. 4: Letter to Martoglio, 29.1.1917

Dear Nino,

Yesterday I received your letter, following the two telegrams from the day before and now today (Sunday), I have received your postcard.

I am delighted that you have decided to do *Darkness (Scuru)*.[10] But everything I hear about the whims of the Milanese audiences and the series of productions that hardly fit in with this serious and splendid work of yours really discourages me. It clinches my condemnation of Musco. And at the same time it's more evidence of the banality of my work. Musco is doomed to farce, and everything you tell me about the massive financial profit from *The last nose (L'ultimo naso)*[11] just goes to reinforce that. What is even more serious though, since it shows Musco's own tendencies and intentions, is the further proof supplied by his insistence on keeping

Giufà's Art (L'arte di Giufà)[12] in repertory because, dear Nino - and you know my sense of brotherly honesty with you - in my opinion that work does you no good at all. It's a patchy play, in which the comic mask never manages to fuse together with the satirical nor with the parody and therefore none of these have any artistic consistency. But though I might be permitted to offer you a friend's advice you have to do as you think fit. Remember, I'm not talking about the type of play, I'm talking about the play itself, which seems faulty to me because it isn't coherent. So far as the type of play is concerned, I find it obvious that Musco has proved that he can't free himself from being the slave of his public, so it is clearly exactly what's needed.

But you know I just don't feel like being something for Musco to parade as his own - and I'm talking about you as well in this, not just myself - I had *Think it Over, Giacomino! (Pensaci, Giacomino!), Liolà, Cap and Bells ('A birritta cui' ciancianeddi), The Jar ('A giarra), Sicilian Limes (Lumíe di Sicilia)*,[13] you had *The Lottery Cheats (Riffanti)*[14] and *Darkness (Scuru)* - just so that Musco can get credibility as an artist every so often and then go back to driving the public and himself mad with his farces. I might have been able to attempt some artistic revival of a new Sicilian comic theatre with you, but I just don't feel like cooperating in trying to prop up a shack full of puppets for farce makers. I can use my talent in other ways and get other kinds of satisfaction.

I'm not telling you this for any immediate reason Nino, I'm telling you for the future. I've gone back to dealing with Simoni.[15] I don't want Simoni to commit me to anything in future in the sense that he might make me write a few plays for Musco every year. I'm not going to write any more. He can keep the ones he has and that's it.

I have to admit that the response to *Liolà* really depressed me. I thought *Liolà* was a joyous piece of writing and I'm sure I won't write anything so pleasant again. But if the result with Musco was that, then what on earth can I write for him in future? The performances at the Diana[16] were cut short, partly because of the quarrelling that took place, partly because of the snow that trapped people at home. But how did it happen that Musco wanted to give you - and rightly so - proof of the pleasure he felt at the reconciliation by taking on *St. John the Baptist (S. Giovanni Decollato)* and *Mainland Air (L'aria del continente)*[17] straight away? And now, instead of giving me just such a tiny sign of pleasure, after *L'aria del continente* and *San Giovanni* and *The best man (Il Paraninfu)*[18] he hasn't done *Liolà* again, he's doing *L'ultimo naso* instead? First he's doing *L'ultimo naso*, then he's doing *Liolà*. And why? It's perfectly obvious: *L'ultimo naso* is a farce and *Liolà* is a work of art; in three nights *L'ultimo naso* will bring in at least 4,000 lire or more and in five nights *Liolà* will bring in - peanuts? I just don't know. I have nothing to complain about. That's the way things are, in view of the way the public feels about Musco and Musco's forgiveness of the public. But I have had enough. O no, Nino, I'm not going to stand for this rejection as well. That among all the new plays Musco has done at the Diana the first one he does again is *L'ultimo naso* because *L'ultimo naso* is a farce, because *L'ultimo naso* as a farce brings in money! First *L'ultimo naso* and then *Liolà* - no! When Musco knows quite well that *Liolà* didn't get good reviews and couldn't do as well as it should have at the Diana because of the terrible weather conditions. In spite of my name, in spite of everything that happened, all the adverse weather conditions that obstructed my work, and in spite of having given you justifiable indications of how pleased he was. And after that heavy-going production of the *Paraninfu,* Musco should have chosen to do *Liolà* first. He didn't and so has insulted me yet again and more seriously in spite of your presence. I don't understand how you managed not to see it for yourself.

One more thing to draw to your attention and then I'll let it be. I have not heard anything at all lately about *The Jar ('A Giarra).* Is it being performed? Is it off? They had me write it in a rush because they wanted to do it in Rome, no less, last October for the evening in his honour along with *Damned smell (Puzzu malidittu).*[19] In Florence, they told me that he was definitely going to do it in Milan at the Olimpia. Now silence reigns. What is that supposed to mean?

Let's abandon this list of complaints and talk about something else. I have resigned myself these days to letting everything be, because otherwise I would have to keep on starting from scratch every two minutes. I'm tired and sick of it all. That's enough.

I'm sending you the script of *Think It Over, Giacomino! (Pensaci Giacomino!)* in Italian for Armando Falconi.[20] I think it's come out better in Italian than in Sicilian, much better in fact. I think Falconi could do it well. It would be better still if Ruggeri[21] were to do it, or De Sanctis[22], but I don't know either of them. I'd be obliged if you would find out whether Falconi likes the piece and whether he will do it before long, if for no other reason than to make sure the script doesn't get lost. Do you realize that three typed copies cost me 20 lire? I'll put a second copy in the post today or tomorrow for Lopez[23], and keep the third copy for publication, firstly in the *Nuova Antologia*[24] and then with Formìggini[25].

I have just received the accounts for the Società degli Autori[26] for the period from October to December 1930, with an intake of L.1571.37. As you see, I am now rich and can stand up to the blackmail you told me about.

All good wishes, Nino.

Document No. 5: Letter to Martoglio, 4.2.1917.

My dear Nino,

Allow me first of all to congratulate you most warmly on your *Darkness (Scuru).* I am assured of its success, and I am sure that the public will respond in the same way as the critics and the play will have a good long run. Please send me a cable and let me know what happens so that I am not left in suspense for the whole day.

Now let me reply to your letter in detail:

(1) I really do not think that Grasso's[27] remarks carry any weight at all regarding the piece as a work of art, even if they may have some value due to his artistic temperament, which in any case is more clearly evidenced by his actions than his words. I just do not feel that there are any tedious passages. The actions and the speeches of the minor characters

are all absolutely necessary, just as the protagonists' are too. Of course the play is written for Musco and I can see that Grasso finds it uncomfortable to be in a role that fits Musco perfectly. I have already stated that I simply cannot feel Grasso, his temperament does not inspire me, it is too primitive, too crude for me, because my work is reflective. So I could never adapt to writing anything for him, nor adapt my plays to the needs of his personality. Consequently it is useless to send me back the script. If he wants to do it, then that is the play and that is how the play will have to remain. I might possibly be able to make a few cuts or reshape a little here and there if you think it necessary once you and Musco have begun rehearsing it, and I have given you my fullest permission to make that kind of amendment. I do not mind such slight changes because they appear to be demanded by the play itself once it is tried out in rehearsal and its life is put to the test, but the kind of changes and cuts that Grasso is asking for would be imposed by him and not by the play at all. They would arise from his particular temperament, which I consider to be antithetical to my artistic conception. *The Vice (La morsa)*, which I shall be sending to you in a few days' time will be ideal for Grasso.

(2) Musco's performances. You have not replied to me about the serious insult caused by the decision to put on *L'ultimo naso* before *Liolà*. In fact you suggest that if you had taken a different stance then neither *Think it Over, Giacomino! (Pensaci, Giacomino!)* nor *Liolà* would have been put on again. And would *L'ultimo naso*? In which case, why does Zerboni protest about that play? Does dear Zerboni want neither the farce nor the serious play? I have to admit that I cannot understand it at all. My complaint was based on what I had heard from you in your previous letter, that is your account of Musco's delight shown to you at the supposed reconciliation by putting on *San Giovanni* and *L'aria del continente* straight away. I do really think that he could have shown some of that pleasure to me too by putting on *Liolà* as principal work in the Diana's season. Instead he did *L'ultimo naso*. And there you are. But enough of that. I repeat that I shall simply let everything take its own course. I notice that *Liolà* was only performed once when it was put on again.

(3) What you tell me about Falconi is fine. My only concern was about losing the script which cost me so much. If he takes it and decides to do it, even on condition that he does a one-off performance, then that is fine too. We shall have to see about setting something up with De Sanctis when I receive the offprints from the *Nuova Antologia*. In the meantime I have sent Lopez another copy.

(4) Box office receipts. I cannot complain, dear Nino, about having taken L.1500 last session. In fact I told you jokingly that I was *rich,* in reply to the playful hint you gave me about the financial flop. The only bitterness to be felt is when comparisons are made with the returns from *L'ultimo naso* which you tell me are tremendous. I do not feel that it can be considered to be a huge financial success when *two new plays*, however difficult, *over a three-month period*, in four cities, Rome, Florence, Bologna and Parma, only make L.1500. But I must be satisfied.

(5) *L'arte di Giufà*. Please do not think for a moment, dear Nino, that I have any objection *whatsoever* to this work of yours being kept in repertory. I know how difficult things are for you and you may imagine

how little I want to make life even harder. I was merely talking about the convenience for you as an artist if you were to drop it. But if you need to use it for the sake of your family, then to the devil with anything else, go ahead and use it without thinking twice. You will have my full approval. Not only that, but I shall admire you greatly because I will understand the sacrifice it will have cost you.

And now let me conclude as I began, by wishing you every success with *Scuru*. I shall anxiously await your telegram and then expect a long detailed letter after the first night.

Do give your wife my best regards.

With all good wishes.

Luigi

Liolà was Pirandello's last play in Sicilian; but the relationship between language and dialect continued to interest him and in 1921 he made a spirited defence of both dialect as a medium for theatre and of Italy's multilinguistic heritage. "On dialect" ("Dialettalità") formed part of the ongoing discussion on the role of theatre in Italy and was published as part of a debate on experimental theatre in *Cronache d'attualità* (*Current Affairs*), August-October, 1921.

Document No. 6: On Dialect 1921 (Dialettalità)

No one could claim that we have not made progress in the field of literature. But as for theatre, I see that we are still discussing Ferdinando Martini's[28] notions about a theatre that does not exist, and can never exist because Rome is not Paris, and there is not a spoken language common to the whole of Italy, and national unity is so recent that it has not yet been able to give to our way of life those customs and particular characteristics which theatre, if it is to be a national theatre, must reflect; the same old story, that is, of the cannon that cannot fire for a hundred thousand reasons of which ninety-nine thousand nine hundred and ninety-nine are superfluous given that there is no gunpowder. That is, that Rome is not Paris.

What a magnificent spectacle of an exemplary faith in one's own opinions! Art as mirror: or rather, life as already formed material, according to those customs and with its fine, indelible and unmistakeable particular characteristics; and art, heigh presto!, like a mirror, that depicts life just as it is, through an almost historical function. Basically the same mentality as those so called *men of the theatre*, who would rather have their throats cut than recognise that theatre too belongs to the field of literature. With this difference, however, that these men of the theatre are at least more logical; for, as far as I know, Martini has never considered the theatre as a separate genre, having nothing to do with the literature of the people; nor, for that matter, has he ever denied that Italy has a literature as far as the other literary genres are concerned, while still not fulfilling those conditions which he considers necessary and indispensable for the existence of a national theatre.

Now how is it that Martini has not noticed that there is no reason why a novel which takes place in Lombardy or the Romagna, Piedmont or the Veneto, Tuscany or Sicily and without any of the habits and characteristics being the same from one region to another and without there being one common spoken Italian language, how is that a novel, then, can call itself Italian and, if it is worthy, become part of what we call our national literature, while a play cannot?

Having acknowledged, but not allowed, this long since superceded art/mirror aesthetic, there remains the question why, in order to produce a national theatre, this mirror of art should necessarily function as it is presumed it does in France, where, that is, appearing before such a great centre as is Paris, it depicts the customs, characteristics, the language and the life of the whole nation; which moreover is not in the least true. And there also remains the question why the customs, characteristics and language of, say, Lombardy, for the sole reason that they are not those of Romagna, Piedmont, the Veneto, Tuscany or Sicily, are not for that reason Italian. And why an art that depicts many small, varied and diverse aspects of a nation rather than one big and common aspect should for that reason cease to be art.

Ferdinando Martini is looking for the common characteristics of a generality and naturally he cannot find it with us here in Italy; because in Italy, of course, and not just now but from way back in time, I mean since the birth of Italian literature, the generality has this special factor: the dialect factor, to be understood as a true and unique idiom, that is, an essential property of expression which, as Dante wrote: "in qualibet redolet civitate, nec cubat in ulla."[29] And this is because there occurred in Italy something that did not occur anywhere else: every region, or in some cases every city, was both small in itself and yet often at the same time a very large nation (and Rome was also the world). But this is not a defect but rather a richness - a richness of history, of life, of forms, customs and characteristics. And it is sheer stupidity of art to want to renounce all of this by envying France for those smooth common characteristics of its generality.

Two distinct and almost parallel strands run through our literary history: two styles, one of things, the other of words, and we can follow them through, close but opposed as they are, right up to our own times: Dante and Petrarch, Machiavelli and Guicciardini, Ariosto and Tasso, Manzoni and Monti, Verga and D'Annunzio. In the former, words indicate things and only have value as words inasmuch as they express things, so that between things and the reader or the spectator who sees them, words disappear and are there not as words but as the things themselves. In the latter, things are not of value in themselves but only for how they are expressed and the man of letters is always there, even if he does not reveal himself, wanting to show you how clever he is in saying this to you. On the one hand then, a construction built from within, things that are born and are placed before you so that you can walk among them, breathe them, touch them; earth, stones, flesh, those eyes, those leaves, that water; and on the other hand a construction from without, words from linguistic repertoires and phrases that know how to tell you these things and which in the end, since you are aware of the game and the skill, leave you tired and satiated.

And if we look carefully into these two strands, or families, or categories of writers, with reference to that hoary old question of the language, seen as it always is from the outside, and not as creation, that is to say sought externally, like an object which naturally nobody manages to find, we see in the second group the written and literary language as it lives - or fails to live; and in the first we taste the flavour of local dialect, beginning with Dante, who saw the vernacular residing in dialects. But how appropriate this flavour of local dialect is in a nation that is only really alive in its variety and therefore in the varied languages of its many regions.

And this dialect factor is not a mirror in writers but a true, real and continuous creation of form.

The life of a region, let us say of Sicily, in the reality that Verga gives it, that is, as he sees it, feels it, as it acts and moves in him cannot be expressed in any other way than how it is expressed by Verga. That language is his own creation, made not with words which are common to everyone and want to be beautiful or ugly for themselves, but made precisely with those things that he wants to say and which he makes live by saying them.

And if writers are able to "create their region" and are in this sense dialect writers it is not some defect in them, nor, I repeat, poverty, but on the contrary, a truly living richness for their literature.

Virgilio Talli and *Right You Are! (If You Think So)* (1917)

After *Liolà*, Pirandello turned in earnest to writing plays in Italian. In 1917 he approached the director Virgilio Talli suggesting that he might like to direct his new play *Right You Are! (If You Think So) (Così è (se vi pare))*. The play was in fact staged by Talli the same year and has subsequently become one of the most popular of Pirandello's plays. In his letter quoted below Pirandello explains that there is no part in the play for Talli's leading actress, Maria Melato, and is clearly aware that this could be seen as a major drawback. He suggests that she might be willing to take the very small but significant part of Signora Ponza, who appears, heavily veiled, at the end of the last act to utter symbolic words that provide the play with its inconclusive conclusion. As will become evident from the following passage taken from Sabatino Lopez, *Dal carteggio di Virgilio Talli*, Talli, who was later to direct the first production of *Henry IV (Enrico IV)* had a different solution.

Document No. 7:   Correspondence between Pirandello and Virgilio Talli

"I have ready for production a three act comedy, or rather, a parable, which is truly original, new in both its conception and development, and very daring, as far as one can tell from a reading, destined to have a definite effect, on account of the intense interest it excites right from the beginning of the first act and which is maintained and increased through the other two. It is called *Right You Are! (If You Think So)* and is based in a strange and unusual way on the validity of reality. *Right You Are! (If You Think So)* or so it is, if it seems to you to be so, which is to say, it's no longer like that if you don't think so.

There is however a problem, a serious reservation. Unfortunately, there is no part in the play for Maria Melato - unless that great actress, in deference to a writer who is not in his first youth would agree to speak, as only she can, and in the way I believe they should be spoken, the last lines of the play which hold all the play's meaning: words put into the mouth of a woman whose face is hidden by a thick veil; a woman who is very much alive in the play, and yet is also a symbol of truth."

In his reply Talli wrote:

"I've at last found an Italian writer who has something to say of his own. Rarely has a dialogue such as the one in your play so raised my spirits and shown me in its writer an outstanding aptitude for writing for the theatre. The philosophic side of the parable is lively and clear and a number of unusual qualities catch the attention in these three acts of yours. I fear only that the psychological sharpness and carefully maintained human aspect of the characters, the totally unconventional development, the simplicity of the language, will not be enough in the public's eyes to justify the overly drawn out tension on which the action depends, nor will they be enough to make the drama of the Ponza family, precisely because of the way the situation is drawn out, credible. I am not making judgments, please understand, I speak only as a man who has experience of the stage and its public. I personally have experienced a real enjoyment in reading *Right You Are!* I will not hide that I was occasionally tired by the flurry of contradictory revelations between Signora Frola and her son-in-law. But the very lively sense of curiosity, so variously presented by the supporting characters, brought to mind writers of other periods, austere, reserved and overly verbose writers, and my attention was immediately revived.

But after I had finished reading I must confess that I could not hide the suspicion that the qualities of *Right You Are!* are those to be enjoyed in solitude, in that absorption that instinctively imposes itself on settling down to read a work whose author can guarantee delight. I was not able to overcome the fear that the work lacks some of the *faults* that would ensure its theatrical success. It is of course the case that the attack on Signor Ponza's secret is constructed with a growing intensity on the part of his persecutors and with a variety of analysis; but it seems also to be the case that the situation remains static. And so what would hold the play together would be its form, that is, that part of theatrical knowledge to which the public has become unaccustomed over the years. And so I do not know how far one can trust that the play would hold together.

Let's do as follows. I will stage the play. I will see how the three acts come out in the early rehearsals and then I will straightaway let you have my definite impressions. I am certain that when the characters are acted I shall be able to understand with greater clarity what hopes and near certainties I should be able to entertain for your work. I want to see my few fears destroyed before giving you a categoric "yes". And I beg you to attribute this caution to my lively admiration for your talent."

Pirandello replied that he was happy with this arrangement and added:

"The public? For my part, I have made my public expect from me all kinds of outrageous things. I have always gone out to offend my public and the public knows it. It is my delight and my pleasure. All my work has always been and always will be like that: a challenge to the opinions of the public and above all a challenge to its moral - or immoral - peace. I will get away with it this time too, you will see. The public will be annoyed, it will complain, but it will be unable to resist being fascinated by what my parable signifies."

When Virgilio Talli cast the play, Maria Melato took the part not of the symbolic character, Signora Ponza, but of Signora Frola, Signor Ponza's mother-in-law, who has a much more substantial role in the play. Since then, other young actresses have distinguished themselves in this role, including Berthe Yolande and Marta Abba. That Virgilio Talli was conscious of breaking tradition with this innovation is evident in the following letter he wrote to another author who was trying to persuade him to cast Maria Melato in the part of an old woman in his own play.

"That part, which you insist on seeing as negligible, was assigned by me to Signorina Melato because I was and still am convinced that only an actress of considerable ability and experience could give to the part those delicate nuances which would retain the *doubt* which is at the basis of the play. And Signorina Melato brought to *Right You Are!* a real personal triumph, especially in Milan. Since I do not believe a young actress does herself any harm playing the part of an old lady I distributed the parts of *Right You Are!* with the absolute conviction that I was doing right without prejudice to any one. But surely you will not tell me that in your play, *Crystal Cranium*, there is a part which involves the same responsibility as Signora Frola. And if you were to say that, I think you would be wrong and I would have to explain your mistake by considering that you were not sufficiently persuaded of the merits of Pirandello's play or that you did not consider it good enough to warrant a break with theatrical conventions as serious as the one I dared to make when I presented Maria Melato in a grey wig. And that would lead to the conclusion that you and I were not agreed on Pirandello's play and that you persist in professional prejudices from which I have freed myself for some time."

Theatre and Literature

The essay on Theatre and Literature takes up once again two of Pirandello's favourite problems - the role of the writer in creating good theatre and the conflicting role of the actor who re-interprets the writer's text. In tone and in content it belongs with "Spoken Action" and "Illustrators, Actors and Translators" but Pirandello now speaks with experience of the theatre world.

The essay ends on a note that seems almost to preface Pirandello's next move towards the establishment of an Art Theatre.

On the whole, as exemplified in his essays up to 1918, Pirandello's views on theatre are fairly conservative and show affinities with the European Arts Theatre movements in general. In his belief in the need for a high status theatre, for a predominantly intellectual theatre with the writer at its centre, he reveals the gap between his own concepts and that of other contemporary attempts to enlarge the frontiers of theatre.

Document No. 8: Theatre and Literature, 1918 (Teatro e letteratura)

Certain distinguished dramatic writers, the *theatre professionals*, reject literary labels altogether because they maintain and indeed affirm that theatre is not literature, it is simply theatre.

It would, of course, be far too spiteful to suggest that the source of their rejection lies in the fact that they earn *serious* sums of money, unlike the *derisory* sums forthcoming to those poor deluded beings who are men of letters.

It is, of course, true that these people have established the theatre business like any other commercial enterprise, able to defend itself against equally commercial enterprises involved within the same company; we have only to think of leading actors as a group, together with theatre owners and managers; or norms established for terminating the contract of a given company; of the distribution of venues; of the percentage on the box office fixed in advance, with so much for the first performance, so much for the second, and so much for all the rest. The collection of this has been entrusted to the *Società degli Autori* in Milan, and at the end of each three monthly period they send their members a breakdown of the intakes, which quite frankly - no matter how badly a play has done - are always far higher than anything which the writer of stories and novels might expect from the sale of his books (not to mention what happens to poets).

There is no doubt that none of this has anything at all to do with literature. We can even allow the fact that *their* theatre, the one they want, which is the production of substantial numbers (or even not so substantial numbers) of comedies and serious plays for the theatrical marketplace is not literature. However, it remains to be seen (since of course it is not literature) quite how and under what new heading their comedies and serious plays should be placed when those scripts become printed texts and pass from the prompter's lips to the bookseller's display window as printed books instead of typewritten manuscripts; when they pass from the lavish profit earned by the voice and gestures of the actors on stage to beg for the miserly three lira quoted on the cover, among all those other beggars seeking public charity, all those novels and stories by the wretched men of letters.

But let us move on from all this talk of finance and come to the present. There is a great misunderstanding that needs to be clarified here, and that misunderstanding is contained precisely in the term *literature*.

Distinguished dramatic writers and theatre professionals write badly, not only because they do not know how to write well and have never bothered to learn, but because they honestly believe that good writing in the theatre is too literary. They believe that you have to write in that conversational mode they use which has nothing to do with literature, because the characters in their plays and in their light comedies - so they say - are not literary people and therefore cannot possibly talk as if they were. They have to speak in the way everyone else speaks, with no literariness.

In taking this approach, they never remotely suspect that they are confusing *good* writing with *elaborate* writing, or rather, they do not perceive that they have fallen into the trap of equating *good* with *elaborate*. They do not realise that the elaborate writing of some false literary figures can be equally criticised as extravagent at the opposite end of the scale that judges their writing bad. Literature that is not art is bad literature, whether produced by those writing *elaborately* or by those writing *badly*, and is therefore to be condemned as such regardless of whether the authors wish to be considered men of letters.

Writing a good play, whether a comic play or a serious one, does not mean creating characters who speak in a literary language, a language that exists only on the page and not in true speech. This kind of writing is elaborate. Characters should speak according to their own personalities, to the conditions in which they find themselves, according to the action of the play. And this certainly does not mean that the result will be an everyday, non-literary language. Because what does 'non-literary' mean to the writer of a work? Language cannot ever be *everyday,* because it will belong to a given character in a given scene, and will be an intrinsic part of that character's passions and games. And if all the characters speak in their own special way and not in the vulgar carelessness of an imprecise language that only denotes the inadequacy of the writer who could not find suitable words because he does not know how to write, then the play will be well written, and a well-written play, particularly if well shaped and well acted, will be a literary work in just the same way as a good novel is, or a good story or a good lyric.

The truth is that these distinguished dramatic writers and theatre professionals have stayed locked inside the blessed poetics of naturalism which confuses the physical, the psychological and the aesthetic in such a pretty way that the aesthetic acquires a character of mechanical necessity and a fixity which belong purely to the physical (at least in theory, because this was impossible in practice).

Now it should be borne in mind that art in any of its forms (by which I mean the art of literture, of which drama is only one of its many forms) is not imitation or reproduction, it is *creation*. There is the question of whether and how language should be spoken, the immense difficulty of finding a language that is actually spoken throughout the Italian nation and the linked question of the lack of a truly national Italian way of life that can provide material and character for an Italian theatre, as though the nature and task of art were the reproduction of that life which anyone can perceive from external factors, and there is the question of all the other distressing trivialities and empty superstitions of so-called technique that ought to reflect action as we see it happen before our eyes in everyday reality (at least in theory, because it is impossible in practice): all of this is a torture filled with the voluntary torments of an absurd system and an abhorrent poetics which is fortunately totally out of date but which, I must repeat, still holds the loyalty of these distinguished dramatic writers.

It is not a question of imitating or reproducing life, for the simple reason that there is no life which stands as a reality in itself and can be reproduced with distinctive features of its own. Life is a continuous, shapeless flow that has no other form than that which at times we give to it. It is infinitely variable, infinitely changeable. In reality everyone creates his own life, but this creation is unfortunately never free, not only because it is subject to all the natural and social needs that limit all things, all men and all their actions and change and deform those actions so that they fail and collapse wretchedly. It is never free because in creating our lives our will always or almost always tends towards ends of practical utility - the achieving of a particular social state, etc. which leads to acts of self-interest and forces us to make sacrifices or to carry out duties which are inevitably a limitation of freedom.

Only art, when it is true art, can create freely. It creates a reality that contains within itself alone all its needs, its laws, even its own end, since the will is not involved elsewhere in overcoming all the obstacles blocking those goals of utilitarian practicality towards which we incline in our creations of self interest, by which I mean everything that we force ourselves to do each day in our own lives. Instead, the will moves inwardly inside the life that we intend shall have a form, and it is this form which is still within us but alive in its own right and therefore almost completely independent of us, which becomes movement. And this, of course, is the only true technique: the will intended as the free, immediate and spontaneous movement of form, when it is no longer ourselves who desire this form to take a certain shape for purposes we intend, but it is that form in absolute freedom, having no other end except itself, which wills itself to be and which evokes in itself and in us those actions capable of putting it in motion in a body, in a statue, a painting, a book. Only then can the aesthetic fact be carried out.

Normally, in the outside world, the actions that throw a character into relief stand out against a background of empty contingencies and ordinary details. Unexpected, base obstacles arise suddenly and knock actions aside, coarsening characters. Occasional small pettinesses often diminish characters altogether. Art frees things, frees men and their actions from these valueless demands, these vulgar details, these base obstacles, these petty accidents, and in a certain way, art abstracts them. That is, without thinking twice, art rejects everything that obstructs the artist's conception and gathers together everything that gives it greater strength and richness in accordance with it. In this way a work is created that, unlike nature, is not without order (at least in appearance) and spiked with contradictions, but which is almost a tiny world in which all the elements reach out to one another and cooperate with each other. In precisely this sense can the artist be said to idealise. Not because he presents types and portrays ideas but because he simplifies and concentrates. The idea that he has of his own characters, the feeling that derives from them evoke expressive images and group and combine these together. Useless details disappear; everything that is imposed by the living logic of the character is united and concentrated in the unity of one being, as we must term it, that is both more true and less real at the same time.

But now here is where the inevitable subjection of the theatre lies, in contrast to the work of art which has had its one definitive expression in the pages of the writer. What is already expression and already is form has to become material - material to which the actors with their own means and capabilities must in their turn give form. Because if the actor does not want the written words of the play to come out of his mouth like sounds from a mouthpiece or phonograph (and he cannot possibly want this to happen), then he has to conceptualise the character as best he can and conceive that character again in his own way. The image that has already been expressed must return and be rearranged by him in order to become the movement which will render it real on a stage and bring it to life. For the actor too, of course, it is necessary that the portrayal should spring from the conception alive, by virtue of that conception, through movements suggested by the image itself, alive and active, not only inside the actor but become one with him and body and soul in him.

Now since it is not born spontaneously in the actor but is suggested in his soul by the expressions of the writer, can this image ever be the same? Can it remain unchanged and unmodified as it passes from one soul to another? It will no longer be the same. It may well be approximately the same image, may be more or less similar, but it will not be the same. The given character on stage will repeat the same words of the written play, but it will not be the playwright's play, because the actor has recreated it within himself, and the expression is therefore his, just as the words, the voice, the gestures, the body are all his too.

The literary work is the play conceived and written by the playwright. What we see in the theatre is not and cannot be anything other than a scenic translation. There may be many actors and many translations, all more or less faithful, more or less successful, but like any translation they will always be inferior to the original.

Because, if we think carefully about it, the actor must of necessity do the opposite to the writer. That is, he must make the character created by the writer more real and at the same time less true. He takes away just so much of ideal, superior truth as he supplies in basic, material reality. He makes the character less real because he betrays that character in the fictitious conventions of the stage. In short, the actor must necessarily give a contrived consistency in an artificial, illusory environment, to people and actions that have already acquired an ideal existence, which is that of art, and that live and breathe in a superior reality.

What then? Can the distinguished dramatic writers who see nothing but the theatre be right, when they argue and insist that theatre is theatre and is not literature?

If by theatre we are to understand the place in which afternoon and evening performances are held, with actors who are given plots and material to shape there and then into scenes of tragic or comic effect, then the answer is yes. But in that case, in taking up a position vis-à-vis art, they must resign themselves to standing in the same rank as those facile versifiers who fire off snippets of rhyme to go beneath cartoons in illustrated magazines. They are writing not for the text itself, but for its translation, and in that case, then truly their theatre has no need for literature. It is material for actors, to which the actors give life and consistency on a stage. In short, something like the scenarii of the commedia dell'arte.

But for us theatre has to be something else.

Notes for Section I

1. Pirandello is referring to Heinrich Heine's poem "Geoffrey Rudel and Melisande von Tripoli" from the volume *Romancero*, 1851. See Hal Draper (tr.), *The Complete Poems of Heinrich Heine*, Boston; Suhrkamp/Insel, 1982, for English version.
2. Gabriele D'Annunzio, 1863-1928, was a poet, novelist, dramatist and politician. Influenced by Wagner, he strove to create a form of tragedy suitable for modern times through poetry and spectacle. Despite his reservations concerning D'Annunzio, Pirandello agreed to direct D'Annunzio's *Iorio's Daughter (La figlia di Iorio)* in 1934. The designs were by Giorgio De Chirico.
3. *Il Marzocco:* a literary periodical founded in 1896 to which a number of the best known Italian men of letters contributed, among them Gabriele D'Annunzio, Giovanni Pascoli and Ugo Ojetti. It ceased publishing in 1932.
4. The ideas Pirandello is referring to here were expressed by Benedetto Croce (1866-1952) in *Estetica come scienza della espressione e linguistica generale* (1902) and *L'intuizione pura e il carattere lirico dell'arte (1908)*.
5. Giovanni Cesareo (1860-1937), poet and critic; his early criticism had positivistic leanings; he gradually adopted a more spiritual and idealistic viewpoint.
6. Giovanni Pascoli (1855-1912) was a major late 19th century poet, classical scholar and literary critic. *Pensieri e discorsi* is a collection of essays first published in 1907. The passage Pirandello quotes comes from his address "La mia scuola di grammatica" delivered in Pisa in 1903.
7. Francesco De Sanctis (1817-1883) was one of the great 19th century Italian literary critics whose *History of Italian Literature* (1870-1) is still a point of reference for students of Italian literature. He was much admired by Croce.
8. Giovanni Grasso (1873-1930), descendant of the Sicilian family of actors and puppet masters, abandoned the puppet theatre to concentrate on acting. Angelo Musco joined his company for a while. A very popular dialect actor both in Sicily and on the mainland, he was criticized for his excessive "realism" by both Pirandello and Verga. Mimì Aguglia was an actress in both Sicilian and Italian who later became a screen actress.
9. Nino Martoglio (1870-1921), man of the theatre, dramatist and poet; see Introduction p.3.
10. By Nino Martoglio.
11. By Francesco Sabato Agnetto. The play was staged for the first time at the Diana Theatre in Milan on 20 January 1917.
12. By Nino Martoglio.
13. All plays by Pirandello. *Cap and Bells* and *The Jar*, at this stage in Sicilian, were later rendered into Italian.
14. By Nino Martoglio. It had its first night at the Olimpia Theatre in Milan on 9 June, 1916.
15. Renato Simoni (1875-1952), dramatist, theatre critic, theatre and film director. His theatre criticism in the Milanese newspaper *Corriere della Sera* was held in respect by his contemporaries and was an important indicator of current trends.
16. Theatre in Milan.
17. Two plays by Nino Martoglio.
18. By Luigi Capuana.
19. By F. Fichera.
20. Armando Falconi (1871-1954), actor.

21. Ruggero Ruggeri (1871-1953), one of the great actors of the time, for whom Pirandello wrote several plays. His most important creation was Henry IV in the play of that name. Ruggeri appeared as a guest actor in Pirandello's company and toured with the company. See also Document No. 17.

22. Alfredo De Sanctis (1866-1954), actor.

23. Sabatino Lopez (1867-1951) prolific dramatist, theatre critic and prose writer.

24. *Nuova Antologia* began in Florence in 1866 as an erudite scholarly journal. It moved to Rome in 1878 and later became a coffee table magazine appealing to the Roman middle classes. It counted leading scientists as well as men of letters among its contributors.

25. Angelo Fortunato Formiggini (1878-1928), writer and editor.

26. As its name implies the Authors' Society, founded in the late nineteenth century, was formed to protect writers. It worked to ensure that the dramatist received a percentage from the plays' takings. It established that dramatists should receive 10% of theatre earnings; of this the Society took a cut of 3%.

27. The Grasso referred to here is Giovanni Grasso jr., the nephew of the Giovanni Grasso referred to in Document No. 3. The play Pirandello is discussing is *Cap and Bells*.

28. Ferdinando Martini (1841-1928), dramatist, theatre critic, writer and politician. Like Pirandello he supported state subsidy for theatre. His love for the theatre had a pessimistic side and he failed to recognize for what it was the new talent that emerged in the late teens and early twenties in Italy, rejecting both D'Annunzio and Pirandello.

29. Dante, *De Vulgari eloquentia*, I, 16: 'whose fragrance is in every city, but who dwells in none'.

SECTION II: INTERNATIONAL DRAMATIST: *SIX CHARACTERS IN SEARCH OF AN AUTHOR* AND *HENRY IV*

Six Characters in Search of an Author (1921)

The play that made of Pirandello an international dramatist is *Six Characters in Search of an Author*. It was first staged by Dario Niccodemi at the Valle theatre in Rome with Vera Vergani as the Stepdaughter and Giorgio Almirante as the Father on 10th May, 1921. This first night has entered the annals of theatre history on account of the play's tumultuous reception (see Introduction "The Years of Success" pp.11-14). Later in the year the play was staged in Milan at the Manzoni theatre, and this time the play was received more calmly, probably due to the publication of the text in between the two productions. In the future, Pirandello was to publish his plays when possible before their presentation on stage, probably to avoid a repetition of the events of the first night of *Six Characters*. By June of 1925, when the play was in the repertoire of his own company, the Teatro d'Arte, *Six Characters in Search of an Author* had been presented in ten countries and in as many languages. The first of these performances was a "green room production" put on in London by the Stage Society of the Kingsway Theatre on 27th February in 1922. The Lord Chamberlain, then empowered to censor plays, refused it a license for public performance; it was, however, reviewed, and we include Desmond MacCarthy's appreciation. In the autumn of the same year, the play was produced in New York, where the Fulton Theatre, under the managership of Brock Pemberton, staged a season of Pirandello plays (including *Henry IV* and *Right You Are (If You Think So)* and had its name temporarily changed to "Pirandello's Theatre" for the duration of the season. It was, however, the French and German productions that are best remembered and that were the most influential. In Paris, April 1923, Georges Pitoëff presented the play at the Champs Elysées theatre in Benjamin Crémieux's translation and this presentation was to have a lasting effect on future French theatre. It also had some effect on Pirandello's own view of the play. Some of Pitoëff's amendments were to find their way into the new Italian version published in 1925 along with the preface. Despite his statements in his theoretical writings that performances are potential travesties of dramatic texts, Pirandello appeared delighted with Pitoëff's production and there followed a long friendship and collaboration. Pirandello was less pleased, however, with Reinhardt's production in late 1924 and some of the alterations to the text (in particular, the more detailed description of the characters and their entry) printed in the 1925 version of the play can be seen as corrections of what Pirandello considered to be Reinhardt's misconceptions.

Six Characters in Search of an Author was quickly followed by *Henry IV*. This was first staged in Milan at the Manzoni theatre on February 24th 1922. It too gained international acclaim, being performed in New York in January 1924, with the title *The Living Mask*, in London in June 1924 and in Paris in February 1925 with Georges Pitoëff in the title role. Between 1921 and 1925, Luigi Pirandello was at the height of his international acclaim. It is not surprising therefore that he thought he would be able to realise at this point in his life his dream for an Art Theatre in Rome.

As the following two documents show, *Six Characters in Search of an Author* was initially conceived as a novel. The letter to Stefano is one of a number sent to his son at the front which provide information about Pirandello's involvement with theatre. The novel he mentions in this letter, *One, No-one and a Hundred Thousand* was not published until 1926 and was the last to be published of the seven novels Pirandello wrote.

The second prose passage is taken from an anthology of fragments of Pirandello's writing written on odd pages put together by Corrado Alvaro and others. These fragments were first published in *Nuova Antologia*, January 1934, with the title "Foglietti" and then reprinted in the *Almanacco Bompiani* for 1938. It is there that the fragment reproduced here is given the improbable date of 1910. This is the only part of the unwritten novel known to have survived, and may indeed be the only part to have been written, though it is well known that Pirandello destroyed many of his drafts. Interesting for an analysis of the future play is the concentration on the sexual shame of the Father and the sense of Pirandello's identification with the Father in contrast to the alienation from the Stepdaughter ("a perfect reality created by me, but who simply cannot involve me"); and in particular, despite the reference to "the scenes of the novel", the growing consciousness that the characters have the necessary autonomy to qualify as stage characters.

Document No. 9 - Letter to Stefano Pirandello, 23.7.1917 (extract)

I finally finished with the exams yesterday. I haven't written a word since June 7: just imagine! I'll get down to work again, but God knows how, as soon as I'm free... I've promised Talli a new play for the new season: *Mrs. Gelli, One and Two* (*La signora Gelli, una e due*), and I must finish the novel during this vacation. But my head is already full of new ideas! Lots of short stories... and a strange piece, which is sad, so very sad: *Six Characters in Search of an Author*: novel in the making. Perhaps you'll understand. *Six Characters*, caught in a terrible drama, who approach me asking to be made into a novel, it's an obsession, and I don't want to have anything to do with them, and I tell them it's useless, I'm not interested in them, I'm not interested in anything, and they show me all their wounds and I send them away...and so in the end the novel in the making will emerge complete. And then I've so many other plans in mind. "The Pain of Living like This" - a long short story. "The Divine Reality", another long short story, almost a novel. But first of all I want to finish *One, Nobody and a Hundred Thousand*.

Document No. 10 - Narrative fragment of *Six Characters in Search of an Author*

The girls' special hour. Madame Pace had told him that one of the girls had said she could not possibly come at any other time in the afternoons except between three and four o'clock and could only stay for that one hour, not one minute more or less, because she was still at school in the fifth form until three, and then after four she had homework to do and then at seven she had to accompany her mother in the carriage to the Pincio.

It was an ordinary five storeyed building in one of the busier new streets of the city. On the first floor there were banking offices, on the second were the rooms of one of the cleanest kind of "family boarding houses". Four rows of gold braid on the doorman's cap testified to the respectability of all the tenants, even the ones up on the fifth floor.

And yet each time he saw the doorman in the distance, he felt overwhelmed by a sense of burning shame, as if all those people who passed him by could read in his face the fact that he was going up to the third floor where a certain Madame Pace, whose establishment bore the outward signs of *Tailleuse pour dames*, performed a service on behalf of certain select clients (and perhaps their husbands too), a quite different kind of service, as so often happens in big cities.

He could not see himself as others saw him, hurrying past him in the street: an ordinary figure, anonymous, tall, large framed, well-dressed, aged about fifty, one among all the other more or less well-dressed unknown passers by. He knew himself; the street stretched before him carrying everything with it, crowded with people, and so it was as though that street and all those people were about to go in through that front doorway with him.

Contrary to the impression he must have given of being an ageing man, he could feel that grotesque, shameless desire shrieking within him, that feeling which would shortly push him in through that doorway. He could see with a brutal, savage nakedness that which was still undeniably young in him moving down that street, hidden by the serious, outer form of the ageing man. He should have been deep in a wood; instead he could see the city all around him, quite clean, with its shining panes of glass. And then, slowly, his glistening eyes began to harden over, and while his temples turned purple, close to blackish round his big, tingling ears, a convulsive shudder sent an almost catlike tremor across his left cheek down to the nostrils and his mouth twisted into a kind of coarse grimace. He stared at passers-by with his hard, glistening eyes and grinned like that to counteract his shame. He did not hear what other people were saying, their conversations, the greetings they exchanged as they walked past, the sound of wheels on tramlines, the buzzing, clanking of the electric tram-bells, cries of barrow boys and newspaper sellers. All that noisy, everyday movement of the street was just a hubbub in his ears, from which he had to tear himself away sharply with a kind of blind violence in order to go through the doorway. There, he had slipped in. The electric trams continued to grind along the tramlines with their bells clanging, the street sellers continued to shout out their wares, the newspaper sellers' cries continued, everyone went on with their conversations along the street, while he climbed the stairs of that building with a fierce, sad effort, trembling all over from the violence with which he had crushed all the noises of the street out of his mind.

What is quite funny really is that they left me and started acting out the scenes of the novel amongst themselves, just as they ought to be acted. They performed in front of me, but as though I were not there, as though they did not depend on me, as though I could not stop them at all.

The girl more than anyone. I see her come in... She is a perfect reality created by me, but who simply cannot involve me, even though I can feel the deep pity she arouses. What about the mother? Do you think about her? Her shame before her legitimate son: not being able to look him in the face, because in order to look at him she would have to cancel out the lives of her other children, the children of her pain and her shame, from another life of hers that he can never share.

Pirandello at rehearsals of *Six Characters in Search of an Author*

There are several reminiscences of Pirandello reading his plays to actors and friends. The one chosen comes from Dario Niccodemi's *Tempo passato*, Milan, 1929: Dario Niccodemi was the director of the first presentation of *Six Characters in Search of an Author* and was himself both a dramatist and director. After a varied theatrical career in Argentina and France, he settled in Italy in 1915 where a number of his plays were successful. Best known amongst these are *Remnant (Scampolo)* and *The Young Schoolmistress (La maestrina)*. In 1921 he established his own theatrical company and presented with considerable success a number of foreign and Italian new plays. The best known of these productions is Pirandello's *Six Characters in Search of an Author*.

In this passage from *Tempo passato* Niccodemi emphasises Pirandello's concentration on the words of the text and his clarification of the meaning of the speeches. It shows Pirandello at work in the theatre long before he took on the responsibility of directing plays himself. An interesting feature of this excerpt is the information it provides about Pirandello's views on prompters. As we mentioned in the Introduction (p. 7) in a traditional Italian production, the prompter spoke the whole play and his voice could be heard by the audience. Pirandello's views on the prompter were a logical extension of his concept of acting. Actors should understand and know their parts so well that they become as one with the character, thus eliminating the need for a prompter. Later, actors who became members of the Teatro d'Arte had to agree to an additional clause in their contracts that they would act without a prompter. Pirandello, however, did not always enforce this clause (see Document No. 34).

Document No. 11 Pirandello at Rehearsal

Pirandello's reading of *Six Characters in Search of an Author* to the company was an unforgettable experience. Admiration began as understanding faded - and that happened after the first few words. It was impossible to keep up with that impetus - or rather, the only way to keep up with it was physically. All of us, breathless and still, were caught up in that rush of words. The actors were deeply and utterly convinced and burst out with their unanimous enthusiasm. We were, all of us, bewildered, at sea.

Light dawned slowly during the many rehearsals. The actors were quiet, deferential and attentive, held in that religious respect which lack of understanding can always inspire. They let themselves be guided along the intricate paths of that weighty and entangled creation, so full of dazzling mental fireworks, imaginative leaps, meditative moments, and fascinating and ingenious theatrical experiments and solutions, all suffused by an atmosphere as enticing as sin. The layers of mist slowly thinned out and the first rays of light appeared, flickered, and then shone more brightly. A moment of clarity was achieved. We all sighed happily, satisfied, as if to say, "We won't let that go". But the actors were still somewhat lost. They were unable to form an opinion about what they were saying. And this just cannot be. An actor without an opinion about the work he's performing in is like a lamp that has gone out or a rowing boat with no oars or a motor with no piston. On stage it is essential to have an opinion about the work one's acting in - whether good or bad is irrelevant. But the days passed by and the mystery remained unsolved.

From the very first rehearsal a simple chair near the prompter's box became Pirandello's seat in the stalls. He directed the play. He revealed an amazing capacity for explaining all the obscurities of the text - indeed, the more obscure the point, the clearer was his explanation. He could plunge into the complexities of certain psychological abnormalities and clarify them. He knew what to ask for and he knew how to get what he wanted. But his personality underwent a strange doubling: he was at one and the same time the author who guided and taught the actors and the spectator who watched and enjoyed the play. For everyone else the structure of the play was still confused, imprecise and formless: for him it was clear and unmistakable. Everyone else felt they were at the sketch stage while he was already at the finished picture: for him, the play was already alive and on the stage. And to watch him follow it through, live it and breathe it, was itself a spectacle of arresting human interest.

Pirandello had a prodigious memory. He repeated the words of his text without forgetting one, or rather his lips mouthed them all in a burning silence. He had an amazingly mobile face. It seemed like a whole crowd of faces at the same time. He copied and corrected the facial expresions of the actors; his eyes darted from one actor to another, giving and taking, sowing and reaping, smiling, quivering, approving. Every muscle was in action: his mouth seemed to become many as it moved through the gamut of expressive possibilities; his chin trembled convulsively, his face would light up in a seemingly infinite number of ways; the enflamed walls of his skull became transparent and seemed to reveal the miraculous workings of that brain, that frenetic motor which emitted sparks and groans in its superhuman effort. One of the scenes would begin to take shape: two, three, four characters would shout at one another and Pirandello was all of those characters. As the scene began to build so did the resources of his expression; he would emphasize with gestures, speed up the pace by twisting his whole body. He would murmur dark words with unspeakable violence, lowering his chin onto his chest and snapping his jaws like a wild animal tossing its meat into the air. His silences were more powerful than any others I've experienced - and his capacity to convey movement while sitting down is unsurpassable. He became the scene. He took it upon himself, into himself and projected it through all the pores of his face, as the gaping mouths of certain rocks along the Sicilian coast - Homeric monsters - draw in the sea with enormous force only to spew it out with the violence of a typhoon.

Then all of a sudden, that uncontrollable human energy would collapse as if struck by a mortal blow. His body would become suddenly still, inert, his arms hanging down, his face expressionless and his eyes lifeless. It was a sign of disapproval. I would interrupt the rehearsal. Then Pirandello would get up, try to explain and put things right. He would be uncertain and hesitant to start with, then warm to his subject; he would confront the offending actor explaining his point with a rush of words. With the tips of his fingers held tightly together, his hands looked like fir cones moved by wind in a storm. "It's not your fault" he would say kindly and gently to the actor concerned. "It's all the fault of the prompter. Everything is the prompter's fault". Pirandello has a deep hatred of prompters. Prompters are his most bitter irreconcilable enemies. He would go on: "So long as there is a prompter there can be no truth or naturalness in acting. The prompter must be abolished." And he would gesture with his hand as if to cut off the prompter's head. "The prompter is the ruin of theatre." He would get more excited and the actors would stand around him, stunned and amazed by the radical revision of all their convictions which were invariably founded in the importance of having a good prompter. "When I direct plays, the actors will have to study their parts and learn their lines by heart." A silent, tentative rebellion from the actors: "They will have to work hard on their lines, in their own homes, in silence - they will have to meditate on them." The actors thought they were dreaming. "And when they come on stage, they must no longer be actors but the very characters of the play they are performing in." The silent dismay of the actors become more obvious. "In that way they will have in themselves not a relative reality but an absolute reality; not the false reality of the stage but the positive and unmistakable reality of life. The actor sees himself reflected in the prompter and naturally feels grotesque in front of the character he has to represent. He cannot be that character. He remains the actor who with more or less intelligence, talent or genius says mechanically the words which the prompter smuggles out of his box. The public nearly always hears the prompter's voice, or if they don't, they guess he is there, which is equally disastrous for the performance." The actors would become more and more bewildered. "And the prompter is not content with merely saying the words; he has his own inflections, his own personal idiosyncracies in the way he says things that can affect a suggestible actor. The prompter is acting there in his lair. You just have to see him in action to realise this. He is like one possessed, who becomes excited, clenches his fists to emphasise a word, who holds his hands to his mouth in order to make a quiet but audible megaphone, who, when all is said and done, directs the performance according to the current state of his nerves, mind and mood." And Pirandello would graphically explain, describing and justifying his theories of the stage.

Luigi Pirandello and Adriano Tilgher

The following review of *Six Characters in Search of an Author* is by Adriano Tilgher and was first published in the newspaper *Il Tempo*, 10th May 1921 and is now in Adriano Tilgher, *Il problema centrale (Cronache teatrali,* 1914-1926), ed. Alessandro D'Amico, Genova, 1973. It is not necessarily the most lively amongst those published at the time, but is is interesting for the light it can throw on Pirandello's relations with this critic and his subsequent influence on Pirandello's work.

Though a writer of criticism himself, and often an incisive one, Pirandello had the traditionally arrogant attitude of the creative artist towards those who criticised his work and did not understand it in the way he thought they should. In the theatre trilogy in particular, Pirandello sets up the critic for satirical treatment. In the second play *Each in His Own Way (Ciascuno a suo modo)*, he went so far as to introduce an actor to mimic a critic he particularly despised who had written a caustic review of the play when it had appeared in book form. It is said that the actor playing the part caught perfectly the Turinese accent of the offending critic, Domenico Lanza. With Adriano Tilgher, however, Pirandello felt an affinity. A philosopher by training, Tilgher was well able to elucidate Pirandello's thought and to express it succinctly. In 1922 when Tilgher's first book of essays on drama came out, Pirandello was grateful for this elucidation. The relationship was to become problematic, however, for after the closure of *Il Tempo* Tilgher went to work on *Il Mondo*, edited by Giorgio Amendola, a leading anti-Fascist, while Pirandello joined the Fascist Party in 1924, after the Matteotti and Casalini murders.

Their political differences also sparked off an arid controversy about who owed whom most: was it Tilgher's formulations that clarified Pirandello's thought and influenced his future plays, or was it Pirandello who gave Tilgher his most important opportunity as a critic?

Tilgher is said not only to have clarified Pirandello's thought (some said unkindly that he clarified it for Pirandello himself) but also to have influenced later plays, such as *Diana and Tuda (Diana e la Tuda)*, a schematised drama about art and life, first published in 1926. There seems no doubt, however, that the review included here influenced the preface to *Six Characters in Search of an Author* and some of the revisions to the play. It is Tilgher who raised the question of "differing levels of consciousness" in the characters, and points out that the characters become "real beings": two points taken up in the preface to the 1925 edition. In the rewriting of the play, Pirandello made considerable revisions to the third act which, in addition to the cuts that Pitoëff made to the text, were probably influenced by Tilgher's strictures.

Document No. 12: Adriano Tilgher's review of Six Characters in Search of an Author (1921)

It is normally extremely difficult to summarize the plots of Pirandello's plays, because what is important about them is never the crude plot line, nor the facts, nor even the action, but rather the process that develops inside the souls of his characters and which manifests itself through a series of reasoned arguments by which they clarify things for themselves and for others, contriving both to explain to others and win for themselves the spiritual position they have reached or at which they have halted. It would be a foolish, vain undertaking to attempt to summarize the plot of the play which was premiered last night at the Teatro Valle. I will therefore abandon any attempt at a summary and restrict myself to shedding some light on the intentions of the author in bringing such an unusual work to life and to discussing how far he may have succeeded. And since I am compelled to trust to memory, besides being constrained by the short space of time available, it is quite impossible to attempt a minutely detailed criticism. In consequence, I shall keep to generalizations and make no pretence of attributing any greater value to my observations than that of critical impressions inspired by an opening night.

Pirandello's main objective in putting on this play can be quickly related. He wanted to represent in stage terms the efforts of artistic creation, the mysterious process thanks to which the tumult of those phantoms which burst out of the artist's imagination, trembling with life but as yet still dark, shadowy, confused, still partially shaped and unformed, can be composed into a harmonious, powerful synthesis, that is at once perfect and complete. The process of creation that coordinates and balances in one luminous, vast, well ordered frame what the artist's imagination has previously only perceived as more or less distinguishable blotches of colour. It is a theme of powerful originality, of indescribable audacity, such that merely having attempted it is a claim to glory. It is a theme that only the weighty intellect of Pirandello could have attempted to devise and transfer into stage terms in Italy today. Anyone who mentioned Shaw last night did not know what they were saying. Not that one could not hear the occasional Shaw-like exchange, especially in the first act, but the ground on which the play was based was totally different to that of Shaw's work. Pirandello was once again attempting to put on a stage the internal processes of states of mind, something that Shaw never even dreamed of doing.

Characters in plays are born just as stones, plants, animals are born. Anyone born as a character does not only have every bit as much life as so-called real, living men, they actually have more than those who are eternally changeable, who are one thing today and another tomorrow, who pass by and die. A character has his own everlasting life that can never decay, fixed for eternity in its essential characteristics. Created as he is, the character detaches himself from his author and lives his own life, imposing his own will on that life in such a way that all the author can do is to observe and leave him be. Now, one fine day, six characters created, or rather sketched out by their author in a roughly drawn episode that does not lead to any conclusion, present themselves on stage to a company of actors and suggest that they might be allowed to enact that drama which is so powerfully compulsive for them.

Not all these characters are equally drawn: two of them, the Father and the Stepdaughter are close to being perfect, finalised artistic creations; another, however, is little more than basic nature, an impression of life that is barely shaped by art at all (the Mother), whilst another has been shaped lyrically and rejects any dramatic realization (the Son). The six characters in search of an author are therefore not all on the same level of consciousness. They are the stage representations of differing levels of consciousness where the author's imagination has come to a halt in a first, incomplete draft. Pirandello's play must therefore be the stage representation of the synthesizing process from which the work of art emerges, of the passage from life to art, from impression to expression. And is the author's intention successfully presented on stage? Let me reply immediately: not completely, as the play proceeds it becomes even less successful. The roughly sketched phantoms are filled with an unrestrainable life given to them by their author. He, however, can no longer control their lives with the result that they play power games with one another, each trying to be the centre and nucleus of the work, and this tumult is rendered very well in the first act through the broken, convulsive, desperate dialogue between the Father and the Stepdaughter, when both tend to justify themselves and so arouse all the interest and sympathy of the author. Pirandello has perceived with profound intuitive feeling that it is precisely in this *eccentricity* (in the literal sense of the word), in this blind rush to follow every motive and every seed of life to its source, that the whole essence of Nature lies, that which distinguished it from the Soul which is coordination, synthesis, discipline and therefore choice and conscious sacrifice. It is that which explains the anomalies, the dysteleologies and the accidents of Nature, and what old Hegel was trying to say when he pointed out that Nature is powerless to render concepts, that the incredible fecundity of Nature is weakness not strength, dispersion not concentration. But this theme, which ought to be the main motif of Pirandello's play and effectively dominates the first act is not adequately developed in the second and third acts. We cannot see the stage representation in these two acts of the movement of the characters from an inferior to a superior level of consciousness, we do not see them moving out of their original confusion into order, out of chaos into the cosmos of art. The one who was nature remains as nature (the Mother) the one who was only conceived of lyrically remains as such (the Son). The play does not come into being. Why not? Because the Son rebels against taking part in the play because he was not born to be on a stage. And so because of this the play fails. Everything remains vague and unexplained. Moreover, the play does not succeed because they try to improvise it and a work of art cannot be improvised. An ordinary director cannot put on a play in half an hour, it can only happen as the result of elaborate effort. But this too is an incidental reason that has no philosophical or universal value and cannot prove anything. We are still faced with the question: Pirandello conceives a truth of universal significance and in order to express it on stage he sets up a particular case, one which cannot possibly assume the necessary universal value. What need was there, what deep necessity was there for the play not to succeed? The figure of the Director is ambiguous: on the one hand, he has to represent the author, the synthesizer on stage; on the other hand, he is the head of the company, the improvised author who lacks any true experience and true artistic depth. From this ambiguity derives a confusion that extends throughout the play and clouds it all.

In the second and third acts the fundamental motif of the play is interrupted by a secondary motif which breaks it up and clouds the issues. We are no longer present at the stage representation of the process of artistic synthesis. The play has moved on to show something much less interesting and much more banal and familiar, that is, that life, if it is lived in the fullest sense of the word, is not art and in its movement from the realm of artistic expression it undergoes a process that must necessarily seem to falsify and distort it in the eyes of anyone who remains on the level of living life. Seeing their gestures and their own words repeated by actors, the characters no longer recognize themselves, they are lost. And unless I am deceiving myself, the author unconsciously turns his characters here into real beings, transferring those characters which, as should be borne in mind, are more or less fully drawn artistic phantoms from the level of the imagination onto the level of real life and so introduces a duality that obscures and disrupts the movement of the play. He is telling us something here that has been known for centuries: that theatre (i.e. art) is not a photograph of real life, but is a reflection of life and therefore a distortion of life. But this was not what he first began to express in stage terms.

Up to now I have pointed to two motifs in this unusual work which overlap and end up by disrupting each other. There is also a third motif less developed than the second, but which also interferes with the other two and so increases the confusion. Each of the characters in search of an author already knows what will happen to them and to all the others even before attempting any stage portrayal of events. They have the fore-knowledge of their own destinies. Each time, for example, the Father and the Stepdaughter take up their story at a given point and try to move it on from there, following the line, the Mother is on stage, and because she knows what is going to happen and through that fore-knowledge cannot remain passively watching events proceed, she is led to plead to be spared from the terrible events that are about to take place. And so sentimental considerations emerge to try and disrupt the architectural structures of a work of art which has its own eternal logic, which is what it is and cannot be allowed to be turned aside out of sympathy for the spectators' sensitive hearts. But this motif needed to be more fully developed and brought into sharper focus.

I could go on indefinitely if I were to try and note all the details which I found striking in this extraordinary play and which I hope to discuss more fully later on if time permits. For the present, I must conclude. In this space, all that can be done is to stress the undeniable genius of intuitive powers and the striking scenic realization of that genius throughout the final act, together with the astonishing technical skill, the brilliant theatrical experience, thanks to which Pirandello has taken a bewildered, confused public by the scruff of the neck and forced it to listen and to applaud, holding it there right to the end which, since it was so utterly absurd, unleashed an absolute storm of protest. We should not forget that the third act does little more than *piétiner sur la place* of the second, and that it ends in a lengthy discussion of a somewhat mundane and ordinary aesthetic theory: that life is not theatre. But due to his astonishing technique, Pirandello walked along the very edge of the abyss and won applause for himself. The play was, therefore, imperfect, but the *idea* was attractive and, in conclusion, it was an attempt that will not lie fallow but which will bear the fruit of timely consequences for our theatre. Any great work of art, if it appears at all, appears after a lengthy, laborious preceding preparation which is necessary. From today, we can say that Pirandello is most certainly among the leading creators of a new spiritual environment, one of the most deserving precursors of tomorrow's genius if tomorrow ever comes.

The Niccodemi company successfully overcame the overwhelming difficulties of this stage experiment. Margheri was an excellent Director, Madame Vergani skillfully rendered all that there was of brutal grace and feline lust for revenge in the character of the Stepdaughter. This young actress is developing her technique before our eyes and is becoming a strong, intelligent, amazingly versatile actress. Mr. Almirante (whom one might have wished a little less servile and downtrodden on occasion) portrayed fairly well the complex, tormented character of the Father. The others were excellent. There were a good many curtain calls at the end of the first act and at the end of the second when Pirandello was called onto the stage I don't know how many times. But, truth to tell, it was a success imposed by a minority on a bewildered, confused public who were basically trying hard to understand. After the third act, however, the weakest act of all which ends so absurdly, a storm of protest broke out that the supporters of the work tried bravely to counter. And so ended an evening that really was a battle for all of us, for the author, the public and also for the critics.

A review of the first production outside Italy of *Six Characters in Search of an Author* (1922)

The following review of the first production of *Six Characters in Search of an Author* outside Italy is by Desmond MacCarthy and was subsequently published in *Drama*, London and New York, 1940.

Document No. 13: Something new

The Stage Society produced a most original play last Monday and acted it extraordinarily well. The play is by Signor Luigi Pirandello, who is one of the leading Italian dramatists and a writer of admirable short stories. It was produced last year in Rome and made a great impression. The Stage Society's programme included a note by A.W. on the play. It was needed; for without some introduction, many of the audience would have been puzzled by this experiment in dramatic form.

> "It is neither a play within a play, nor yet a play in the making. Rather it is a trial - possibly an indictment - of the modern theatre. The author has created Six Characters and imagined for them a situation of poignant intensity. And then, doubtful of the theatre's adequacy for his intentions, he abandons his play - it is not to be written. But the characters remain; he has endowed them with life and they refuse to relinquish his gift. A theatrical stock company meets to put another Pirandello play into

rehearsal, and as they begin their work, the six characters arrive, and demand that their story shall be given the dramatic representation for which it was destined."

What an extraordinary plot for a play! How can a play be made out of such a situation? It certainly required considerable cleverness to do it, but Signor Pirandello is clearly endowed with a quite enormous amount of ingenuity. This is how he did it.

The curtain did not go up. It was up when we assembled; we found ourselves sitting in front of the dark empty stage, and presently, one after the other a number of actors and actresses in their everyday clothes walked on. The humorously-strident voice of Mr. Alfred Clark was heard giving directions for a rehearsal, and the lights were turned up. A slightly quarrelsome, snappy-chatter followed, and the rehearsal was just getting under way, when at the back of the stage appeared a gloomy procession of figures dressed in deep mourning. An elderly man in immaculate black, a woman, presumably a widow, in streaming weeds, a tiny girl, a young girl about eighteen, a youth, say twenty-two, and a little boy about twelve. These people are "Characters" in a play Signor Pirandello intended to write.

The rehearsal stops; the actors turn and stare, and Mr. Alfred Clark naturally asks the intruders what the devil they want. Diffidently the Father (Mr. Franklin Dyall) steps forward. It is quite easy to state why they are come, but not so easy to convince the assembled actors that the visitors are not lunatics. What these portentously grave intruders want is to be given the opportunity of living through the story for which their creator created them. At present they are hanging in a miserable sort of void; they are real - there they are, solid human beings, men and women, boys and girls - but there is nothing for them to do. Politely, but with a certain insistence which gradually mesmerizes the matter-of-fact, dumbfounded Mr. Clark (call up the image of a man vigourously, not to say blatantly, matter-of-fact), the Father explains that such a condition of nebulous unattached existence has become intolerable. They must fulfil their destiny; would the company kindly impersonate them and thus bring rest to their perturbed spirits? (No one can act better than Mr. Clark that frame of mind which is expressed by the simple words, "Well I'm blowed.")

Interrupted by the titters of the actors and the passionate corrections of his family, each of whom has his or her version of their terrible story, the Father actually succeeds in getting the idea lodged in the producer's head that the terrible events through which his family have lived might make a better play than the exceedingly doubtful stuff Signor Pirandello has actually provided. Their story intrigues him.

The father explains that he married beneath him. "You see this poor woman?"

"But she is a widow, and you are alive."

"Yes, but listen. I married her. I had a secretary; they loved each other; they were continually signalling to each other with their eyes for fear they should wound me by their words; it became intolerable. I let them go off together, and with them went my son - the young man over there."

Here the Stepdaughter (I have not seen Miss Muriel Pratt act so well before) breaks in with a passionate accusation against the Son, describing his intolerable icy contempt for the rest of the family...

Confusion...

The father resumes his story. He had no idea that, after the death of his wife's lover, the family had fallen into poverty...

More passionate family recriminations...

He had lost sight of them; he is a man not old enough to be indifferent to women and yet too old to be loved by them: a very humiliating condition... in short he has recourse occasionally to... well, he buys his love.

Now, it is very unfair to think that the whole of a man in all his actions; yet others always judge him as though that were the case. A most terrible thing happened. He went to a certain house which under the pretence of being a dressmaker's was a house where these sort of bargains are struck, and there without recognizing her, he met his wife's daughter, "the girl you see over there". They were interrupted by the cry of the Mother who had come to see her daughter. Imagine how terrible her predicament is now. The girl only sees him in the light of the interview; he is to her merely that man...

More interruption from the Stepdaughter, who expresses her loathing and contempt...

Agonized distress on the part of the Mother.

This is the situation which precedes the climax. It rather takes the Producer's fancy, who suggests that the Characters should reproduce what happened before the actors and a shorthand writer. This is just what the Characters want, but they are terribly disappointed when they see themselves afterwards impersonated. They come out completely different characters; there is something fatally wrong with the stage version. What we see is the contrast between "actuality" as an author imagines it and what actually gets across the footlights.

Signor Pirandello has illustrated what every profound dramatist must feel when he sees his characters on the stage; his sufferings at the inevitable distortions due to the substitution of the personality of the actor for that of his character as he imagined it. But he has done more than that. He has suggested the inevitable limitations of the modern drama, the falsifications which result from cramming scenes into acts and tying incidents down to times and places. And he has done more yet; in an odd way he has suggested that the fate of many people is not unlike those of the "Characters" in the play; that many of us are in their predicament, namely, like them, real enough people, for whom fate nevertheless has not written the plays in which we might have played a part.

Mr. Franklin Dyall's performance was of the first excellence; it was difficult to pull it off and he succeeded triumphantly.

The 1925 Italian Version of Six Characters in Search of an Author

It should be borne in mind that the play that was received so controversially at the Teatro Valle in May of 1921 and then presented in theatres all over the world, was not identical to the play that is now read and staged. What might strike the English reader or spectator as the most innovatory and theatrical aspects of the text were not in fact present in the version of 1921. In this text the whole play was staged behind the proscenium arch. There were no steps linking the stage with the auditorium, the Characters, unmasked, appeared from the back of the stage, as did the Leading Lady, and the Director never left the stage to take a seat in the auditorium to see how the play was progressing. In other respects, too, the text of the play differed. The third part and hence the play, finished with the Director sending his actors and actresses home: there were no silhouettes, no final presentation of the surviving nuclear family and no exit of the Stepdaughter through the auditorium. Furthermore, Pirandello rewrote parts of the play for 1925, cut some of the speeches, in particular some of the Father's "philosophical" ones, and re-arranged some of the material. These additions and alterations were inserted into the fourth version of the play and were presented for the first time on stage in the production directed by Pirandello himself at the Odescalchi Theatre, Rome, in the spring of 1925. The text with the preface were printed the same year. English readers can consult the 1921 version of the play in Edward Storer's translation and the 1925 text in Frederick May's, John Linstrum's and Felicity Firth's translations (see Appendix 1, Some Translations into English of Plays by Pirandello, pp. 185-87). The preface is in Luigi Pirandello, *Naked Masks*, ed. by Eric Bentley, Dutton, New York, 1952, and translated by Felicity Firth, in Luigi Pirandello, *Collected Plays*, vol. 2, John Calder, London, 1988. There were two intervening versions of the play in 1923 and 1924, each containing some of the alterations that were to find their way into the 1925 text; these have not been translated into English and were probably never performed in Italian.

Although in his theoretical writings Pirandello made it clear that he considered the stage rendering of a play as a potential travesty of the dramatist's "holy writ", it seems equally clear that as well as Adriano Tilgher's criticism mentioned in the previous sub-section, three theatrical experiences influenced the revisions to the play. In 1923 Georges Pitoëff directed the play at the Champs Elysées theatre in Paris with himself as the Father and his wife Ludmilla as the Stepdaughter. A number of the cuts and amendments made to Crémieux's translation found their way into Pirandello's 1925 text. From extant photographs of the production, it appears that although he did not use the auditorium, Pitoëff put some of the action on broad steps leading to the proscenium arch, was the first to establish that the flats used for "the scene" in part 2 should be striped, used stylised make-up for the Characters that came close to the masks recommended by Pirandello in 1925, and introduced a backdrop into the garden scene. His cuts to the text were also close to those made by Pirandello in 1925. Pirandello did not include, however, Pitoëff's most famous amendment to the text: the introduction of the Characters by means of the stage lift.

The second theatrical experience that contributed positively to the textual revisions was Pirandello's own production of the play. It was he who first used the steps at the side of the stage thus linking stage with auditorium. This device was initially used in the opening production in the Odescalchi theatre which had been redesigned to suit Pirandello's purposes by the architect Virgilio Marchi. It was while redesigning the stage that he and Pirandello decided to place two moveable flights of steps which could be used either together at the centre of the front of the stage or singly at either side. Having experimented with the steps in his first production in the theatre, Pirandello then incorporated them into this play later in the same year.

The success of the play owed much to Ruggero Ruggeri's interpretation of the major role. As can be seen from the letters that follow, Pirandello wrote the play with Ruggeri in mind, and although other actors have successfully offered different interpretations, Ruggeri's was the one best remembered, particularly in England, where he appeared as guest actor with the Teatro d'Arte in the summer of 1925. Ruggeri had previously played the major role in *The Rules of the Game (Il gioco delle parti)*, *The Pleasures of Respectability (Il piacere dell'onestà)*, and *All for the Best (Tutto per bene)* and would later take the lead in *Six Characters* and *No-one Knows How (Non si sa come)*. Though a very popular actor in Italy, Ruggeri was sometimes criticised for not having a definite repertoire and for ignoring certain major contemporary dramatists, such as Shaw; but his restrained acting style which allowed for sudden outbursts of passion, giving the impression that he spoke the words as he thought them, made him an eminently suitable actor to interpret Pirandello's characters.

Document No. 17: Letter to Ruggieri, 21.9.1921

Dear Friend,

I am replying in haste to your letter of 19 September, for which I was deeply grateful.

I told you last time in Rome that I was thinking over something for you. I have followed up those thoughts and now finally worked out a play which I think is one of my most original works: *Henry IV*, tragedy in three acts by Luigi Pirandello.

I'll tell you briefly what it is about. The background to the story is as follows: about twenty years earlier some young aristocratic men and women decided to hold a "procession in fancy dress" at carnival time in one of their country houses. Each of them chose an historical character, a king or a prince that they could portray, each with his lady alongside, a queen or princess, riding horses saddled in full period harness. One of these young men chose the character of Henry IV, and had taken immense trouble to study every minute detail in order to make the portrayal more authentic, so much so that he had been virtually obsessed by it for about a month.

Tragically, on the very day of the procession when he was riding with his lady alongside in that magnificent cortège, the horse stumbled suddenly and he fell, hitting his head. When he recovered from the concussion caused by the blow, he was still locked into the character of Henry IV. There was simply no way at all of releasing him from that fixation and persuading him to give up the costume he had dressed up in, and the "mask" which he had studiously contrived in minutest detail with such obsessive care became the "persona" for him of the great, tragic Emperor himself.

Twenty years have now passed.

He is still living - as Henry IV - in his lonely country house, peacefully mad. He is nearly fifty years old. But for him time has not passed (or rather for his mask, which is his self), he can neither see nor feel it passing, and time is therefore fixed with him. Although he has grown old, he is still the young Henry IV of the procession.

One fine day a psychiatrist turns up at the villa and introduces himself to Henry's nephew, who is very fond of his uncle and helps keep him in his harmless madness. There may be a way to cure the madman by giving him back "an awareness of the distance of time" with a violent shock. Now the tragedy really begins and I think it has an unusual philosophical depth even though it comes to life through a sense of the dramatic that is not without its own unusual effects.

I won't tell you what happens so as not to spoil the impressions of your first reading. Given the situation, really unexpected things happen, if you think that the man whom everyone believes to be mad has in fact not been mad for years. He is simply feigning madness philosophically so that he can laugh at all the others who believe that he is mad, and also because he likes the garish representation of his imperial status that he plays out for himself and for others in that villa which is decorated with all the imperial trappings fit for Henry IV. And then if you consider that he doesn't know that the doctor has put his plan into operation and, fake madman as he is, is so terrified that he thinks for a moment that he *is* mad and is about to disclose his own pretence and then suddenly manages to pull himself together and revenge himself by ... well, yes, I shall not tell you how he does it, in order to leave you with a few surprises.

Leaving aside all false modesty, I really do think that the subject is worthy of you and of your great talent. I do hope that you will be able to take it on, because my imagination is working so well at the moment and is more lively and vital than ever. But before settling down to work I would like to hear your views, whether you like it and think it is any good.

Did you see *Six Characters in Search of an Author*? If only you know what pain it caused me when I was not able to give you that play, since you were on tour with *Sly*,[2] not because I was displeased with the way in which Niccodemi's company interpreted it, but because I had envisioned *you* and not Giorgio Almirante in the role of the Father. So be it.

Do please give my best greetings to our dear Virgilio[3] who was kind enough to send me a friendly telegram of sympathy when poor Nino Martoglio died so tragically.

I hope, dear friend, that your friendship and Virgilio's will go some way towards easing a certain coolness that signora Alda Borelli[4] quite justifiably feels for me at the moment. I will tell you about that next time.

This letter has become too long, so I send you all my good wishes.

Luigi Pirandello

The first reading of Henry IV

Carlo Tamberlani belonged to a family of actors and his memories of his theatre days and of acting in Pirandello plays in particular provide valuable insights into the theatre world of the twenties. (Carlo Tamberlani, *Pirandello nel "teatro che c'era"*, Rome, 1982). This reminiscence of the first reading of *Henry IV*, however, is taken from the *Atti del Congresso di studi pirandelliani*, Florence, 1967. It provides information about the tradition of the first reading of a play and some indication of how young actors of the time viewed authors. Interesting too is the mention of the pleasure Pirandello took in Olivieri's interpretation of the Doctor.

When Wanda Capadoglio's company presented the play in Rome, she recalled that Pirandello was eager for the character to be played with the same accent.

Document No. 18: Carlo Tamberlani recalls the first reading of *Henry IV*.

The reading of a new work had its own traditions and customs. It was nearly always done by the prompter who read out the work in a semi-didactic way, hence with few changes in intonation and so leaving a lot of opportunity to the imagination of the actors.

For those of us like myself, for whom it was merely a question of finding out at the end of the reading when the parts were distributed whether there were any minor parts that could attract attention on to us, the reading of the work in its entirety, that is, following the main parts, was really always put out of focus by our hopes that we would get a small part. For us young actors the first reading was a bit of a bore. That need not seem in any way iconoclastic for, after all, in order to enjoy a theatrical work the actor must be able to enter into the play. The actor first of all quickly transforms the written word inside himself into impassioned action. From this process, perhaps, come those complete marriages between written work and interpretation; because from the moment of the reading itself the actor has already glimpsed and begun to live his professional life.

On that morning *Henry IV* was to be read by Pirandello himself who already had his supporters and opponents, and who, in *Six Characters in Search of an Author* was thought to have taken things a bit far. An author, that is, of a certain reputation but certainly not as experienced as Butti[5] and Praga[6], and whose theatre, pundits predicted, would have a brief and ephemeral life, depending as it did on the attitude of mind of an acrobat who always prefaced his new trick with a gesture which said, "Look! this one is even more difficult!" A theatre, in fact, which would leave nothing that would last.

On that January morning of 1922, the Company sat on the stage of the Manzoni theatre in the traditional way: in a circle, in front of the proscenium arch with a table in the middle on which there was a reading light for the reader. The system of providing each actor with his own chair with fitted desk had not yet been introduced. In those days parts weren't even distributed to the actors, and even when they were, after the reading, they didn't contain the cues from other actors in them. After he had read the work, the Director would stage it, by giving moves and positions to the actors and by establishing the style of the play; in fact, by bringing it to life in its artistic environment and not by deadening it with literary research.

When Pirandello came on stage he appeared a very ordinary person, just any author. He smiled good naturedly at all of us and greeted Ruggeri warmly. He sat at the table and read *Henry IV.*

Did I have a proper understanding of the work? I don't know. I was very young and still very much in the mould of traditional theatre. But the impression I received was a lasting one, one of those indelible impressions that form a reference point in later life. Pirandello's reading had little change of tone it it, which I, used to the vocal colouring of the time, did not find particularly attractive. And Pirandello spoke with a dialect accent which made me look down on him rather, as his diction was so far from the pure diction of our teachers. We young people began to exchange a glance or two. The older and more experienced among us were quicker on the uptake and were attentive from the beginning. As the reading progressed, I, too, became impressed. By what? By hearing new words, sentences with unexpected conclusions; you heard the word or image you least expected but which turned out to be the most logical one, the right one. In every exchange his dialogue and action were different and I couldn't define or label it. I followed the whole reading, which is all the more suprising for Pirandello never attempted anything more than a reading.

I'll explain what I mean. I remembered how the year before when I was with Ruggero Ruggeri, Forzano came to read *Sly*. His vocal range was excellent, and you experienced the play as he read it. The play was interpreted as he saw it on the stage. He revealed then those qualities he had for directing plays which I was to admire at other times when he directed *Peter the Great* with Zacconi[7] in 1928 and the films I took part in later. Pirandello did not alter his tone in this way. His words were always his own, alive and intimate, rather like one of Plato's dialogues read from a lectern. The regional accent made Pirandello's reading so personal that it discouraged any interpreter, even the most frank, from thinking he could translate that "truth".

We felt that all the approximate interpretation that an actor easily puts into a first reading of a part to be quite inadequate. Our tonal range was of no use. We just were not interested in using that easy ability to make a part feel our own by meeting it with our limited resources of perception.

The small range of the impassioned phonetic world communicated nothing and there came into being that separateness typical of Pirandello's work to which every effort must contribute in order to reveal him. That we understood straight away.

Those teasing words were not thrown down by chance, but were quickly directed towards strange solutions. Forzano *was* Sly, he was the innkeeper, he was all the drunkards of the inn; he was the beautiful, gentle romantic lady. Pirandello was always Pirandello. You could say he read in a most individual yet impersonal way. Forzano gave us a theatrical interpretation. Pirandello gave us the author's. The first was interpreter of himself, the second the unique revealer of the author, entirely faithful above all to his own inner world, to his rhythm, to his style which came through clearly in his particular and essential use of commas, full stops.

But that minute and precise faithfulness to the text in his reading could have deceived us into thinking he would be an inexorable and dissatisfied author. He knew how the interpreter can never identify completely with the image in the author's mind, and he had shown this in the play *Six Characters in Search of an Author...* and so he only concentrated on details with the actors and hardly ever with the more experienced, leaving them free to develop. At the very first rehearsal Ruggeri, with the author's approval, gave to his part a characterisation which he kept at the triumphal first night. Olivieri[8], on the other hand, took longer to hit on the Neapolitan character which so delighted Pirandello that it has fixed that part in that form for future interpretations. And so with Calò[9], who played Belcredi, Tòfano[10] who played Bertoldo and Gilda Marchiò[11] who took the part of the superficial Marchionness of Canossa. The respect for other people's living words was truly a reality for Pirandello.

An earlier version of Henry IV

Not much remains of Pirandello's drafts as he tended to destroy them. Earlier versions to the published text of *Henry IV* remain, however, and have been published. The following extract comes from *Un manoscritto autografo inedito dell'"Enrico IV". Di Luigi Pirandello*, ed. Livia Pasquazi Ferro Luzzi, Rome, 1983.

Document No. 19: Three versions of a speech from *Henry IV*.

Fools! fools! fools! - Did you see that? Did you see her? - A keyboard of colour! - The moment I touched her, she played red, white, blue and yellow. - What a nerve! And that other one who was afraid to step in front of me... - Pietro Damiani ... oh, - he looked like a character from a book ... a colouring book for kids ... and he was frightened to come back in front of me. Fool. - But look at this idiot here with his mouth open ... Don't you understand anything? ... Can't you see how I set them up and dress them and make them come before me for my amusement, so I can play the madman! But I'm the tyrant here. They think they're doing this out of pity, so as not to upset a poor sod who is out of this world, out of time, out of life ... But the real tyrants are out there amongst them in their world ... the people who impose the world they have inside them onto others ...

Second version

Fools! fools! fools! A keyboard of colours! The moment I touched her she played red, white, blue and yellow ... And that other one ... - Pietro Damiani - perfect! I've got him! - He was afraid to step in front of me. (*He says this with frenzied exuberance, rolling his eyes, moving edgily, until he suddenly notices Bertoldo who is not just dumbstruck but is terrified by this sudden, unexpected change. He stops in front of him and points him out to the other three, who are all bewildered in amazement*) - But look at this fool here standing watching me with his mouth open ... (*Takes hold of his shoulders and shakes him*) Don't you understand? Can't you see how I set them up and dress them and make them come here before me (*referring to the Visitors*). Frightened fools that they are - because you know what frightens them? Just this: that you might rip off their comic masks and show them to be disguised, as if it had not been me who had forced them to dress up for my entertainment here, so I could play the madman! - They think they're doing this out of pity, so as not to upset a poor sod who is already out of this world, out of time, out of life! - They wouldn't put up with this unless that were the case, would they? Such tyranny! They're the kind of people who expect everyone else to be exactly as they see them, every day, at every moment.

Third version

Fools! fools! fools! - A keyboard of colours! The moment I touched her, she played red, white, blue and yellow... And that other one, Pietro Damiani - perfect! I've got him! - He was frightened to step in front of me ... (*He says this with a rush of frenzied exuberance, moving about rapidly, rolling his eyes until he suddenly sees Bertoldo who is not just dumbstruck but is terrified by this sudden change. He stops in front of him and points him out to the other three who are all bewildered in amazement.*) But look at this fool here standing watching me with his mouth open ... (*Takes hold of his shoulders and shakes him.*) Don't you understand? Can't you see how I set them up and dress them and make them come here before me, frightened fools that they are. And all that frightens them is this: that you might rip off their comic masks and show them to be disguised, as if it had not been me who had forced them to dress up for my entertainment here, so I could play the madman!

Letter from Silvio d'Amico to Virgilio Talli

Virgilio Talli, to whom this letter is addressed, was a respected and prolific director. He concentrated almost entirely on modern plays, largely French and Italian ones, and was responsible for the first productions of Henry Becque in Italy. He also directed the première of D'Annunzio's *Iorio's Daughter (La Figlia di Iorio)* (1904), and, after considerable persuasion from Pirandello, two plays by the Sicilian dramatist, Rosso di San Secondo, *What Passion, You Puppets! (Marionette che passione!)* and *The Sleeping Beauty (La bella addormentata)*. He was respected by actors he directed for his sensitivity to the text and for his flair for knowing what would be well received by contemporary audiences. Before directing *Henry IV*, he had presented the première of Pirandello's *Right You Are! (If You Think So) [Così è (se vi pare)]* (see Document No. 7).

Silvio d'Amico was a critic and theatre historian. His books include *Storia del teatro drammatico* (1940) and *Il tramonto del grande attore* (1929). He founded and directed the many volumed *Enciclopedia dello spettacolo*. From 1918 he fought for an improved theatre in Italy: for a non-commercial repertoire, the establishment of the director, and for a better cultural and rhetorical preparation for actors. To this end he founded the Academy of Dramatic Art in Rome which still retains his name.

The National Theatre company had delayed its production of *Henry IV* for so long that the question of its eventual appearance was put in doubt. D'Amico had supported the granting of State aid to the National Theatre company, the first new company to be formed in the post-war period, but instead of something completely new, the companies of Ruggero Ruggeri and Alda Borelli, two star actors, merged with Virgilio Talli's company and many of the old "mattatore" problems remained. In this letter, d'Amico reminds Virgilio Talli of the problems and comments with enthusiasm on *Henry IV*.

Document No. 20 Letter from Silvio d'Amico to Virgilio Talli, Director of the National Theatre (13 December 1921)

Dear Friend,

I hope I may call you such? I ask you this because if you do not permit me to address you in this way, then it were best for you not to read this letter. Since I have no right at all to send you critical comments through the post, this letter of mine should be seen quite simply for what it is - the expression of a friend's pent-up feelings.

Yesterday evening I saw Pirandello's *Henry IV*. It is quite fantastic. Absolutely unlike anything that has been seen in the theatre before, and there is no doubt that it is a work of major importance. So how on earth could a company such as yours, with your high moral standards, disposing of the only actor capable today of performing in that play and having had the last act since the 2nd of this month, not realize that *Henry IV* offered the fortunate means of enabling you to have the great triumph that everyone expects? How could Alda Borelli have had any doubts about accepting such a part? And how could the Company Management not realize that its greatest novelty, in the true sense of the word, was this play?

I would like to point out that I am writing this with my customary detachment, out of simple love for the theatre and the hopes that so many of us had placed in that company. - I have a personal involvement in the fate of your enterprise; I have had an old belief for which I have fought now for many years, demanding that, in the absence of anyone else, the State at least should become the supporter (not the director) of a truly great Art Theatre. The first step towards realising that dream can be seen in the albeit modest grant made to the Company. But, as everyone now knows, as has been discussed "in high places", as has already been stated in the press and will certainly be openly printed in a fortnight's time, during the first two months of its life, the Company has hardly done anything except try things out. There has been a lot of Ruggeri's personal repertoire, a lot of Borelli's personal repertoire, very little ensemble work, a mediocre revival, no new plays. Because it is obvious that the Company's enemies will hardly fail to note that the *Parisina*[12] - a work which had to be done, in view of the author's reputation, but not on its own - is not a new play, neither in fact, since it has been around for several years, nor in spirit, seeing the kind of theatre to which it belongs. In this last month they had to make an effort at all costs and do something new, at least, with *Henry IV* and *Caterina Ivanovna* (by Leonid Andreev).

This would still have been a minimal programme, but it would have been respectable. Instead of which, the public are starting to ask what has been done so far to justify the bringing together of the former Ruggeri, Borelli and Talli companies under the goodwill of the government.

I should like to have said all this to you myself. That I cannot do, since I am forced to remain at home to fulfil publishing commitments that must be finished within the week. Therefore I wrote to you instead. I also wrote so that, when I find myself compelled to say these same things in my paper, in the most friendly way possible, you will not be totally unprepared.

I am yours ever,
Silvio d'Amico

Document No. 21: Review of the first night of Henry IV (1922) at the Manzoni Theatre in Milan

Henry IV, a tragedy in three acts by Luigi Pirandello, was performed for the first time in Milan on 24 February and received an enthusiastic response from the audience in the Manzoni theatre. In spite of the fact that the play is not one that can be easily assessed nor does it have mass appeal, the audience were deeply moved by it on more than one occasion, particularly at the end of the first act and halfway through the second. The play compelled the audience not only to admire the writing skills of the author through the strength of the protagonist, but to feel the passion that gradually built up in the strange atmosphere of the drama being performed on the stage in such an unusual way. There were several people in the stalls who enjoyed some of the most significant exchanges of dialogue immensely, actually emphasising them with half-audible comments. This was such an extraordinary occurrence that it can only be explained by the audience being utterly gripped by the content of the play they were watching. For the exchanges were not cleverly rhetorical, like some of those that make vulgar audiences burst into applause, but rather elegant philosophical speeches, subtle logical reasoning building up to a final quick phrase or image, paradoxes shaped with such naturalness and precision that the audience was left stunned and won over at the same time. The success of *Henry IV* represents above all else the success of the lyric-philosophical mode of expression that Pirandello has been emphasising in his most recent plays, particularly in *Six Characters in Search of an Author* and in this play. Of course the drama is determined by an "external situation", but it is immediately incorporated into the spirit of the characters where it originally existed; in other words, it once again becomes interiorized and is developed in depth. What are termed "situations" in a play are here developed in a parallel manner, but independently to the development that the play follows in the inner mind of the characters. And when this form of mutual independence is absent and the characters are compelled suddenly to adapt to an external situation and resolve it, then there arise those undreamed of, devastating catastrophes of which the crime committed by Henry IV is the prime example. This play, like other plays by Pirandello, can be described as a drama not of character but of situation. But we should not be so far from the truth were we to state the opposite.

Leaving aside details of general consideration, since time presses, *Henry IV* with all its great virtues also possesses all the defects of a work that acquires its life and form in the structures proper to theatre without having the almost physical means required to ensure that its life may be perfectly complete. It is not difficult to uncover, act by act, through the structure of the tragedy, the places where it develops through natural processes and those places where it develops through contrived processes. The most suitable, albeit vulgar, image to describe this fundamental flaw in the tragedy would be that of a mutilated body that a capable surgeon has been able to repair by adding artificial limbs. The two first scenes of the first act come into this category, together with the first scene of the second act. In general, when the protagonist is not on stage, *Henry IV* moves slowly and clumsily, the audience loses interest and Bertoldo's foolery, the Doctor's caricatured verbosity, the back-biting between Belcredi and Donna Matilde whose words and actions are all too obviously intended as a comment or an explanation or a preparation for the situation in which the protagonist will find himself when he comes on, all of this is not sufficient to fill the void left by the absence of Henry IV from the stage, even before he first appears to the audience and increasingly once he has gone. But the moment he does appear, then immediately one can feel a formidable dramatic strength in the midst of those clumsy, weak characters. If, in discussing a play that is so intensely modern, so dominated by spiritual forces, we can talk about a *deus ex machina*, then such is Henry IV. Although he appears to be so mysterious and contradictory, the sole fact of his presence illuminates and clarifies the world of the play in which he stands at the centre, and with a single word he can render superfluous the wordy explanations that the others around him are all too quick to offer on his behalf. He shares this power with another great tragic figure of a few centuries earlier: Prince Hamlet. And in this power lies the secret of his appeal to the audience.

It is hard to recount the plot of *Henry IV*, nor does it serve to explain the true meaning of the play or to emphasise the most typical and most vital elements. It is a tangled web, that on retelling does not offer any approximate idea of what is seen on stage, and even less of what is heard. Henry IV is a gentleman of the present who fell from his horse and has been suffering from a strange kind of madness. He has lived alone in his castle for twenty years, believing himself to be Henry IV of Germany whose clothes and lifestory he has taken for himself. But for the past ten years, without letting anyone else suspect, he has merely been pretending to be mad as before, and although now sane, he has continued to live cut off from the world and undisturbed, acting out the role of the historical character whose disguise he has assumed, together with his servants. When some of his relatives and friends with the aid of a doctor want to try to bring him back to sanity through a trick that makes the figure of the Princess Matilde of Tuscany seem alive in a double image, then since he is sane he runs the risk for an instant of going mad again. But he does not go mad. Instead, he rebels against a certain Belcredi who, twenty years previously, had been the cause of his ruin and had then become the lover of the woman that Henry had loved. And in a sudden burst of fury, he kills him.

This is the "story". But the tragedy of *Henry IV*, as I have tried to show, does not lie in the plot. And if one wants to determine precisely how Henry IV relates to his own past and to his own former madness and to the people who surround him and to his present clarity of mind, and what state of mind is created in him when he reveals his true self and kills Belcredi, then the tragedy must be heard or at least read. I say, at least read because undoubtedly in performance it acquires a focus that, without the stage interpretation, not everyone would know how to bestow on the characters and their words. In this respect, Ruggero Ruggeri is unquestionably a worthy, distinguished collaborator of Luigi Pirandello's. With great depth, he has analysed the character that he had to portray and has then brought him to life with amazing dramatic intensity. The audience received him enthusiastically, together with the author who took about fifteen curtain calls. Among the secondary figures, Mr. Calò, Mr. Olivieri and Mr. Tofano all deserve mention. The expert hand of Virgilio Talli was evident in the sensitivity of the whole production.

Document No. 22 - The Pirandello Play: The Living Mask (Henry IV) by Luigi Pirandello, translated by Arthur Livingston, Forty-fourth Street Theatre, January 21, 1924, by Stark Young

The Pirandello play at the Forty-Fourth Street Theatre is important not by reason of any display or novelty or foreign importation but through the mere occurrence on our stage of a real intellectual impact, a high and violent world of concepts and living. So far as the practical end of it goes Pirandello's *Henry IV* is difficult for our theatre. Its range and complexity of ideas are made more difficult by the presentation that it gets now and that it would be almost sure to get one way or another from any of our producers.

The play is fortunate in its translation, certainly; Mr. Livingston's rendering is both alive and exact, and expecially in the second act, where the thought is more involved, Mr. Livingston achieves an unusual quality of distinction. Mr. Robert Edmond Jones' two settings - save for the two portraits in the first scene, which obviously should be modern realistic in the midst of the antique apartment - are ahead of anything Pirandello would be apt to get in Italy, more precisely in the mood and more beautifully and austerely designed. Otherwise the trouble begins with the acting. Bad Italian actors would, congenitally, if in no other way, be closer to this Italian play and its necessities than many actors of our own would be. The actors in the opening moments at the Forty-Fourth Street Theatre could not even cope with the necessary delivery of the words. They not only could not whack out the stresses needed for the mere sense of the lines, but had no instinct for taking the cues in such a manner as would keep the scene intact. All that first part of the scene Pirandello means to keep flowing as if it were taking place in one mind; and the actors should establish that unity, speed and continuity by taking fluidly their lines as if from one mouth. Miss Lascelles' portrayal of Donna Mathilde is not definite or elegant enough; it is muffled and it is not full enough of a kind of voluptuous incisiveness. Mr. Louden's Doctor is wrong, too flat and narrow; the part is rough and tumble - out of the old commedia dell'arte very nearly - and a satire on specious scientific optimism and incessant explanation. And Mr. Korff's troubles with the language make his lines, which are hard enough already to grasp, confused and elusive.

Much of the meaning of *Henry IV* will depend of course on the actor who does the central character. Mr. Korff is a very good actor indeed in a certain style. He has a fine voice and a good mask in the manner of the Flemish or German schools of painting. But his portrayal of Henry IV lacks most of all distinction and bite. It is too full of sentiment and too short of mental agitation; it has too much nerves and heart and too little brains. The average audience must get the impression from Mr. Korff that we see a man whose life has been fantastically spoiled by the treachery of an enemy, that the fall from his horse began his disaster, which was completed by the infidelity and loose living of the woman he loved. But this weakens the whole drama; the root of the tragic idea was in the man's mind long before the accident; Pirandello makes that clear enough. The playing of this character which is one of the great rôles in modern drama, needs first of all a dark cerebral distinction and gravity; the tragedy, the irony, the dramatic and philosophical theme, depend on that. Mr. Korff has theatrical power and intensity, but too much waggling of his head; he is too grotesque and undignified vocally; he has too little precision and style for the part; and not enough intellectual excitement and ideal poignancy. And the very last moment of the play he loses entirely by the rise that he uses in his voice and by the kind of crying tumult that he creates. Pirandello's idea cannot appear in such terms as Mr. Korff's. Pirandello is concerned first and last with a condition of life, an idea, embodied in a magnificent personage, not with personal ills and Gothic pities.

A man dressed as Henry IV of Canossa fame rides beside the woman he loves, who goes as Mathilde of Tuscany. His horse is pricked from the rear and lunges; the man when he comes out of his stupor believes himself to be the real Henry IV. For years the river of time flows past him; his beloved marries and has a daughter, she becomes the amante of his rival. He chooses, when his reason returns, to remain in the masquerade of the character that for an evening's pleasure he has put on. Life has cheated him, made a jest of him; he gets even with life by remaining permanent in the midst of everlasting change. All men play a part in life; he plays his knowingly. And the people who come out of life to him must mask themselves before they are admittted; he makes fools of them. The woman he has loved comes with his nephew and the doctor to see him, bringing also her amante - well played by Mr. Gamble - with her and her daughter, who is the image of what she herself was in her youth. They are the changing Life brought now against the fixed Form in which the supposed madman lives. Driven by the sense that years have passed and are recorded on these visitors from his past and that he has not lived, he tells his attendants of his sanity and his masquerade. They betray his secret. In the end he sees that in the young daughter alone can he recognize his renewal and return to life. There is a struggle when he tries to take her, and he kills the amante. Necessarily now, after this crime, he remains shut up in the mask under which he has masqueraded.

With this the Pirandello theme appears - the dualism between Life on one hand and Form on the other; on the one hand Life pouring in a stream, unknowable, obscure, unceasing; on the other hand forms, ideas, crystallizations, in which we try to embody and express this ceaseless stream of Life. Upon everything lies the burden of its form, which alone separates it from dust, but which also interferes with the unceasing flood of Life in it. In Henry IV this man who has taken on a form, a fixed mask in the midst of flooding, changing Life, remains in it until the moment when his passion and despair and violent impulse send him back into Life. But only for a moment: the impetuous violence of the Life in him expels him into his masquerade again: in the struggle between Life and Form, Life is defeated, Form remains.

Nothing in town is to compare to Pirandello's Henry IV - well or badly done - as worth seeing. If there is a tendency in many of his plays to think, talk, analyse, without embodying these processes in dramatic molds that carry and give them living substance - and I think that is one of Pirandello's dangers, his plays too often when all is said and done boil down too much to single ideas - this fault cannot be laid on his *Henry IV*. In this play Pirandello has discovered a story, a visual image, and a character that completely embody and reveal the underlying area. This drama has a fantastic and high-spirited range in the spirit of the Italian comedy tradition; it has also a kind of

Shakespearean complexity and variety; and in the second act, at least, something like a poetry of intellectual beauty.

Pitoëff's Production of Henry IV (1925)

The best known production of *Henry IV* outside Italy is Pitoëff's in Paris in February, 1925. Pitoëff had been attracted to the play considerably earlier; in July of 1923 he wrote to his manager, Jacques Hébertot, saying that he had re-read the play finding it "an extraordinary thing - even better, perhaps, than *The Characters*, and I believe it absolutely essential to stage it". It might have been better if Pitoëff had followed this hunch and included the play in the next season's programme, for the delay until early 1925 contributed to its mixed reception. Both French critics and French public were suspicious by then by what was referred to as "Pirandello mania". As had become the pattern in Pitoëff's company, the major part was taken by Pitoëff himself, and his wife, Ludmilla, took the part of Frida. *Henry IV* was one of Pitoëff's major roles and his performance was well acclaimed. He made of his face a mask, meticulously following the stage directions about this in the play, and created from the text an intense, inward character (a number of critics mentioned Dostoyevsky in this regard), who was always teetering on the brink of an all-consuming madness. Pitoëff's set design, however, was not appreciated. Critics did not like, and said so with some emphasis, his geometric set which totally abandoned any pretence to naturalism.

With the foreign productions of *Henry IV* Pirandello had consolidated his position as international dramatist. While Pitoëff was presenting *Henry IV* in Paris, Pirandello and his colleagues were preparing for the opening night of the Teatro d'Arte in Rome. In the summer of the same year, Pirandello brought his company to Paris and they performed, along with other plays, the two which had brought him greatest renown, *Six Characters in Search of an Author* and *Henry IV*. Ruggero Ruggeri accompanied the company as guest actor and took the role of Henry IV which he had created in Italy. French reviewers were quick to comment on the totally different interpretations and acting styles of the Italian and Russian actor. Antoine, for instance, wrote in *L'Information*, July 25, 1925: "There is no link between Ruggeri's Henry IV and Pitoëff's. Pitoëff stretched the play to the limits of nightmare, while Ruggeri leaves it in the realm of waking consciousness. Why does Henry continue to feign madness when he is cured? Pitoëff explains this by leaving the unfortunate man always teetering on the brink of madness; Ruggeri lucidly explains it by giving emphasis to the fine reply that having been distant for so long from the world, it is impossible for him now to find a place for himself within it." By contrasting Ruggeri's performance with Pitoëff's, the critics established Pitoëff as a leader of what they referred to as the "northern" interpretation of Pirandello and thus contributed to the European stature of the Italian dramatist.

As the document for this section, we include a translation of Jacqueline Jomaron's reconstruction of the set.

Document No. 23: Pitoëff's set for *Henry IV*.

The design shows a backdrop on which is painted a schematic representation of a throne over which are also painted oriflammes whose long poles cross one another to form a decorative background of irregular triangles. On the floor of the stage are two benches obliquely placed. The stage set followed very closely this design with its emphasis on geometric composition. In the performance, Pitoëff kept the idea of a painted backdrop and canopy, but, abandoning any representational intent, he replaced the flags by triangles and curves. The chair on which Henry was to sit was backed up against the painted throne and rested on a triangular base; and the obliquely placed benches marked out a triangular acting space. The two portraits, representing Henry IV and Matilda of Tuscany on the day of the carnival, were placed on slanting supports in front of empty niches, and, in the angular treatment of the faces, rather in the manner of El Greco, were reminiscent of a triangle. There were no three-dimensional effects in the set, no sense of architectural realism, or *trompe l'oeil*; doors, furniture, rostra existed in lines and surfaces and colours. For Pitoëff, this design was the design of the theatre in which twenty years ago Henry had imagined his masquerade. The image corresponded to Henry's words at the end of the play "everything is mask here, including the throne room and the four secret counsellors". With his set Pitoëff emphasised that in a certain way *Henry IV* too was theatre within theatre.

The design for the second act ("another room in the villa, next to the throne room and furnished in an austere and old style") was realized in the same spirit of systematic stylization. The backdrop was firmly divided into two parts of different colours on which were boldly painted windows looking out onto a garden. This time the dominant motif was the rectangle: acting space, table, door, armchairs and stools.

In accord with the sets, the interpretation and stage business of the play was designed to underline the essential ideas of the play. Two instances will clarify this. When Henry IV made his entrace in Act I, the four counsellors and the two attendants formed a line parallel to the footlights, two sets of three men, one behind the other. Henry advanced majestically towards them as if they were a crowd, stopped at the end of the line, did a right-angle turn, turning his back on the audience and facing the throne, while the same line reformed, this time perpendicular to the footlights and the throne, which the madman now approached. By this stage business, Pitoëff underlined visually the derisory and fictitious nature of the ceremony. The end of the production is famous. Pitoëff visualized in a stunning way the disassociation of a sick mind. While the madman, announcing himself to be sane, made his re-entry into life by killing his rival Belcredi, the support on the court side of the stage fell on the characters on stage. After the exit of the other characters, Pitoëff, by now alone on the stage, lifted the flat onto his shoulders, trying to put it back in position along the wall and the false madman appeared to be walled in as if in a cage.

Notes

1. See Introduction to Document No. 28.
2. By Giovacchino Forzano. It was first staged on 20 November 1920 by Ruggeri's company at the Olympia Theatre in Milan.
3. Virgilio Talli (1858-1928), director and actor dedicated to the fostering of good theatre. He was well known for his excellent ensemble work. See Document No. 20.
4. Alda Borelli, actress. Pirandello wrote *Clothe the Naked (Vestire gli ignudi)* for her.
5. Francesco Annibale Butti (1868-1912), dramatist.   *Flames in the Shade (Fiamme nell'ombra)* is usually considered his best work.
6. Marco Praga (1862-1929), prose writer, dramatist, director and theatre critic.
7. Ermete Zacconi (1857-1948), stage and screen actor, best known for his sensitive acting in the realistic mode.
8. Egisto Olivieri, actor, was probably best known for the quality of his diction. He joined Pirandello's company in 1925.
9. Romano Calò (1883-1952), actor who was also a playwright.
10. Sergio Tòfano, actor, played in other Pirandello plays: *Clothe the Naked (Vestire gli ignudi)* in 1923 and *Each in His Own Way (Ciascuno a suo modo)* in 1925.
11. Gilda Marchiò later became a member of the Teatro d'Arte during the 1927-1928 season. She took the role of *madre*.
12. By Gabriele D'Annunzio.

plays were presented at the little theatre, among them Pirandello's *The Man with the Flower in his Mouth (L'Uomo dal fiore in bocca)* in February 1922. None of these ventures, however, combined a theatre with a touring company, none of them had a figurehead as prestigious as Pirandello and none of them had attempted mixed funding on the same scale.

The approach to the government for a subsidy came at the time when Fascism in Italy was at its lowest ebb. The murder of the socialist deputy Matteotti on 10 June 1924 caused a number of people to hesitate in their allegiance to the party as it seemed all too clear that the Fascist hierarchy was implicated in the crime. The later murder of Casalini on 11 September was thought by some to be a retaliation from the opponents to Fascism. There were fears of instability, possibly anarchy. It was at this juncture that Pirandello joined the Fascist party. His involvement with Fascism and his relationship with the party is a complex issue but one that cannot be separated from his activities as a man of the theatre. In October of the previous year, Pirandello, along with others, had written a highly rhetorical piece in the *Idea nazionale (National Idea)* congratulating Mussolini on the first anniversary of the march on Rome but had made no move to join the party at this point. On 12 September 1924, that is one day after the murder of Casalini, he applied for membership by sending a telegram to the editor of *L'Impero (The Empire)*. This was followed up by an interview with the editor, Telesio Interlandi, which was published in the paper of 19 September. The letter we include from Stefano Pirandello to Claudio Argentieri (Document no. 24), which mentions the successful visit to Mussolini on behalf of the Teatro d'Arte is dated 1 October. As Giudice has indicated, Pirandello joined the Fascist part as ostentatiously as he could so that he could gain maximum advantage and credit for his act; and throughout his life, he made a point of making public statements and gestures that emphasised his allegiance to the party and its policies.[1] For instance, he made certain he was in Italy at strategic moments, such as at the declaration of the Ethiopian war, and gave his Nobel prize gold medal, along with other pieces of gold, to be melted down for the cause. Furthermore, though it would be difficult to see any play, novel or short story as a direct apology for Fascism, there is evidence from newspaper articles and interviews that Pirandello liked to be thought to hold anti-democratic views. After his return from the United States in early 1924, he said in a much quoted interview with Villaroel for *Il giornale d'Italia* (8 May 1924) that he considered the American way of life too democratic, that the masses needed someone to guide them, and he himself was anti-democratic par excellence; views he repeated more than once during his lifetime. On the other hand, his wishes and instructions concerning his death (that there be no public funeral, that his body be cremated and the ashes scattered) seemed a gesture to thwart the fascists from gaining any advantage from his death. Though a few of his plays found favour with the hierarchy, for instance *The New Colony (La nuova colonia)*, Pirandello had to tread very carefully both at home and abroad; a number of statements he made indicate that he knew he was being watched. As the letter from Salvini to Interlandi (Document no. 45) implies, Pirandello found it difficult to barter his prestige for the funds he wanted, and though on that particular occasion in 1926 he did not carry out his threat to leave Italy, he later went to Germany on a fairly permanent basis and his last years were spent for the most part living in hotel rooms in foreign cities with only occasional visits to Italy. And no less than six of his premières were presented in foreign cities.

In October of 1924, however, as Stefano Pirandello's letter to Claudio Argentieri suggests, all seemed possible. The exitement of transforming the Odescalchi theatre where Podrecca had shown his famous puppet company before he began his world-wide tour in 1924, into an intimate, well-furbished theatre remained high during the winter and spring of 1925. All the reviews of the opening night indicated that the venture was a success and had won approval from a number of people both at home and abroad. However, only a few months later, while the company was gaining acclaim in London and Paris, Renzo Rendi, the man left behind to look after the administration of the theatre, was having anything but a happy time. Debts were mounting, the subsidy had been spent. Mussolini entrusted one of his higher officials, Count Giacomo Suardo, Undersecretary of State for the President's Office of the Cabinet, with the task of raising money from individual patrons and firms; he also received an investigatory report from D. Razza, General Secretary of the National Theatre Guild, on how the money had been spent so far. By 1 September 1925, Pirandello had agreed to continue to take artistic responsibility for the company but wanted nothing more to do with the administration. Although the indefatigable Suardo managed to raise some funds, it was only possible to keep afloat the theatre company. Apart from the short 1925 season before the company left for London and Paris, the beautiful little Odescalchi theatre was not used by the Teatro d'Arte. The company continued to tour, nevertheless, and became in effect what Pirandello had wanted to avoid, a travelling theatrical group. They were in demand in many cities of the world and took their repertoire to Germany, where they performed in fourteen cities, to Switzerland, Hungary, Austria, Czechoslovakia, Argentina, Brazil as well as touring within Italy itself.

Letter from Stefano Landi [Pirandello] to Claudio Argentieri (1924)

The letter that follows is from Pirandello's eldest son, Stefano, better known as Stefano Landi, himself a playwright and poet. The letter is addressed to Claudio Argentieri, one of the founding members of the Teatro d'Arte, a publisher living in Spoleto. The group that went to see Mussolini were mostly literary men. There was one actor among them, Lamberto Picasso, who was to take leading roles in Pirandello's plays. He had already submitted a plan to Mussolini for an Art Theatre but then decided to join forces with Pirandello. Orio Vergani (1899-1960), brother to Vera Vergani, who took the part of the Stepdaughter in the first performance of *Six Characters in Search of an Author*, was a journalist and dramatist, one of whose plays *The Walk on the Waters (Il cammino sulle acque)* was performed by Pirandello's company in 1925. Massimo Bontempelli was a composer and dramatist, whose best known work is *Our Dea (Nostra Dea)*, first presented by Pirandello and the Teatro d'Arte company in April, 1925, and providing Marta Abba with her début for the company. Antonio Beltramelli was a novelist of nationalistic persuasion.

A number of the people mentioned in the letter were to become key members in the Fascist Party. Balbino Giuliano was a deputy in 1924, Under-Secretary for Education and then Minister of Education in 1929, Luigi Federzoni was a founding member of the Fascist Party, editor of *Idea Nazionale*, in which Pirandello published. Dino Grandi was also one of the founding members of the Fascist movement. By 1925 he was a member of the Council (Gran Consiglio) and Under-Secretary for Home Affairs. Alessandro Casati, on the other hand, though a senator in 1924 and Minister of Education for a short while in 1925, left the government and party before the end of the year.

Document No. 24: Stefano Landi [Pirandello] to Claudio Argentieri, 1.10.1924

Dear Argentieri,
The constitution of the Society has been again deferred until next Saturday. It is very important that you are here for it. The notary public, Mencarelli, has examined the powers of proxy you have given me and finds them inadequate and imprecise; inadequate because, since you are to be president of the administrative council, I ought to have the authorization to accept this nomination on your behalf; and imprecise where it says, "The Society which will operate from the former *Teatro dei Piccoli*". Even the notary public says it is strange in comparison with other similar bodies that the person who is to administer and represent them is not present at the act of constituting the society. I am returning the document of authorization to you, but not for you to alter it: you must come in person.

Personal

Our affairs couldn't be going better. We've been received by Balbino Giuliano, Cremonesi, Mussolini and Casati. The two decisive interviews were the latter two. Papa, Beltramelli, Bontempelli, Vergani, Picasso and I went to see Mussolini. We were received most warmly. The Duce had heard all about it from Federzoni and Belt [ramelli]. He anticipated all our requests; and assured us that the Government would assume the entire financial responsibility for the enterprise with a grant of 250,000 lire. He gave us 50,000 there and then from his personal wallet, so that we could get on with the construction work; another 50,000 lire will come in a few days' time, a further 50,000 he will get the City Council to give us, and the last 100,000 will come from the Ministry of Education which will return to its budget sheet for us an annual prize of 100,000 lire for Dramatic Art which has not been removed this year. In addition we will definitely have a further 50,000 lire from S.R. Grandi.
To get the enterprise going (which will then sail along without need of further support) we need roughly 216,000 lire (I want you to bring it up to 250,000 lire). We have 250,000 lire from the Government and City Council, the other 50,000 lire, our own 60,000 lire and 5,000 from the theatre corporation: 365,000 lire in all, without counting the strong probability of soon having two life members at 25,000 lire each, Cesano and Mercadante. As you can see, after months of dogged work, we have fully overcome our problems.
Yesterday we signed the new contract of agreement with the new proprietor of the Teatro dei Piccoli (because you must know that yesterday evening

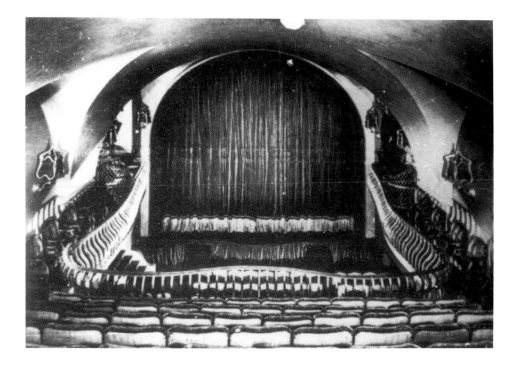

1: The Teatro d'Arte stage and auditorium

2: *The Festival of Our Lord of the Ship* at the Teatro d'Arte, 1925.

3. The striped flats of Pitoëff's production of *Six Characters in Search of an Author*, 1923.

4: The cast of Salvini's production of *Tonight We Improvise, 1930*.

5: **Egisto Olivieri, Marta Abba and Lamberto Picasso in Pirandello's production of** *Six Characters in Search of an Author,* **1925**

6: *Egisto Olivieri, Marta Abba, Lamberto Picasso and Gino Cervi in Pirandello's production of Six Characters in Search of an Author, 1925*

7: **Ruggero Ruggeri in *Henry IV*, 1922.**

8: **The end of Pitoëff's production of** *Henry IV*, **Paris, 1925.**

9: Virgilio Marchi's set design for Dunsany's *The Gods of the Mountain* at the Teatro d'Arte, April 1925.

10: Enrico Job's set for Mario Missiroli's production of *The Mountain Giants*, 1979.

11: Puppets in Missiroli's production of *The Mountain Giants*, 1979.

12: The funeral of Ilse (Valentina Cortese) in Strehler's production of *The Mountain Giants*, 1967.

the separation of the Podrecca-Fidora Society took place with the ownership of the hall remaining with the latter). Rent and surety have the same conditions as the contract with Podrecca. That means that from today, 1st October, we are in our own place in Via Santi Apostoli, and it's almost certain that construction work will begin on Monday, due to be finished within twenty days, which we can pay for with the first grant already allocated to us.

As you can see, we are on the right road.

Please confirm that you're coming on Saturday morning and that you will also stay on for a few days for the Assembly and the Elections. Orio [Vergani] sends his greetings too and is looking forward to seeing you.

Yours affectionately,

Stefano

Documents proposing the Teatro d'arte (1924)

The following three documents are all taken from Alberto Cesare Alberti, *Il teatro nel fascismo, Pirandello e Bragaglia*, Rome, 1974. The first is the legal document, dated 6th October, by which the Teatro d'Arte came into being; the third is a letter from Pirandello to Mussolini, impressing upon him the importance of their enterprise and repeating his invitation to the opening night. Mussolini was in fact present at this event, as is clear from Corrado Alvaro's review of the occasion.

Lamberto Picasso, the author of the second document, which puts forward a proposal for an art theatre on which the Teatro d'Arte was based, was a distinguished actor who had already directed an art theatre company from 1920-24, during which period he staged plays by Andreev, Crommelynck and Molnar, and also presented the première of Pirandello's one-act play *At the Exit (All'uscita)* in September, 1922. In addition to bringing new foreign works to the Italian stage, he was also a firm supporter of an Italian repertoire and staged successful productions of works by Chiarelli, Bontempelli and Betti. The following quotation, take from a *causerie* given to the Accademia Teatrale degli Indipendenti on 17th January, 1925 entitled "I, You, and the Theatre" (and now held in the Fondo Picasso in the Museo-Biblioteca dell'Attore in Genoa) illustrates his views on the relationship between text and actor which are similar to those of Pirandello as expressed in his theoretical writings. "The actor must serve the work of art and hence the author who has conceived and determined it. And his only concern must be to make the character entrusted to him live, as the imagination of the author has created it, and not in a different way. The actor must be a faithful and scrupulous interpreter of the author before an audience and he must know how to free himself from every preconceived preference or sympathy which often comes from reading the play before working on the text in rehearsals." Lamberto Picasso joined the Teatro d'Arte company as a leading actor, but also co-directed a number of the company's productions.

Document No. 25: The constitution of the Teatro d'Arte

Victor Emmanuel III
by the grace of God and the will of the Nation
King of Italy

In the year Nineteen hundred and twenty-four this day the sixth of October, in Rome in my rooms in Vicolo Sciarra, 61.   In the presence of Dr. Metello Mencarelli, myself, Notary Public resident in Rome, registered with the Collegio Notarile dei Distretti of the aforesaid city, without the assistance of witnesses, whose presence has been deemed unnecessary by all the parties together unanimously.   The following have constituted themselves:

1.   Argentieri, Dr. Claudio di Giovambattista[2], born in Correto di Spoleto and resident in Spoleto;
2.   Pirandello, Stefano di Luigi, freelance writer, resident in Rome and domiciled in Via G.B. De Rossi, no.23 in his own name and in the capacity of special attorney for Mr. Beltramelli[3], Antonio of the late Francesco, freelance writer and resident in Forlì, by virtue of the attached special commission received by me dated the third inst. and for Mr. Giovanni Cavicchioli di Alfredo, born and resident in Mirandola, freelance writer, by virtue of the attached special commission attested by Dr. Borellini, Giuseppe, Notary Public in Mirandola dated October third, 1924;
3.   Bontempelli, Massimo[4], son of the late Alfonso, freelance writer, born in Como and domiciled in Rome, Viale Giulio Cesare, no, 51;
4.   Celli, Maria Letizia[5], daughter of Luigi, spinster, of independent means, born in Rome and domiciled in Via di Santa Bonosa, no.22;
5.   Cantarella, Pasquale, son of Francesco, clerk, employed in the State Archives of Salerno and domiciled in Rome in Via Muzio Clementi, no.18;
6.   Picasso, Lamberto, son of the late Luigi, actor, born in Genoa and domiciled in Rome by choice with Enrico Bises, Enrico, solicitor, Via Borgognona, 7;
7.   Prezzolini, Giuseppe[6], son of the late Luigi, freelance writer, born in Perugia and domiciled in Rome in Via Brescia, 29;
8.   Rendi, Renzo [...] freelance writer, born in Milan and domiciled in Rome, Salita S. Nicola da Tolentino, 1B;
9.   Vergani, Vittorio (known as Orio)[7], son of the late Francesco, freelance writer, born in Milan and domiciled in Rome, Via Boezio, no. 8;
I declare as Notary Public that I am assured of the identities of the parties who in this present act agree and stipulate the following;

Article 1

An anonymous society is hereby constituted to be known as TEATRO D'ARTE DI ROMA.

Article 2

The object of the society is to carry out the following programme devised by Luigi Pirandello;
1. The management of a public theatre in Rome;
2. The management of an independent dramatic company to perform in Italy and abroad;
3. Associate management of the "Corporazione delle Nuove Musiche".

Article 3

The Society shall be governed by a single public statute, composed of thirteen articles to be read and approved by all parties and signed by them and by myself, Notary Public and attached to the present document under the letter C, whereby it will then become an integral part of the said document.

Article 4

The public capital of the Society is 55,000 lire, divided into eleven shares of nominal value of 5,000 lire each.
The shares are named and cannot be sold without approval by the Executive Council.
An Assembly can be called to hear appeals.
The shares cannot be placed in the name of any single person.
The aforesaid capital has been underwritten as follows;
Argentieri, Claudio, 5,000 lire
Pirandello, Stefano, 5,000 lire
Beltramelli, Antonio, 5,000 lire
Cavicchioli, Giovanni, 5,000 lire
Bontempelli, Massimo, 5,000 lire
Celli, Maria Letizia, 5,000 lire
Cantarella, Pasquale, 5,000 lire
Picasso, Lamberto, 5,000 lire
Prezzolini, Giuseppe, 5,000 lire
Rendi, Renzo, 5,000 lire
Vergani, Vittorio, 5,000 lire
Three tenths (16,500 lire) have been deposited in the Banco di Napoli on 4th October, 1924, as shown by the bank's receipt, an original copy of which is attached under B.
The remaining seven tenths will be deposited when requested by the Executive Council.

Article 5

The society will continue in existence for three years from the date of ratification of the Constitution and may be prolonged further if so determined by the Assembly.

Article 6

The organs of the Society are:
a)   The Executive Council consisting of three members;
b)   The College of Auditors consisting of three working members and two
       deputies;

Article 7

The results of the elections for public appointment are as follows:
Claudio Argentieri
Giuseppe Prezzolini
Orio Vergani
Working members:
Dr. Giovanni Balella di Dario
Furini, Romeo
Rendi, Renzo
The deputy members:
Cantarella, Pasquale
Preti, Amilcare
All parties have agreed to accept their respective appointments.

Article 8

The first period of operation will terminate on 31st December, 1925.

Article 9

The parties delegate Dr. Claudio Argentieri to investigate all legal formalities required for the legal constituting of the Society and empower him to make any necessary amendments to the Statutes and to this present document if so requested by the Court of Rome for the required ratification, and furthermore empower him to make withdrawals from the Banco di Napoli, once legal requirements have been met, of the three tenths of the capital deposited in the aforesaid bank.

Article 10

All parties concerned in the present act agree to be domiciled in Rome on the premises of the said constituted Society.

Article 11

All expenses incurred in drawing up the present act and all following papers are to be met by the Society and will be included in the general expenses of the first period.
The parties declare that they have all read this document and the attached papers and accept my statement of their reading.

The present act, written by a person known to me on three sheets of paper, covering approximately eight sides has been read by me to the parties who have declared that it is in keeping with their wishes.

Signed by: Claudio Argentieri - Stefano Pirandello in his own name and in the two names declared - Massimo Bontempelli - Celli Maria Letizia - Pasquale Cantarella - Lamberto Picasso - Giuseppe Prezzolini - Renzo Rendi - Vergani Vittorio - Dr. Metello Mencarelli, Notary Public.

Registered in Rome on October 21st, 1924 having the number 7497 Reg. 436 Public Acts

Costing 303.75 lire

Senior Attorney [illegible signature]

Document No. 26: Lamberto Picasso's Proposal for a Small Theatre (February, 1924)

Among the many and varied causes of the crisis of the Italian theatre, the principal one and also the most obvious one is certainly the continued gypsy wanderings of our companies from one city to another, which leads to various problems, not least of which is the use of non-artistic criteria in the choice and preparation of new works, and even more so in the staging and acting.

The particularly unstable conditions in which companies find themselves do not allow directors to use a sense of decorum and artistic taste in staging works in general, especially in presenting works with special features that require the creation of an atmosphere and environment corresponding to the spiritual values of the characters. This contrast between the recreation of the environment and the performing of a play is precisely what prevents the public from understanding certain works which are presented to them in such a strange and crudely unfinished way. On the other hand, especially in recent times, the public has shown its interest by attending with increased enthusiasm, keenness and sympathy, the performances of those very few companies which follow the principles of their art in matching the uniqueness of every play with its own special environment and which try to stage plays in accordance with those principles, even though the costs which are quite incompatible with their touring budget mean that they are unable to present a wide and eclectic repertory. The public by now has well understood the need for stagings that are tasteful and in keeping with a play, and demands such from all companies, so that any performance which falls short of these expectations and principles arouses a chorus of protest immediately confirmed by the reviewers.

Another obvious cause of the present crisis in the theatre derives from the physiognomy and irrational composition of the present companies. They have completely lost all pretence of homogeneity and are now nothing more than hybrid organisms created purely for business speculation in the theatre for the vanity of a single, self-made actor-director, around whom exists a vast group of mediocrity. And since in modern theatrical works it is rare to find the greatly famed "big part" in which such an actor can excel and stand out above all the others, the result is that he all too readily rejects any works that do not allow him to be a star.

The creation of special theatres in Paris such as the Vieux Colombiers, the Chimère, the Théàtre des Arts, and the Kammerspiels in Munich, Berlin and Dresden, besides the art theatres in Prague, Moscow, Riga and in America is primarily due to the reasons outlined above. With the founding of these permanent theatres for permanent companies, it has been possible to cut off at its roots that same evil which threatened those countries with the destruction and sterility of all modern theatrical production, which must be and is a faithful mirror to the times and the outcome of the changed spiritual needs of the post war period. Precisely because they could attract a select, well-educated public and an elite circle of scholars and intellectuals, those theatres have immediately enjoyed great success and vastly reverberating approval in all the other countries, and have effectively contributed to the development of a new, noble form of intelligent theatre. And the Italian public, the intelligent, educated public which knows about these foreign initiatives through magazines, newspapers and intellectual exchanges and can estimate their importance in international artistic circles, deeply regrets that it is not seeing similar artistic criteria applied in Italy.

For these reasons and for this truth that everyone believes, a group of daring, willing persons have proposed the idea of instituting a Modern Theatre in Rome, the Italian Capital, that would accord with the said principles and to that end it is in the process of gathering together all the elements to render the attempt worthy and well executed, following foreign models but improving the criteria so that this enterprise will be a genuine national endeavour.

A plan of campaign, a crusade will be fought by these young people on behalf of art, that art which they hold uppermost in their brave hearts where they have always believed the stage to be a place from which truth, intelligence and beauty cannot be excluded.

The Theatre will be based on the following principles:

1. There will be a general management which will maintain the artistic aims established in the programme and will have full control of all activities together with artistic responsibility.

2. An organic company made up of experienced, well-tried actors appointed by the artistic director so as to create a group that will be ideally suited to the diverse and particular needs of the varied artistic programme.

3. A repertory that will cover revivals of Italian and foreign plays that are new to Italy, together with musical comedies and folk plays, will aim primarily at presenting a select, accurate series of new works, so as to become a complete whole, a kind of performing review of the entire vast theatrical movement of the world.

4. A well-chosen administration which, in agreement with the Artistic Director, will have the joint task of administering the Theatre finances together with those of the company and any other duty that the ordinary Administration shall think fit.

THE ACTING SCHOOL

Alongside this unit which shall have a maximum commitment to the art, there will be an acting school dedicated to modern training methods. In addition to classes, students will be expected to take part in evening performances, under the guidance of the artistic director, in small parts that will be assigned to them without payment. There will be a monthly experimental matinee performance during which a complete play will be performed by the students under the guidance of the Artistic Director. They will receive no financial recompense, but will bring some profit to the organisation through admission charges and the attendances at acting classes. These courses will be taught over three terms and will last until the future actors have been fully trained and, with the stage experience they have acquired, they will be able in a short space of time to understand in full the techniques of acting, without which any theoretical school can have no practical effect.

OTHER ACTIVITIES OF THE ORGANISATION

1. The Management will organise concerts of Italian and foreign classical music to be performed by well-known musicians: there will be "afternoons", following a preannounced programme, with artistic dances performed by well-known Italian and foreign artistes, that will reflect all the newest and most original developments in the contemporary plastic arts.
2. There will be a direct relationship and a programme of intellectual exchanges with similar organisations in France, Germany, Russia and America and elsewhere. Works which have been successfully received in the theatres of those countries will be introduced to our own audiences and Italian plays favourably received in performance in our own Theatre will be performed in theatres abroad.
3. Art exhibitions in the Theatre will be encouraged, together with similar artistic displays.
4. There will be a reading room and a library for all contemporary works, established through agreement with the publishing houses, and this will be open to the public.
5. There will be exhibitions in the Theatre of set designs created by our own designers and photographs of performances.
6. Every month the Theatre will publish a newsletter in which details of the activities of the Theatre will be set down, together with the programme of plays offered in the following month and the new activities planned. In this newsletter, in agreement with the holders of the copyright, it is planned to publish the plays in the repertory of the Theatre for which there is the greatest demand, following the objective criterion of critical acclaim and public appreciation. There will also be interviews with the most fashionable authors written by the best critics.

THE BUILDING

The Theatre requires a cultured, gracious location in which there should be no more than 400 seats. The sale of tickets will be organised alongside concessionary tickets, so that it will be possible to have an audience able to follow the development of the programme of repertory with interest and intelligence and which, although it will differ at every performance, will nevertheless comprise a group of constant, faithful attenders.

The Company, the performances outside the repertoire, the students' monthly experimental performances, the dance performances, concerts, exhibitions and all the other activities of the Theatre will be rigorously controlled by internal general rules of the Theatre, to which everyone will be expected to adhere, without exception, and this shall be established at the moment of signing the contract.

Document No. 27: Letter from Pirandello to Mussolini, Rome, 19.3.1925

Your Excellency,

Our theatre will open on the evening of Thursday, 2nd April. We have made every effort to ensure that the event will not only reflect well on the founding fathers, that is, on the National Government and the Italian artistes, but also on the Nation itself. However, up to now everything has rested on our communal efforts, since those who could have allowed us to work without worries have not reacted adequately to the national importance of that work.

Allow me to point out to your Excellency the fact that we have been aware of the expectations of the whole world concerning this project of ours. Knowing this, and having the responsibility of being virtually officially commissioned, since our theatre is regarded as the Italian State theatre both at home and abroad, we have been compelled to underwrite the sum of six hundred and fourteen thousand lire (264 thousand more than estimated) for everything - theatre, Company, stage props - so as to operate on that level of dignity and artistic propriety that might allow us to withstand the strain of so much responsibility and the shock of such huge expectations. We have not spent a single penny in luxury trimmings, to satisfy egoistic desires or whims for external pomp. As Your Excellency will see and ascertain, we have been motivated by what was necessary not by any vain pride. Our work and our efforts have been bold and long drawn out, but today we are able to say that we have given Rome a theatre which, both as a locale and in terms of stage machinery, may be envied by any other capital, and we have given to this theatre a group of actors able - as the first performance will demonstrate - to perform any kind of work without any kind of limitations.

As I have already indicated to Your Excellency, the cost so far is 614,500 lire.

Contributions are as follows:

L. 100 thousand from Your Excellency

L. 100 thousand from the Ministry of Education, from which 10,000 were deducted as tax = 90 thousand

L. 50 thousand from the City Council of Rome

L. 30 thousand from the Provincial government (which has not been paid in, but which we managed to obtain through the bank)

L. 26 thousand (!) from private contributions

L. 55 thousand from social capital

L. 5 thousand contributed by the New Music Corporation

L. 53 thousand 500 from subscriptions

Total contributions 1.409 thousand 500.

The deficit has been covered by assistance from the bank with some of the committee members standing surety, together with *my own anticipated income*. I myself, in fact, although I do not receive any profit at all from my work, have not been able to restrict myself to merely giving the theatre all my time, effort and the guarantee of my name; I have also given it all my liquid savings, that is, 65 thousand lire.

We had hoped for much from industry, not only because of the quality of our enterprise but also because of the favour shown to industry by the National Government. Instead, as will be seen by the sorry details of the contributions, industry has assisted us in the most paltry manner: Riccardo Gualino gave us 5,000; Senatore Borletti gave us 5,000; Max Bondi gave us 5,000[8]. Out of all the banks to whom approaches were made, only the Banco di Roma responded with 5,000 lire and the Banco di Santo Spirito with 1,000 lire. Although all the others were approached, they nevertheless not only refused outright but also declined to permit us even the smallest amount of credit.

This closing of the doors is not unconnected with the sorry experiences most of our possible contributors had with the "Teatro degli Italiani"[9], together with the distrust aroused by the failure of the three art theatres in Milan. We were not able to persuade them that the life and prosperity of our enterprise is assured, since it is based on the certainty of being able to recover rich profits from our foreign tours.

We are being invited by all countries; all the major theatrical bodies are offering us contracts: in South America, in Spain, in Belgium, in France and in Germany. I have given serious consideration to these offers since I propose to accompany the Company abroad where, through conferences and public interviews on contemporary Italian life, I propose to undertake a propaganda exercise for the State, as I did last year in North America. This is the real way in which I can have a direct political impact that is not entirely wasted, and putting my efforts into such an undertaking is not only a source of lively moral satisfaction, it is also the fulfilment of a mission that I feel I have been appointed by Your Excellency to undertake.

The Teatro d'Arte of Rome, fired as it is by my passion and by the skill and interests of my friends is now a lively, vital organism. All that is required is the assistance of one who could help it be born without the pangs of too long a labour, thus sparing its parents from the danger of losing their economic livelihood in that labour.

For that would not be fair.

I shall therefore wait for Your Excellency to grant us supreme, definitive assistance so as to resolve this situation which embarrasses me and is an obstacle to the free movement of my activities just at the moment when I have the greatest need. I hope for further contributions and trust that the authority and prestige of Your Excellency will encourage rich industrialists such as Rotellini, Borsalino or Treccani, for example, among others, to contribute a worthy sum and thus uphold the decency of the Italian industrial class.

I trust that Your Excellency will be present on the evening of 2nd April for the inauguration of *our* Theatre. In this way our efforts will be rewarded and we shall rejoice in this manifestation of Italian life that is so largely due to Your Excellency. Please accept my most respectful and cordial greetings,

Your servant, Luigi Pirandello.

Virgilio Marchi's memories of the early days of the Teatro d'Arte 1924-5

Virgilio Marchi's first assignment as a theatre architect was to redesign the Odescalchi theatre for Pirandello's Teatro d'Arte. Later he redesigned a number of theatres, including the San Marco theatre in Livorno and, as his last work in this field, the Cinema-Auditorio Odeon at Livorno.

Before concentrating on designing theatres, Marchi began his career as an architect and was a member of the futurist movement. He was also a stage and costume designer for Anton Giulio Bragaglia's Teatro degli Indipendenti in Rome where he held an exhibition of futurist architecture in 1922.

The passage that follows has been selected from pages Marchi left which were intended to become his memoirs and which are now published in the periodical *Teatro Archivio*, May 1981. In addition to redesigning the Odescalchi theatre, Marchi was also one of the stage designers for several of Pirandello's productions. He combined spatial imagination with considerable techical skills. His *pièce de résistance* as a designer was the earthquake at the end of *The New Colony (La nuova colonia)* in 1928. Reproductions of a number of his designs for Pirandello's plays can be seen in Richard Sogliuzzo's book, *Luigi Pirandello, Director,* Metuchen, N.J. and London, 1982, and Alessandro d'Amico and Alessandro Tinterri, *Pirandello capacomico*, Palermo, 1987.

Document No. 28: Virgilio Marchi on the Teatro d'Arte

Once the Teatro dei Piccoli had been sacrificed and the beautiful dark red curtain had come down (grade one velvet, which I acquired, and I still have bedcovers that to my everlasting delight belong to theatre history) and the auditorium had been reduced to a vast hole in order to create the gradient in the auditorium, the noisy, smoky, hard-working builders' yard only lasted a few months. They worked desperately hard day and night with fanatical zeal, adding yet another plank to the building of the new Italian theatre, watched over benignly by Luigi Pirandello who was

watching the growth of his own child that he would be leading down
unsuspected streets. Such is the unknown whim of tomorrow even for men
of genius. I will pass over technical details and focus on those particulars
which come to mind whenever I think of the Odescalchi. I forget
professional details, but trivia stay in my mind because unquestionably they
represent the real life that was lived in there better than anything more
significant could do. And I shall only add this. The all-seeing, anxious,
curious gaze of the overseer was still represented by those twelve associates
amongst whose names, unless I am mistaken, we find Pirandello,
Bontempelli, Beltramelli, Landi, Vergani, ... Cavicchioli[10], Pavolini[11] and
yours truly.

In fact there were eleven. They were never able to find a twelfth
shareholder, but since eleven did not sound right, they said they were
twelve: the eleven twelve. Which means, that if you ignore me, there were
twenty eyes overseeing what went on, ten people in all, who invariably
turned up, quite separately every day, wanting to be told details of the
progress of the work. If you think that these people came back several
times a day, accompanied by friends or sending friends and acquaintances
along, then you can work out that every twenty four hours I had to explain
the same things about twenty or twenty-five times. For me that was a great
trial and very irritating, the worst thing that could happen to me in the
builders' yard. There is a useful notice: "only site personnel permitted to
enter". But there were people with a vested interest, famous people,
theatre people and they all had to be handled carefully, touchy people who
were extremely useful, not forgetting the ladies, writers who were well-
known or total unknowns, famous actors, small-time actors, gossip
columnists and journalists looking for hot news.

No builders' yard was ever so visited and so honoured by such a
fashionable intellectual crowd. The workers hated it. The visits were a
danger to the curious. One lady had her dress soaked by a sudden spurt of
liquid of doubtful origin from up above; a disgusting habit the builders had
when they did not want to climb down the scaffolding. One unfortunate
gentleman - a very important person - slipped and fell into a trench of
quick lime. We barely saved him. He was wearing a blue suit and had
turned into a ghost. He was a famous university professor and had a
lecture to give. We sent him home in a taxi. His students waited for him
in vain that afternoon.

Luigi Pirandello spent hours in the room they had turned into an
office. He liked to look through the plans, sketch out details, give orders
for the creation of his theatre - I see someone who is always working - he
used to say. And he would smile kindly. I was flattered by his trust; it
increased my energy, which was linked to my sense of responsibility and
my pleasure at being important and able to play a significant role in the
whole enterprise. And there was my ambition to begin to realise an idea
that had been haunting me for a long time, inspired by the Italian tradition
of Renaissance masters: "To build a theatre specifically for a stage. To
finish the building work and not leave it to ready made things but to stay
involved in the creation of scenic representation." [....]

[...] Now my ambition to make theatres for specific stages played me
the tricky card of double responsibility: responsibility for the opening night

and for the *mise en scène*. Concern for this latter really caused problems in the smooth running of things. There were rehearsals with actors and crowds in a theatre that was still in the process of being transformed from a builders' yard. The first night was decided, with a new play by Pirandello, *The Festival of Our Lord of the Ship (La sagra del Signore della nave)* and a three acter by Lord Dunsany, *The Gods of the Mountain*. The first piece was very complex and involved a procession across the auditorium, a peasant celebration with a crowd, shouting, gunshots and general mayhem. The second had a huge crowd of actors in showy Indian-Persian costumes. When you think about the size of the stage (no more than seven metres by five), then you can understand the difficulty of putting on a performance of this kind, especially in a place that was still being built. No matter how well all the details had been thought through, we fell into the trap of over-elaborateness through trying to do too much, partly due to practical exigencies and partly due to the fashion for detailed theories at that time.[12] Biagini sculpted the figure of Christ on the cross that was carried in the procession,[13] and then its head was broken off when it passed underneath the concrete architrave in the passage. The set for *The Festival* was designed by Oppo[14] and built by Bianchini[15] with a solid church door in the realist mode, but proved to be quite inadequate for the demands of theatre and the proportions of the stage. Pirandello made his debut as director with this mass piece in particularly difficult conditions and he must have wondered more than once about the kind of inferno in which Pirandello the writer was about to expose himself, since he had never wanted to be bothered with the problems of staging.

The experience grew harder for him every day, as we shall see, until he was overwhelmed with debts, but there was a toughness in him that helped him to overcome this and worse [....]

[...] The Theatre opened on April 2nd at 9 o'clock. There was enormous interest and curiosity. The theatre was decorated in purple and silver. Young ladies who had heard whispering about the colour scheme came dressed in outfits that toned in, created especially for the occasion. The narrow hall was packed like a royal box (there was even a tiny royal box) and gleamed with sophisticated elegance. It really was the auditorium of a high quality theatre where our greatest playwright was the host. At 9 o'clock precisely M.[ussolini] came in. He was escorted to the left flank of the sloped stage. I was presented to him after the first act of *The Gods of the Mountain*. He admired the transformation of the theatre and the staging effects. He said: "I often used to come to this theatre of Podrecca's." The Marquis Paulucci de' Calboli tugged my jacket to indicate that the conversation was at an end. (I was to feel the familiar signal of the tugged jacket, the usual sign apparently, on two other occasions during ceremonial diplomatic encounters. The second time was in Siena, when I accompanied Prince Umberto along the battlements of the Medici Fortress on the occasion of the first exhibition of typical wines and it was the Prefect who did it. He did not tug a sleeve, but pulled my coat-tail.) Next morning Antonio Beltramelli confirmed the official approval of the previous evening "for the style of the staging". All the press noted it as one of the most important theatrical events of the day. Go and check it out, you'll find I am right. In fact in those few days a new Pirandello was born.

As for what might have been the architectural significance of that theatre - which has now been destroyed and transformed into an ordinary vulgar cinema - that is not for me to say. The ancient princely stables of the Odescalchi, that were probably designed by Bernini, were revitalised by flowing, curving lines inspired by the model of the corbel of the vault. Orio Vergani had given me a sketch showing the sinuousness of the rhythm and I still have it. Parapets, cornices, footlights, balusters, etc. all flowed in S curves that recalled the baroque, cushioned by the welcoming modernity of the textiles and the silvery gleam of the borders. The wall lights shone with a calm, warm light like candles. Tradition was joined with the new in such a welcoming elegant combination that it resembled a small court theatre, in camera. You would have thought that the twentieth century had never arrived. [..........]

How many afternoons and evenings and entire nights did we spend in those readings and rehearsals, those infuriating rehearsals! Pirandello used to stay in the theatre even when the actors had gone home and I was still there with the technicians putting the lighting equipment away. He relished the feel, the atmosphere. With me he used to get worried about the defects in technical apparatus of Italian theatres. We used to dream together about the ideal theatre which would have magic keyboards, the fantasy theatre that would make dreams come to life. Nothing infuriated him more than the nerve-wracking waiting around while the lighting men fixed up wires and cables and equipment and hooks, whereas everything ought to have fallen into place instantly at a nod of the head or at a command. Long half-hours went by, full hours before a certain effect could be seen and he used to think that the lighting men were doing nothing. Nights flew by. To our eyes, tired as we were and confused after so many heavy hours of work, the real dawn light outside became muddled with the multi-coloured glimmerings of the projectors.

I can still see the side entrance of the Teatro Argentina, on Via Barbieri, when we used to go down the sloping corridor together, tired out with the effort that had begun the morning of the previous day, obsessed with living those dramatic realities and stunned to discover that the dawn was touching the cornices of the buildings with the first rays of sunlight. That unexpected light on the rooftops, on the gables, on the edges of the guttering, had us dazzled with exhaustion. We used to go with the Maestro to Piazza Arenula where he got his taxi. In the silence of the city there was the occasional delayed spray of water from the street cleaners, a piercing call from the first swallow, and I used to go on seeing the lights getting bigger as though they were behind frosted glass, because of the life of the stage at night that kept all the sensitive fibres of my body still throbbing. I used to cross the Via Ripetta and walk on to my office on the Via Flaminia.

The Odescalchi had been a small venture, and had come after the even more modest although much talked about Indipendenti[16] project. This project had made me think that one day - perhaps even with Pirandello himself - we would have reached the goal of having a great theatre that was truly ours; a sort of Wagnerian dream of Bayreuth for prose theatre and for

Pirandello's directorship.   (And Oh, how many useless projects were drawn up, only to collapse through discussion, bureaucracy, doubts and the inevitable meddling of politicians.)

Document No. 29: Corrado Alvaro's account of the first night of the Teatro d'Arte, 2.4.1925

The opening night of the Teatro d'Arte of Rome directed by Luigi Pirandello took place last night at the Teatro Odescalchi in Via Santi Apostoli.

Appearing innocently happy in evening dress, Pirandello first of all made a short speech to the assembled audience. He began by saying that the Teatro d'Arte had come into being in Rome with the help of the Fascist government, of the local government and a group of theatre lovers.   It aimed to follow a programme which was unaligned to any school, trend or political creed. He spoke briefly and simply. The theatre was filled with Roman high society, displaying sumptuous furs, resplendent jewels, well-groomed heads set elegantly on tall white collars. Pirandello said: "With the help of the national government, our expression of the youth of Italy". Fortunately in such gatherings it is not customary to burst into thunderous applause - or even to applaud at all. The Hon. Mussolini, together with the Hons. Grandi and Suardo, were present in the box opposite the Royal Box in which sat a representative of the King.

On show in the stalls were members of the Roman aristocracy, many representatives of the official world, in addition to a great number of foreigners, writers and Italian and foreign journalists.

The performance consisted of two plays of the most exquisite scepticism. The first was *The Festival of Our Lord of the Ship (La sagra del Signore della nave)* by Luigi Pirandello.   In this one-act play, the brutish nature of crowds was given a full treatment: a greedy, loud-mouthed, festive and sceptical crowd that grabs at the first symbol that speaks of some kind of mystery that we all harbour within us. In this work the animal nature of human beings finds a comforting portrayal both in its brutality and in its aspiration towards something higher and divine. It is only a matter of degree. The other play, *The Gods of the Mountain*, shows how people can become false prophets and false gods, and casts a shadow of doubt on all revelation. What is serious is that punishment is meted out to the sacrilegious and to the usurpers of divinity. At the end the false gods are turned into statues of green jade: a magnificent destiny for all imposters.

But we will return to this later.

The two plays chosen for the opening night of the Teatro d'Arte are among the most choreographic and visual available. With these two plays the theatre is able to manifest all its resources and possibilities. Footlights have been abolished. Lighting is effected by means of a series of spots in five colours, placed both front of house and on stage. These spots plunge the stage into pools of colour. With careful control amazing effects of proximity and distance can be obtained. The actor is not highlighted by a shadowless light, like little figures under a stereoscope, but immersed in a warm and general light that can change tone by minute and imperceptible degrees. Provided that it is not abused, this method of lighting could be used to compensate for shallow but wide stages like the one at the Teatro Valle. The setting is created emblematically. A large piece of cloth, called a cyclorama, covers the three walls of the stage. Against this, lit by spots of different tonal colours, are placed a few pieces of scenery so as to create the character of the setting. This is a method widely adopted by art theatres abroad. Purple and grey are the informing colours of the whole auditorium, which is raked towards the stage and accommodates three blocks of grey seats on grey carpet; above a dress circle six rows deep in silver. A grey curtain with silver edges opens on to the purple carpet of the stage. The walls covered in grey material are lit by baroque lamps, and indeed the whole design of the theatre by Virgilio Marchi could be called baroque. The silver of the decorations, the mother-of-pearl and dove-coloured grey of the wall hangings and velvets, give a soft tone to the whole theatre. The golden heads of the ladies in the stalls seemed balanced on an antique jewel case.

The lamps cast a prism of light on the grey wall hangings. In the auditorium there is a lyrical quality that is even better discovered on going out into the foyer. There, windows, lamps, gratings, blinds form an orchestra of silver, emphasised by the brick yellow of the plaster and by the gleaming muted red of the curtains. The design of the whole theatre, with its system of levels, loggias, balconies, has a musical movement.

It was difficult to stage the two works we saw yesterday in a theatre as small-scale as the Teatro Odescalchi. The productions turned out to be rather like those opening performances of dance companies that make a point of presenting the whole company. They were well done and worth seeing.

The Festival of Our Lord of the Ship (La Sagra del Signore della nave) by Luigi Pirandello belongs to that class of popular mime of which we have recently seen a charming example in *The Jar (La giara)* presented the other evening by Luigi Almirante[17]. It is the feast of Our Lord of the Ship in a village. We are in the church square. The feast day coincides with the day on which pigs are slaughtered. People come from all parts and among them is Signor Lavaccara who has just sold his pig called Nicola. He arrives at the square just in time to hear the pig give out its last squeals. He was very fond of his pig, which, he said, was as intelligent as any man. At this point a dispute arises. The Young Pedagogue gets up. If the pig were so intelligent, it would have refused to get fat, because it would understand that it was being fattened for the butcher. As the discussion proceeds, the whole theatre becomes a stage. Emerging from the doors at the back, a crowd rushes through the stalls: drummers, thieves, women of low repute, the devout and officials. The festivities have reached their peak. You can hear the noise of fireworks, the rolls of drums, the church choir. Meanwhile the discussion concerning the nature of the pig continues, foul-smelling, dirty and greedy. The wine flows freely around the innkeeper's tables and goes to peoples' heads; quarrels begin, the atmosphere is heady and smoke-filled. It's midday at the fair. Suddenly, amidst the noise and singing and firework explosions, the religious procession appears on the church steps, as if bearing upon itself all men's derision. The crowd falls to its knees, in a froth of wine and devotion. The men pass from drunkenness to compunction as if struck by an aspiration born from their very brutish nature.

The programme note explains that this one-act play is a conflict between the flesh and the spirit, between matter and an aspiration to something higher. It seemed to us to be a mime redolent with a bright and brutal colour like the images of village festivals. Pirandello shows a considerable theatrical talent in this little piece. By calculating exactly the length of the dialogue, the discussion on the nature of the pig reaches such an obscene level that the appearance of the wounded Christ could not be more terrible or impressive. It seems much less effective when you read it. The colour used on stage last night is not in the text and the stage directions that are in the text are convoluted as Pirandello's so often are. But last night Pirandello, the man of the stage, took the upper hand by the way he directed each actor and each group scene. More than 120 people take part in this one-act play, and it is very impressive to see how each scene is directed with clarity and a real flair for the visual effect of grouping. There were women stretched out on the ground wracked with devotion before Our Lord of the Ship, as they can be seen in certain paintings, more for visual effect than for devotion. We would like to mention that these visual mimes by Pirandello could be a starting point for a colourful Italian theatre which falls into none of the traps of folklore, regionalism and the short sketch. They remind you of certain aspects of Verga's theatre.

There were four curtain calls for this one-act play and Pirandello was called to the stage twice.

Oppo designed the set: a curtain and a backdrop, rather charming and pleasing in themselves, but too much like the scenery for Russian ballet productions. Those painted figures looking out of windows are like the curtain settings by Sudeikin[18] and Picasso[19]. Perhaps a more Italian and diffused popular spirit was required here. With all that hullaballoo on stage the painted curtain taken from the world of dance was too light without managing to be either sceptical or ironic. There is a man at a window on this curtain who has turned-up mustachios looking for all the world like some Russian gentleman out of the most authenic Russian ballet.

The crowd scene worked perfectly. Lighting played a major part in this production and it gave a sense of space and emphasis to moments of psychological significance. Sometimes, perhaps, the effects were too complex and contrasting and the chromatic effects ended by making the stage look like a shopwindow of sweetmeats. However, a fountain of blue light that transformed the backdrop into a great sea was a beautiful effect, as were certain sudden dimmings of the lights, when Christ appeared, for example, and a catastrophic sadness permeated the stage.

The Gods of the Mountain by Lord Dunsany is a strange work. This too has something of the ballet and cinema about it, in no way detrimental to the work. Moreover, certain experiments with form and style unrelated to the text, which could have seemed cold and distant, conveyed nevertheless inspiration and artistic results. It brings to mind that the formal problem of a work of art is a very important constant factor, that it can produce of itself an artistic emotion and a warmth of inspiration.

We are in the East. Four beggars at the city gates complain of lack of alms. The Gods have forgotten them. A mysterious man, followed by a servant, arrives at the city gates. He is the most able beggar of the East, Agmar, a man of extraordinary resources, of compelling logic, born to understand men and to take advantage of them. He suggests to the four beggars that they go into the city, having first got his servant to announce that the Mountain Gods, the seven jade idols placed in the valley opposite the hills, will move and go into the world. They need two further people: these are found, a thief and another unfortunate wretch. The seven, dressed like beggars, reveal green garments beneath their tatters. They will not say they are gods; they will let the people say that. And they are indeed taken for mysterious beings disguised as beggars. The voice of the people turns them into gods. They acquire the bearing of the Mountain Gods. They go into palaces, they sit on high-backed chairs, accept sacrifices. In truth they are hungry. Only Agmar, as crafty as a false god, acts his part well. His logic sounds like a profanation of every style of every prophet of every religion. When questioned, he replies with symbols, threatens punishment and withdraws punishment when men are prostrate before him. Forced to perform miracles by raising the dead he announces even more terrible punishments in order to get the present mourning accepted as a lesser evil. Instead of replying appropriately to every question, he questions the questioner and breaks the weapon of the questioner's enquiry with further questions of a divine flavour. In short, everyone adores these seven beggars who devour offerings and get drunk on good wine.

But now a rumour spreads through the city. Some pilgrims who had gone to see whether the stone gods of the valley were in their places have found the niches empty. This seems to confirm the divinity of the seven rogues. But only for a little while. Mysterious figures are already appearing in the desert and people are dying as they pass. They are the Mountain Gods who have come to punish the false gods. In the palace where the seven beggars sit on their seven high-backed seats posing as gods are heard the heavy footsteps of the real gods of stone. They appear. The seven beggars are magically turned to stone as they sit on their high-backed chairs.

The work received ten curtain calls.

There is little to say about this play. It is interesting, it is at times dramatic. Its success lies in its intricate blending of travel curiosities, theological doubts, echoes from fables and its ballet setting. Despite the presentation of this work, its author remains as shrouded in mystery as before. The material of this play, even at its most moving, seems organised for the sole purpose of conveying some grotesque and purely theatrical effects.

The set was designed by the architect Marchi. The first act is composed of white surfaces looking like walls sloping towards a source of green light, conveying a desolate feeling, dark and sterile, like the space in front of the walls of a city. The setting for the other two acts, made up of panels with an indication of a door, is less impressive. It has no style. The lighting effects were beautiful, however, especially those of the last act when the men were turned to stone.

In this play too the group scenes were perfectly arranged and the speaking well enunciated. It would be difficult to pick out individual members of the Company for special mention.

And so the Art Theatre of Rome was born. Time and future experience will say what fortune it deserves.

From yesterday's opening night one had the impression that something new could come of it. Although the stage will not allow stage designs which are complex from a purely architectural point of view, without the intricate symbolism too often excessively exploited in this kind of theatre, it might nevertheless be possible to develop a stage design with its own innovations and originality. We do not believe that theatre can move far from its origins and essence, and in any case we see no reason for making theatre into a pulpit for the recitation of fine literature. That was all right for France with its kind of protestant chapel which was the Vieux Colombier, because there an overskilled theatrical technique was threatening to destroy the art of theatre. Here in Italy, where we are still hoping to develop such skills, theatres must not be restictive. There exist in Europe about a dozen plays in which theatrical reforms can be renewed. They offer a pretext for innovation in interpretation and theatrical solutions. We hope to see them on the stage at the Odescalchi theatre. That would be both good for the public and bring credit to the new theatre. Rather than follow experiments already tried in other experimental theatres, we need an Italian theatre that follows a programme of innovation and renewal that will place Italy in the European theatrical context which began, after all, with the simple travelling players whose efforts, it must be said, made it possible to have today a modern theatre in full development.

This evening the same programme will be presented as a first performance for subscribers and the general public.

Marta Abba

Marta Abba was not part of the cast of the two one-act plays that were presented on the opening night at the Odescalchi theatre. She made her début with the company on the evening of 22 April in the première of Massimo Bontempelli's *Our Dea (Nostra Dea)*. The play concerns a woman with identity problems - her character changes with every change of dress - and was an excellent medium through which Marta Abba could reveal her sensitivity and range. The play and her performance were well received and was the only play not by Pirandello which remained in the repertoire during the life of the company. Having praised other members of the cast, Silvio d'Amico wrote in his review in *L'Idea Nazionale*, 24th April, 1925: "But the long awaited revelation of the evening was Marta Abba: this young actress, whom the Teatro d'Arte has introduced to the Roman theatre-going public and who presented herself with such assurance and ease, and such a variety of tone and colour, which were admirable in every way. And one must bear in mind that if there were ever a part in which it is possible to judge the formal qualities of an actress, then undoubtedly it is Dea: in which we have in turn seen Marta Abba as *gamine*, and as a passive, gentle, dreamy, treacherous, remorseful, imploring woman."

Marta Abba began her career as an amateur actress. Her first major professional success was as Nina in Chekhov's *The Seagull* in Virgilio Talli's production in Milan in April 1924. It was reviews of this performance, and in particular Marco Praga's in *L'Illustrazione italiana*, 13 April, that initially attracted Pirandello and other founding members of the Teatro d'Arte to ask her to join the company. We include an extract from Marco Praga's review in *L'Illustrazione italiana*, later published in *Cronache teatrali* for 1924 (Milan, 1925).

As his satirical presentation of the Italian company in *Sei personaggi in cerca d'autore* shows, Pirandello took issue with the role system in Italian theatre. In May 1924 when interviewed about the Teatro d'Arte project, he was clearly considering the possibility of jettisoning the role system altogether and employing actors for each individual play. However he must have soon abbandoned this idea for his actors were issued with normal one-year contracts for specific roles. Marta Abba was employed as leading lady (prima attrice). Although only recently recognised as a potential leading lady, she charged a high price and was, in fact, the highest paid member of the cast, receiving 170 lire a day, while the considerably more experienced actor, Lamberto Picasso, who had run his own company, was paid 160 lire. Under "Additional Clauses" in her contract, Marta Abba was allowed a travelling companion at the company's expense and three trunks of personal luggage.

Marta Abba was the only member of Pirandello's company who stayed with him for the full two-and half year's of the company's life, from April 1925 to August 1928. During that time she took a major female role in thirty-eight plays (Document 31). Three of these, *Diana and Tuda (Diane e la Tuda)*, *The Wives' Friend (L'amica delle mogli)* and *The New Colony (La nuova colonia)* were inspired by and written specifically for her. (She was also the inspiration of other plays not performed by the Teatro D'Arte: *Lazarus (Lazzaro)*, *As You Desire Me (Come tu mi vuoi)*, *Finding Oneself (Trovarsi)* and *When One is Somebody (Quando si è qualcuno)*.) Apart from the reviews of *The New Colony*, some of which were less than enthusiastic, Marta Abba's acting was well received by contemporary critics. In addition to Bontempelli's *Our Dea*, particularly notable among her performances were The Stepdaughter in *Six Characters in Search of an Author* and Ellida in Ibsen's *The Lady from the Sea*. Eleanora Duse had created this role in the first Italian presentation of the play three years earlier to enormous acclaim. Clearly Marta Abba was inviting comparison with the legend in her presentation of Ellida and the critics responded positively to her challenge.

In his book *Maschera nuda di Pirandello*, Luigi Antonelli, playwright and theatre critic, who recalled seeing Marta Abba as an amateur actress in Milan, had this to say about her effect on Pirandello the playwright. "Certainly Marta Abba has given a human face to Pirandello's plays and theatre. Indeed, since she joined the company and interpreted his work, his art began to lean towards the character. His female characters grew in consistency and meaning. They had the voice, nerves, gestures and the very movements of Marta Abba. The sudden movement with which she animated words, the magical atmosphere which bestowed a mystery to her stillness, the gleam of tragedy which at times lit up her face, still belonged to that young woman who acted in the Company of Art and Delight in the little theatre in Milan, but it was all transformed miraculously into Pirandellian art."

After a period with the Teatro d'Arte, Marta Abba formed a company of her own which was largely dedicated to staging plays by the *maestro*, as he was known to friends and theatre colleagues. In 1938 she married S.A. Millikin, a nephew of the steel magnate and resolved to sever all connections with the theatre, but subsequently both produced plays in the U.S.A. and published translations of Pirandello's plays. In his will Pirandello left her one sixth of his fortune and the rights to a number of his plays. Marta Abba, who later returned to Italy, was one of the longest surviving members of the Teatro d'Arte. She died in 1988. Pirandello's letters to her, the cause of considerable controversy, are now held in the library of the University of Princeton in the U.S.A.

Document No. 30: Extract from Margo Praga's Reviews of *The Seagull*, 13.4.1924

I have already mentioned that Virgilio Talli has staged *The Seagull* in his own way. Wanda Capodaglio[20], who has a walk-on part, Calò[21], Campa[22], Olivieri[23], Scelzo[24], Biliotti[25] and Miss Custrin were all impressive. But Miss Abba was a revelation; a young actress who has been acting professionally for only a few months, I am told. She was a magnificent Nina - particularly considering she is so young and at the beginning of her career. There is a fine actress in this young woman, and, I'm willing to add, a leading actress. Her stage presence, her make-up, her voice which is of the sweetest timbre and at the same time very warm, the intelligence she brought to this leading role, her assurance and ease, show her to be made for the stage, and already sufficiently mature to tackle a major role. And so I point her out to directors and actor-producers - if there are any - who are looking for a leading actress to develop, an actress who is free from all false allurements and stage conventionalisms as well as from exaggerated and vulgar traditional traits.

Document No. 31: Marta Abba's Repertoire
(Place and date refer to first performances.)

Dea in *Our Dea (Nostra Dea)* by Massimo Bontempelli (Rome, Odescalchi Theatre, 22.4.1925)

Paolina Bonaparte in *Paulette* by Eugenio Giovannetti (Rome, Odescalchi Theatre, 6.5.1925)

The Stepdaughter in *Six Characters in Search of an Author* by Luigi Pirandello (Rome, Odescalchi Theatre, 18.6.1925)

The typist in *The Chief Thing (Ciò che più importa)* by Nikolai Evreinov (Rome, Odescalchi Theatre, 29.6.1925)

Ersilia Drei in *Clothe the Naked (Vestire gli ignudi)* by Luigi Pirandello, (London, New Oxford Theatre, 23.6.1925)

La signora Frola in *Right You Are (If You Think So) (Cosi é (se vi pare))* by Luigi Pirandello (London, New Oxford Theatre, 25.6.1925)

Agata Renni in *The Pleasures of Respectability (Il piacere dell'onestà)* by Luigi Pirandello (Paris, Edward VII Theatre, 12.7.1925)

Evelina in *Two in One (Due in una)* by Luigi Pirandello (Florence National Politeama Theatre 13.3.1926)

Violetta in *The Madmen on the Mountain (I pazzi sulla montagna)* by Alessandro De Stefani (Florence, National Politeama Theatre, 18.3.1926)

Emma in *The Walk on the Waters (Il cammino sulle acque)* by Orio Vergani (Rome, Valle Theatre, 29.3.26)

Eugenia in *The Volcano (Il vulcano)* by Filippo Tommaso Marinetti (Rome Valle Theatre, 31.6.1926)

Silia in *The Rules of the Game (Il giuoco delle parti)* by Luigi Pirandello (Milan, Filodrammatici Theatre, 19.4.1926)

Marcella in *Dancing Tonight (Qui si balla [Ici l'on danse])* by Benjamin Crémieux (Milan, Filodrammatici Theatre, 24.4.1926)

Gasparina Torretta in *But It Isn't Serious (Ma non è una cosa seria)* by Luigi Pirandello, (Bergamo, Teatro Nuovo, 30.5.1926)

Anna Luna in *The Life I Gave You (La vita che ti diedi)* by Luigi Pirandello (Turin, Chiarella Theatre, 18.6.1926)

La signora Perella in *Man, Beast and Virtue (L'uomo, la bestia e la virtù)* by Luigi Pirandello (Turin, Chiarella Theatre, 25.6.1926)

The Woman in the Blue Fur in *What Passion, You Puppets! (Marionette, che passione!)* by Rosso di San Secondo (Turin, Chiarella Theatre, 29.6.1926)

Beatrice Fiorìca in *Cap and Bells (Il berreto a sonagli* by Luigi Pirandello (Florence, National Politeama Theatre, 24.8.1926)

Ellida in *The Lady from the Sea (La donna dal mare) [Fruen fra Havet]* by Henrik Ibsen (Florence, National Politeama Theatre, 28.9.1926)

Fulvia Gelli in *As Before, Better than Before (Come prima, meglio di prima)* by Luigi Pirandello (Padua, Garibaldi Theatre, 27.10.1926)

Tuda in *Diana and Tuda (Diana e la Tuda)* by Luigi Pirandello (Milan, Eden Theatre, 14.1.27)

Solange in *The Romantic Bourgeois (Il borghese romantico) [Le Bourgeois romanesque]* by Jean Blanchon (Turin, Carignano Theatre, 12.2.1927)

Bellinda in *Belinda and the Monster (Bellinda e il Mostro)* by Bruno Cicognani (Rome, Argentina Theatre, 23.3.1927)

Cloe in *The Skin Game (La casa difesa)* by John Galsworthy (Rome, Argentina Theatre, 31.3.1927)

Barbar in *The Labyrinth (Il labirinto)* by Solomon Poliakov (Rome, Argentina Theatre, 7.4.1927)

Marta in *The Wives' Friend (L'amica delle mogli)* by Luigi Pirandello (Rome, Argentina Theatre, 28.4.1927)

Anna in *The Southern Cross (La croce del sud)* by Telesio Interlandi and Corrado Pavolini (Rome, Argentina Theatre, 11.5.1927)

Giulia in *The Vice (La morsa)* by Luigi Pirandello (Montevideo, Urquiza Theatre, 18.8.1927)

Livia Arciani in *Other People's Reason (La ragione degli altri)* by Luigi Pirandello (Naples, Mercandante Theatre, 8.10.1927)

Giulia Yanez in *A True Man (Un vero uomo) [Nada menos que todo un hombre]* by Miguel d'Unamuno (Naples, Mercandante Theatre, 22.11.1927)

Dady Norel in *The French Doll (La bambola francese)* by Yager Schmidt (Messina, Mastrojeni Theatre, 10.12.1927)

Laura Banti in *The Grafting (L'Innesto)* by Luigi Pirandello (Catania, Sangiorgi Theatre, 17.12.1927)

Delia Morello in *Each in His Own Way (Ciascuno a suo modo)* by Luigi Pirandello (Naples, Politeama Giacosa Theatre, 26.1.1928)

Hedda in *Hedda Gabler* by Henrik Ibsen (Florence, Pergola Theatre 4.2.1928)

Anna in *Outward Bound (In alto mare)* by Sutton Vane (Rome, Argentina Theatre, 6.3.1928)

Paolina in *The Virgins (Le vergini)* by Marco Praga (Rome, Argentina Theatre, 13.3.1928)

La Spera in *The New Colony (La nuova colonia)* by Luigi Pirandello (Rome, Argentina Theatre, 24.3.1928)

Countess Teresa in *Scrollina* by Achille Torelli (Milan, Manzoni Theatre, 25.4.1928)

Reviews of The Teatro d'Arte on tour in London (June 1925)

It is sometimes thought that Pirandello set up his company in order to present his plays as he thought they should be performed, that is, that the Teatro d'Arte was the practical consequence of his views on theatre expressed in the theoretical essays. The fact is, apart from the opening night, the intention had been to present contemporary works of high quality by Italian and foreign dramatists, but with no particular brief to include plays by Pirandello. However, when plans were broached for the company to tour, theatre managers from abroad wanted the company to perform Pirandello's plays. It was C.B. Cochran who first insisted on this condition. From the summer of 1925, when the company visited London, Pirandello's plays remained the most important part of the company's repertoire.

The Teatro d'Arte came to London in June 1925. In addition to the permanent members of the company which included Marta Abba, Lamberto Picasso, Enzo Biliotti and Egisto Olivieri, Ruggero Ruggeri came as guest actor for the title role of Henry IV, a role which he had created when the play was first presented in Rome, 1922. The other plays presented in London at the New Oxford Theatre were *Right You Are (If You Think So) (Così è (se vi pare))*, *Six Characters in Search of an Author (Sei personaggi in cerca d'autore)* and *Clothe the Naked (Vestire gli ignudi)*. We include reviews from *The Times* of three of these performances and a review article by Francis Birrell in *The Nation and the Athenaeum* on the visit of Pirandello's company.

It will be seen from these reviews that Pirandello took the opportunity of addressing audiences personally, either during an interval, or after the performance. This became a custom of the company and allowed Pirandello the opportunity of both expounding his views on the play and explaining the political situation in Italy, as he indicated he would do in his letter to Mussolini of 19 March. It will also be noted that despite his strictures on the role of the prompter (Section II, Document No. II), a prompter was very much in evidence on this tour.

Document No. 32: The review in _The Times_ of _Sei personaggi in cerca d'autore_, 16.6.1925

Well, we have all seen the great Pirandello and discovered that he is, as they say, no chicken. He came on between the first and second acts of his _Sei Personaggi_ and made a few exegetic remarks which didn't much help us of the audience, but which absolutely stumped the interpreter. A baffled interpreter was an unhoped for addition to the joy of the evening. "Mr. Pirandello says" the poor man would begin, but what it was that Mr. Pirandello said proved nearly always too much for him. The crowded and brilliant house evidently thought this interlude immense fun.

The _Sei Personaggi_, it will be remembered, has already been done in English - and in the English fashion - by the Stage Society. It is another, a different, play done in Italian by Italians. Everything is a little "more so". The tragic personages are more tragic, the squalid personages more squalid, and the comic remnant more emphatically and volubly comic. Benissimo!

As everybody knows - for a typical Pirandello play is known all the world over - the _Sei Personaggi_ presents a play within a play. Not in the old-fashioned way of one little crowd of actors playing before another crowd, representing an audience; the two crowds are antagonistic, the one - six characters in a play which, they say, the author has never completed, characters who want to act out a play for themselves - the other a set of professional actors at a rehearsal, who scoff at these amateurs, and want to show them how to act their parts. The six are a family, father and mother, son and stepdaughter, with a small boy and girl who do not speak. But the small girl, the bambina, who was assigned by the programme to "_N.N._" did better than speak. She sat immovable throughout the play, with a fixed stare, and a look of utter boredom. Not exactly a pretty child, but her immobility was so fascinating that it was impossible to take your eyes off her. Brava, bravissima, "_N.N._".

The father (abject in appearance, with hair of a carroty tinge) is at once the villain and the raisonneur of the sordid and tragic little play which the family, with many interruptions from the audience of professionals and from themselves, proceed to present. The father is guilty of the worst offence and of the most frequent interruptions. The offence - or intention - resembles that of the father in _The Cenci_. In a house of ill-fame or, rather, "of accommodation", he encounters his own step-daughter. It is a terrible scene as they act it - terrible chiefly for the depravation and mocking laughter and self-loathing of the girl - but we may be excused for not dwelling upon it here.

What is even more remarkable about the father than his sinister misfortune is his enthusiasm for philosophic curiosities. Thus, in the midst of his histrionics, someone calls him and the rest of the six "illusions". This at once sets him off distinguishing between illusions and realities. He explains that the six are more real than the people round them, for they have been created and fixed by their author, whereas the others are constantly changing throughout their lives, and who shall say that their old selves are not "illusions" to their new? Nay, he goes further than that, and says an author's creations have a life of their own, independent of him, and can be imagined in all sorts of situations that he, the author, never thought of. We should like to talk that point over with him - but must postpone discussion to a more convenient season. It is the father who will never postpone a debating point. When the professional actors start rehearsing the scene of his daughter and himself, he cannot refrain from laughter: as though actors, with their own temperaments and individualities, could hope to be anything like the six, who are the characters *themselves*, the characters the author has conceived. And so on and so forth. And the result is the peculiar mixture of quasi-philosophy, psychology, and dramatic action which goes to make up a Pirandello play.

Call it Pirandellism and you have a name for a new theatrical amusement. For it is certainly amusing to see characters disintegrated, as it were, on the stage before you, wondering how much of them is illusion and how much reality, and setting you pondering over these perplexing problems while enjoying at the same time the orthodox dramatic thrill. For, if we have used the word amusing, it must be understood in the widest sense. Nothing could be more impressive than the solemn procession on to the stage of the Six (all in deep black), with their pale masks and their tragic eyes; they seem like some accursed family from the Aeschylean stage. And they are truly tragic in their acting. Marta Abba the daughter and Lamberto Picasso the father. But our last word of commendation must be reserved for that astonishing little silent immovable mite, N.N.

Document No. 33: The review in *The Times* of *Enrico IV*, 19.6.1925

"ENRICO IV"
by LUIGI PIRANDELLO

Enrico IV	Ruggero Ruggeri
La Marchesa Matilde Spina	Jone Frigerio
Frida, sua figlia	Jone Morino
Il Barone, Tito Belcredi	Enzo Biliotti
Il giovane Marchese Carlo di Nolli	Gino Cervi
Il Dottor Dionisio Gennoni	Egisto Olivieri
Landolfo (Lolo)	Arnoldo Montecchi
Araldo (Franco)	Umberto Ferrari
Ordolfo (Momo)	Carlo Simoneschi
Bertoldo (Fino)	Mario Bettini
Giovanni, vecchio servitore	Aristide Frigerio
Due Valletti in costume	N.N.

The story of the Italian nobleman who went mad and supposed himself to be the Emperor Henry IV of Germany, became sane, and then went mad again, or pretended madness, is almost as puzzling to follow on the stage as it is in the study. The Emperor who went to Canossa is a familiar historical figure to few playgoers, and the temporal colour, which Signor Pirandello has laid on with a trowel, only elucidates the matter on the principle of *obscurum per obscurius*.   Then, of course, there are his customary Pirandellisms - curious points in the psychology of insanity, and in the debatable borderland between the insane and the sane - to make confusion worse confounded.   The precise nature of the sentimental relation between the madman and the Marchesa was another riddle. Decidedly, *Enrico IV*, cannot truthfully be said to be as plain as a pikestaff.

But it is nonetheless affecting to see, because madness, whether treated poetically as by Shakespeare, or ironically, as by Pirandello, is always a moving spectacle.   It becomes terrible in the hands of Signor Ruggero Ruggeri.   His voice and glance and gestures hover on the outer edge of the uncanny.   When his mind is restored to him he towers superb over the technically sane inferiors - petty in their loves and hates, in their pedantry and folly - who huddle round him.

Ruggero Ruggeri is a great tragic actor.   And Signor Pirandello, in acknowledging his debt to him in a short curtain speech, did what we all felt to be not only a graceful but the right thing.

Document No. 34: The review in *The Times* of *Vestire gli ignudi*, 25.6.1925

"VESTIRE GL'IGNUDI"

by LUIGI PIRANDELLO

Ersilia Drei	Marta Abba
Franco Laspiga	Gino Cervi
Il Console Grotti	Lamberto Picasso
Il Romanziere Ludovico Nota	Egisto Olivieri
Il giornalista Alfredo Cantavalle	Enzo Biliotti
La Signora Onoria, affittacamere	Gina Graziosi
Emma, domestica	Maria L. Fossi

Pirandello might have taken for epigraph of his *Vestire Gl'Ignudi* a saying of Anatole France.   "I love truth.   I believe humanity to have need of it; but assuredly it has much greater need still of the lie that flatters and consoles it, and gives it infinite hope.   Without the lie, it would perish of despair and boredom."   *Vestire Gl'Ignudi* is the story of a woman who seeks to cloak her despair under lies, and who, stripped of them, is again plunged in despair, so that "her only refuge is to die."

Act I. A novelist, Ludovico Nota, brings to his lodgings a young girl, Ersilia Drei, pale and obviously ill, in whose sad case he is interested, partly out of honest pity, partly perhaps on the off-chance of an "adventure" (for the girl is pretty), but chiefly with the idea that her case will help him to some good "copy" for his next novel.   Her case has already supplied abundance of "copy" to the Roman newspapers.   She had been governess in the family of the Italian Consul at Smyrna, and had there been seduced, under promise of marriage, by a young naval officer, one Franco Laspiga, who promptly deserted her, and who, it subsequently appeared, was already affianced to another woman. It never rains but it pours. Through the alleged fault of the governess the Consul's child fell from the roof and was killed. Ersilia, dismissed by the Consul's wife without a farthing, tried to poison herself, but was rescued from death and taken to the hospital, whence Nota has now brought her. He tells her something of the story he has already constructed about her case. His heroine was, in her poverty and despair, to have gone down into the street and offered herself to the first man she met - who refused her. Well, the novelist has guessed right. Ersilia says that is exactly what she did, and it was not only Laspiga's desertion, but her own self-disgust, that had driven her to attempt suicide. The girl is, somehow, comforted by the prospect of figuring as the heroine of a novel - in fiction she may hope to escape the ugliness of fact - but is depressed by the thought that, after all, the heroine will be another woman than herself. (A characteristic Pirandellian subtlety. Would such a girl in such circumstances concern herself with such a point? Nor can Pirandello leave the matter without a touch of irony. Ersilia "adores" Nota's novels - most of all one that he didn't write, but is the work of an author he particularly detests.) But the novelist himself is beginning to feel not quite so happy about his novel. The reporter who had worked up Ersilia's "story" for his newspaper arrives for further details, and incidentally lets out that there is a terrible fuss over it in the town, not to mention the threat of a libel action. Altogether, there is a little too much publicity for Nota's taste.

At this juncture Laspiga rushes in - bursting with news and good intentions. The girl to whom he was affianced, on learning the scandal, has broken off the match, and he is free to marry his Ersilia, the only woman he ever really loved, etc., etc. But, strange to say, Ersilia refuses all "reparation" and even declines to see Laspiga. She is left, moaning and wringing her hands. Just before the act-drop falls you get a hint. Ersilia mutters something about "that other man". Mystère!

In Act II the mystery is soon cleared up. "That other man" was the Consul, who now arrives, furious with Ersilia. She and he, it appears, as soon as Laspiga's back was turned, had become lovers. There is a violent scene of recrimination between the pair. Whose fault was it? The man says the woman led him on; she declares that she was practically a victim to his violence. Anyhow, they were discovered together on the roof by the Consul's wife - it was just then that the child fell. So Ersilia, then, had less romantic reasons for her attempted suicide than she had given out: not a broken heart at her sweetheart's desertion, but the ignominy of a disgraceful intrigue discovered.

It now only remains for the unhappy Ersilia - stripped bare of the poor fictions in which she had tried to dress up the ugly facts - to complete the frustrated suicide. And so, in a brief third act, she takes another dose of poison and pathetically dies, humiliated, exposed, and, as she declares with her last breath, naked. All your sympathy is for Ersilia, for, as Signor Pirandello somewhat superfluously explained in a short speech at the end, this was not a play about the detection of a lie, but about the tragic consequences which may ensue from the revelation of the truth. As Anatole France says, humanity has need of the truth, but still greater need of the lie, to save it from despair.

Marta Abba, who had already made her mark as the daughter in *Sei Personaggi*, profoundly impressed the house with the poignancy of her acting as the wretched Ersilia. Pathos and passion were alike at her command, and with them went a "petitionary grace" which is peculiarly her own. Gina Graziosi was droll as a termagant landlady. The men, at least according to English standards (which, perhaps, are out of place), lacked distinction. And, as usual with these Italian companies, the prompter kept up a kind of hissing commentary on the play throughout the evening.

Document No. 35: Pirandello at the New Oxford by Francis Birrell

Two years ago very few people in England had heard of Pirandello. One of his plays had been performed by the Stage Society, on which, naturally enough, the Censor stepped in and banned a public performance. This act of bureaucratic folly was about the first warning the public had received that a new artist of importance had arisen in the theatre. Even the very bad translation of "Three Plays by Pirandello", published by Messrs. Dent, failed to attract the notice of reviewers. But then suddenly everybody, in a confused way, began muttering about Pirandello. The Cambridge Marlowe Society twice played *Henry IV* for a week, while other people went over to Paris, where he had taken the town. Finally, Mr. Cochran, a most sensitive observer of the movements of straws, has brought over Signor Pirandello and his own company to act in four of his best-known plays.

However bad one may be at the language, it is always interesting to see a play acted by the compatriots of the author, and it is difficult to say how much we have lost by never seeing Ibsen in Norwegian or Chekhov in Russian. We may find fault with native productions, but we must assume that the producer and actors probably understand their author better than we do. Which of us can say we have met a foreigner who seems to "understand" Shakespeare?

Were it only for the opportunity of seeing Pirandello, acted in Italian, we should be grateful to Mr. Cochran for his venture, though as a matter of fact we have had every reason to be delighted with the performances as well. For we have now seen Pirandello on his native heath. Foreigners acting him are bound to be a trifle self-conscious, to become weighed down by their mission of introducing an unknown artist to an unsuspecting audience. They will probably labour all sorts of points, which compatriots will take for granted.

The difficulty of seeing Pirandello acted had already made him a sort of recondite figure, adopted by enthusiasts and persons suffering from excessive sensibility. The depth of his philosophy and the beauty of his conceptions have been almost unwisely lauded. The practical dramatist and the theatrical craftsman have been neglected. The Italian players have put this right once and for all. They are not taken in by their author, and the play shows him for what he is - one of the most brilliant play-makers (in the good sense of the word) that have appeared in Europe. Italians, when they are clever, are cleverer than anybody else, and the Commedia dell'arte is the witness of their cleverness. Pirandello is of this lineage, but has added to his heritage a tremendous power of suggesting emotion. In all the four plays that have been running at the New Oxford, the excitement is intense throughout. The interest is never allowed to flag. The marvellous naturalism, the apparent ignorance that such a thing as an audience existed, made of *Six Characters in Search of an Author* a tremendous evening's entertainment. The bizarrerie of the Six Characters themselves shone out in dazzling contrast to the dull vulgarity of the "real" actors in the theatre. I did not myself enjoy *Henry IV* so much, as I thought I saw theatrical cabotinage sticking out all through Signor Ruggeri's performance. I am told, however, he was tired and acted far better on the second night. He has in any case a magnificent presence and a fine voice.

On the whole, these performances tend to put Pirandello in his proper perspective. He is not a profound and original thinker, and if he were, play-writing would not be a suitable method of expounding his views. But he has taken over a certain amount of Bergsonian and Freudian philosophy and welded it into plays as enthralling as any which modern Europe has produced. He has been called the Bernard Shaw of Italy, a nomenclature that is absolutely fantastic; for whereas Mr. Shaw spends his whole time airing his opinions on all sorts of subjects, Pirandello's opinions, if he has any, never emerge for an instant. He simply builds up a design round a neurotic situation. All his main characters in fact reach the last word of neuroticism. They pass their time continually in acute nervous conflict, and Pirandello is a great dramatist because he is able to communicate this neuroticism to the public, till it leaves the theatre as shattered as characters in the play. He is, in a way, an Elizabethan who has taken a course of Freud, a writer of intellectual melodrama, who can at any moment bring a new rabbit out of his hat. All through *Henry IV*, it seems impossible that the situation can be kept going an instant longer. Then the unfortunate "Emperor's" mentality is given another twist, and we are once more jolting along the switchback of his agony.

Pirandello is not a revolutionary in theatrical technique, and in this way is more conservative than Chekhov. He starts his play by presenting us with some startling incident, the arrival of the six characters, the palace of Henry IV, etc., and then in the way elaborated by Ibsen observes the unities by writing the play backwards in time. This method reaches its highest point in *Naked*. This is now, I think, a more hopeful way of approaching Pirandello than is concentration on his supposed theory of the Universe, which even if it be his own, is largely irrelevant when we are considering him as a dramatist.

Letters to and from Claudio Argentieri (1925)

The following letters, held in the Burcardo Library in Rome, are all addressed to Claudio Argentieri. Two were written by Giuseppe Prezzolini, who had a considerable influence on early twentieth century Italian culture. With Papini he founded the periodical *Il Lionardo* (1903-7) and later edited the more famous *La Voce* (1908-1915). Although he held no specific function in the government, he supported the régime and among his many publications (on syndicalism, Italian contemporary culture and Italian Renaissance culture), is one translated into French, written especially to explain Italian fascism to foreigners (*Le fascisme*, traduit par Georges Bourgin, Paris, 1925).

The rest of the letters were written by Renzo Rendi, Prezzolini's secretary, who was acting as administrator in Rome for the Teatro d'Arte while the company went on tour.

The letters indicate some of the reasons why the Teatro d'Arte venture was short-lived. Although the productions staged by the company were, on the whole, well received, it is clear that there were internal difficulties and problems with the actors and organisation that led to excessive spending.

Document No. 36:   Guiseppe Prezzolini to Claudio Argentieri, 18.5.1925

Telef. 31.457 - Telegr. Forpress-Roma
Rome (34) 29, Via Brescia

Rome, 18th May 1925

Dear Argentieri,

The situation of the Teatro d'Arte seems to be getting worse, because the famous promises of hundreds of thousands of lire have come to be a few thousand, which come through in dribs and drabs, and don't cover the basics. Furthermore, there is an open disagreement between Salvini[26] and Beltramelli.

I have called the Assembly for the 5th of next month, with the proposal of liquidating the Society. Whatever happens, I cannot continue to be part of the Council of the Assembly, both because I have to be out of Rome, and because I do not consider it possible to direct a concern whose survival depends on grants raised by others.

I'll be out of Rome for a few days. I am going to Paris with Pirandello. When I get back around the 6th I hope to see you again in Rome.

With best wishes,

G. Prezzolini.

Document No. 37: Renzo Rendi to Claudio Argentieri, 19.6.1925

Joint Stock Company for the Art Theatre of Rome
Director Luigi Pirandello
Odescalchi Theatre
SS. Apostoli, 19
Tel. 11.3.51
Claudio Argentieri
Publisher,
Spoleto.

Rome, 19th June 1925

Dear Argentieri,

With reference to the Fabbrica Italiana Mobili business, I had a long session with the partner Moroni a few days ago and I think I've calmed him down. You can reply that "following verbal explanations that took place between Mr. Moroni and the deputy councillor, R. Rendi intimates that the affair will have a rapid and satisfactory conclusion". But how it will really turn out is another affair.

It is certainly the case that due in part to the stories of the bouncing cheques and in part to letters such as the one sent to FIM, we are somewhat discredited in the market and we are now experiencing the consequences as no one wants to give us any more credit.

In general, I'm working in various ways to obtain money, but it is a long business, as Salvini must understand and, indeed, could help from London. On the contrary, however, I have had no news from him apart from the early telegram which informed me of the first night's fifteen curtain calls. Salvini left, leaving me a note of urgent creditors, but forgetting to mention others that popped up hardly had he gone. And, please note, creditors of the Company, not of the theatre. Just imagine: of the 189,000 lire which have come to us as donations this last month, only about 50,000 have been used to pay the theatre's creditors. The rest has been absorbed by the Company.

The Company uses up an immense quantity of funds. In fact, it costs us more today than the construction of the theatre. This is due to real problems but also in part to the fact that estimates are made by guesswork and so many elements are left out that the bills when they come are real surprises.

The tour is the last example of this. If all goes well the only gain it will make is to cut the debt to Fidora by about a half. The tour accounts have been put together like this: for example, travelling expenses of the Company, from Rome to London, estimated at 15,000 lire. In actuality it cost them 36,000 lire to go and 36,000 lire to come back. With 25,000 lire for the scenery, that comes to just about that 100,000 lire which had been roughly estimated as profit. We will have to be grateful if we don't have to send them further funds. Then, overall, there is a tendency to lower the estimate considerably: for example, 3,000 lire for photographs alone.

These are matters that are the Company's concern. But since there are two societies but only one source of cash and since up till now the tendency has always been to put off getting the theatre finances straight in order to sink money into the Company, I feel I must raise support for an attempt to change policy. Once the theatre is in order and has enough to keep it going, even without profit, we can concentrate on the Company. If we don't do this, both societies will collapse.

It would be a good idea, if you have the time, for you to make a short visit to Rome soon. There are things to discuss in committee and to put a stop to on paper.

With best wishes,

Renzo Rendi

Document No. 38: Renzo Rendi to Claudio Argentieri, 30.6.1925

Joint Stock Company for the Art Theatre of Rome
Director Luigi Pirandello
Odescalchi Theatre
SS. Apostoli, 19
Tel. 11.3.51

Claudio Argentieri
Spoleto

Rome, 30th June 1925

Dear Argentieri,

I have received your letter enclosing one from a bank asking for 900-plus lire for expenses and renewed interest. I enjoyed your advice "that at least these trifles can be paid". You tell me how I can pay 900 lire and more with only 43 lire to our name.

But this is not all. I've finally had a letter from Salvini and it now seems clear that in the fourteen days of the London tour they lost £380, that is 50,000 lire and that to meet such a deficit, Salvini has set in motion a banker's transaction involving the prize of 100,000 lire from the Ministry of Education; the prize, furthermore, that is already pledged to the National Institute of Insurance and which I had hoped to cancel or at least renew as a loan so as to have at my disposal a certain sum which could have served to silence some of the suppliers of the theatre.

Amongst these, the one that is shouting the loudest is the one who provided the stalls, who is making use of that wretched letter which you also signed which marked the beginning of one of Salvini's worst bungles - his notion of letting Fidora understand that the stalls were already paid for. Now both Fidora and the supplier are having a fine time sending registered letters, full of angry threats, insisting on having the money straight away. And I have 43 lire. And the actors are threatening to go to the theatre corporation. So Salvini advises me to pay the actors. And you ask me to pay "trifles" of a thousand lire. And Fidora is making a fuss because the rent of 4,300 lire is now due.

Whatever happens, we must save the theatre. If we can get the theatre out of debt and functioning properly, it could be the source of assets worth about 50,000 lire a year which added to the 100,000 lire from the Ministry would provide a good basis from which to run the Company. If they go on as at present they will end up devouring us all: company, theatre, subsidies, loans, grants, the lot - and us with them.

With best wishes,

Renzo Rendi.

Document No. 39: Renzo Rendi to Claudio Argentieri, 6.7.1925

Joint Stock Company for the Art Theatre of Rome
Director Luigi Pirandello
Odescalchi Theatre
SS. Apostoli, 19
Tel. 11.3.51

Dear Argentieri,
    We expected you on Saturday because we wanted to put you into the picture concerning an exchange of letters between Pirandello and us.
    Following the decisions taken at the last meeting of the council, I have written that famous letter which you felt able to sign, of which I enclose a copy. The letter has been sent in your name too. Pirandello has replied after several days with the telegram I also enclose. Prezzolini then compiled the enclosed letter, which you will please read, *sign* and send direct to Pirandello.
    As you see, all this is far from satisfactory. But the news I have indirectly received from Paris is worse. Apart from the London loss, there is a further debt Salvini has contracted with Pirandello of 27,000 lire, which brings the loss entailed in 14 days' stay in London to 100,000 lire and perhaps more.
    They reached Paris without a penny in their pockets, and since they had to pay a deposit for the rent of the theatre, they contracted a further loan of 7,000 francs with a bank. And, of course, having undertaken to do the full administration for the performances (and who knows why) and not having a penny, they couldn't do any publicity or any other preparation. So, from the three performances, Wednesday to Friday, they took 7,000 francs in all. And they have to pay everybody, agents who will have swindled them (and who knows what use they are anyway) - suppliers of little things, etc.
    I only know these things indirectly, because after our famous letter, they don't trust us any more. I know that Salvini is counting on remittances from Italy. He must have written a desperate letter to Vergani, because the latter went to see Mussolini at 4p.m. on Saturday. I don't know the outcome of the conversation. Either he got nothing, or having got something, he doesn't intend to communicate this to us, so that he can help Salvini in this tragic situation. But I do know that both Salvini and Pirandello are thoroughly depressed - and Pirandello must be doubly depressed by the disastrous outcome of the tour and by the loss of the money he put into it.
    From all this you will understand that it is not possible to go on in this way. It is the system that is fundamentally wrong. It is also an attitude of mind totally blind to necessity. Just imagine: they didn't distribute the playbills to the hotels until Saturday evening - a distribution done at the last moment. This small detail is characteristic of the system adopted up till now.
    From some figures I have managed to see, it is the case that the theatre has given the company 320,000 lire. They have consumed 90,000 in two months. Add to that the loss on the tour - over 500,000 lire swallowed up

by the Company in about three months' activity: on that basis, 2,000,000 lire a year...

With best wishes,

Renzo Rendi

Document No. 40: Renzo Rendi to Claudio Argentieri, 10.7.1925

Ufficio Prezzolini,
Via Nazionale
Telegr. Forpress
Tel.65.15.89

Claudio Argentieri
Publisher
Spoleto

My dear Argentieri,
    Thank you for the papers you returned to me.
    The matter of the accountant is not important and is now closed. I have some understanding of business matters, both because I think what is important in such matters is to have a certain common sense, and also because I have had some business experience in my time, such as with *La Voce* when it was in Rome in 1919-20. And it's my view that the publishing business is still one of the most difficult to manage.
    Don't concern yourself about coming to Rome. Prezzolini is away. He is returning on the 14th to go away again on the 15th until the end of the month. I do not know when the Company will be back in Rome.
    The expiry of Fidora's bills came out in his favour. On the 11th, that is tomorrow, we have to give him his promissory notes. You just have to refuse to sign the new bills and everything is done. On their return Salvini and Pirandello will arrange to find a substitute. Meanwhile, try to get yourself substituted in this messy business. There's no hurry to find someone to substitute you on the council. My own mode of conduct is clear and simple: if I haven't any money I don't pay out any - I don't want to be involved in any more muddles.
    I don't know whether I mentioned to you that Pirandello wrote a pitiful letter to Forges Davanzati[27] saying that if he doesn't get back the 80,000 lire he lent in Rome and the 30,000 lire he lent in Paris, he's ruined because he hasn't any money to go on with to keep the four walls of his house together, either for himself or for his children. Forges has reservations about such a poverty-stricken condition and he also has something to say about the tour which seems to have been less one of the Teatro d'Arte than of Mr. Pirandello himself, who receives all the honours and benefits, if only in an indirect way. Forges went to see Mussolini to present the piteous case. Mussolini was surprised that the 90,000 lire received in June had already disappeared and expressed the view that perhaps the money had been spent too easily. Since he had been told that

the tour had produced a heavy loss, M. had asked: 'But weren't you insured or guaranteed by the theatre manager in any way?' All in all, he has his suspicions too and I don't know how long we can go on having his support. But in any case, he promised to give us 100,000 within the week.

When Pirandello received the news, he telegraphed to say deposit the money with the Commercial Bank, into his account, because he had already disposed of it in part. In the first instance Stefano[28] was of the same view but on reflection overnight advised that the money should be given to the Council, to prevent the latter from resigning. But the fact is that up to yesterday there's been no sign of the money.

I only know all of this indirectly because there is no direct communication between me and the Company; and, incidentally, it's worth pointing out that the Society of the Company acts as it pleases and as it has the right to do, except that, when things go wrong, it comes running to the Society of the Theatre for support, and the Society of the Theatre looks after not only its own responsibilities but also those of others over which it has no influence.

I will summon a meeting of the Assembly of members at the appropriate time and meanwhile I am racking my brains trying to write a long report in which I'm trying to demonstrate that the Council is resigning, not because of difficulties which are inherent in any organisation, but in protest against a system that runs counter to all the most elementary laws of organisation. We are speaking two languages with no understanding between them, and the Council, not having the power to silence the other, prefers to resign.

Away with all these problems! I'm thinking of the possibility of taking a break in Spoleto while Prezzolini is away. I don't know Umbria at all and I'd also like to take a look at your office. As in the past I too have spent some time trying to make volumes out of manuscripts, I'm feeling rather nostalgic about it. In any case, I'll let you know so that you don't run off the very day I can come.

With best wishes,

R. Rendi

Document No. 41: Guiseppe Prezzolini to Claudio Argentieri, 9.8.1925

Prezzolini
Tel. 31.487
Telegr. Forpress - Roma
Rome (34) 29 Via Brescia

Rome, 9th August 1925

Dear Argentieri,

I've given Rendi some holiday as he needed it. I have received your express letter which did not contain Vergani's telegram after his telephone call, so I do not understand very much of it. In any case, you must come over on Thursday, above all to cheer up Pirandello, who says we are all deserting him and who needs continual injections, and then in your own interest, to make every effort to shore up the ruin compromised by the tour. When all's said and done, it's a matter of getting from Fassini[29] or Treccani[30] or from others or from all of them together a sum of 100,000 lire with which, if administered prudently, the Company can function again, using the prizes and some other monies to pay the Theatre's debts. Fidora already has his eyes on you. I cannot approach the Fascist Party and its men; you, on the other hand, could and you could encourage Pirandello to do so too. You must get them to understand that a failure would be a serious business and could easily become a political issue, though it has nothing to do with politics. I must go on the 14th to see some friends in Perugia or Assisi, so you could take my place in Rome for a while and on my way back I could perhaps stop for an hour or two at Spoleto; though I don't actually see how, because I would like to be back on the 15th and you will still be in Rome that day. I'll expect you on the 13th; I'll be at home until half past eight and in the afternoon from 1 until 4 and then at the office at about 5 as usual.

Affectionately,

G. Prezzolini.

Document No. 42: Renzo Rendi to Claudio Argentieri, 12.9.1925

Ufficio Prezzolini   Tel.65.15.89
Via Nazionale
Telegr. Forpress

12th September 1925

Dear Argentieri,
    First of all thank you very much for the design: just what I wanted. As to the Theatre, you already know that the meeting of the Assembly is on 19th September to vote in a new council. The meeting is called for 9 but will be at 10.
    The shares have not been yielded to Fidora because another arrangement or complication has occurred and we are now waiting for Dr. Razza of the Theatre Corporation to come up with a solution.
    Salvini has gone to Berlin to set up a tour in Germany. Pirandello is in Milan to bring the company together for Germany. Here there's only us and the empty dirty theatre which has been partly seized through the initiative of a creditor.
    I don't understand anything any more and have neither the strength nor the will to understand. I feel as if I have been caught up in some tornado and just hope to get out of it with as few bruises as possible.
    Greetings to both you and your wife,

    R. Rendi.

Problems with Playing Places

The following two telegrams and letter come from the Salvini collection in the Museo-Biblioteca dell'Attore in Genoa, Fondo Salvini, 1357/446 and 1359/447. They were all written by Guido Salvini, descendant of the famous actor family, one of the Teatro d'Arte stage designers and general assistant to Pirandello (and who was later to become a director in his own right), who was in Rome trying to secure good playing places for the company for the following season. The letter is addressed to Telesio Interlandi, editor of *L'Impero* and influential with the Fascist hierarchy. This little collection of documents reveals something of the problems Pirandello suffered as director of an arts theatre, compounded with the intricacies of living and working in Fascist Italy. Giuseppe Paradossi, mentioned in the first telegram and letter, was the President of the Association of Theatre Owners (Presidente della Associazione Proprietari di Teatri) and responsible for the allocation of playing places to theatre companies.

Pirandello believed that Paradossi was using his power to allocate inferior playing places to the Teatro d'Arte. He was also suspicious of the Society of Authors, which, as a southerner, he tended to regard as a northern clique. These documents give a clear impression of Pirandello fighting with his last card, his reputation, in an attempt to gain the power and freedom both to run a theatre company and to have his own plays presented in Italy. In the event, Mussolini intervened and Pirandello did not leave for Germany at this time. However, Pirandello carried out his threat in part; the première of *Diana and Tuda (Diana e la Tuda)* took place in the Schauspielhaus Theatre in Zurich on 20 November, 1926. This was Pirandello's first new play to be presented since *The Festival of Our Lord of the Ship (La sagra del Signore della nave)* on the opening night of the Teatro Odescalchi on April 2nd, 1925.

Document No. 43: Telegram from Salvini to Pirandello, from Rome to Ferrara, 26th January, 1926

To Pirandello at Teatro Verdi, arrived 24.20.

Lengthy favourable interview Paradossi received categoric orders playing places Italy Spain Portugal stop my impression Paradossi convinced president to give up America this year if no reply from theatre stop tomorrow further interview vital importance with important person please wait for me before taking decision hope to leave tomorrow reaching you Brescia stop Paradossi by order of president will see you soon as possible

Salvini

Document No. 44: Telegram from Salvini to Pirandello at Brescia 28th January, 1926

Guido Salvini to Pirandello Teatro Sociale Brescia, 28th January, 1926.

Interview Beppe Morello[31] by order from on high excellent results I leave this evening after definitive decision maximum confidentiality please

Salvini

Document No. 45: Letter from Guido Salvini to Telesio Interlandi, Brescia, 2nd February, 1926

Dear Interlandi,
    After a dramatic session this evening, Paradossi and I tore up these four telegrams from Pirandello. I will transcribe them for you.

To His Excellency Mussolini Rome
    Since enemies whom I consider also to be enemies of Your Excellency remain unpunished for their reprisals, abuse, slander and defamations, neither wishing nor having to submit to such injustice, I leave Italy for ever. In departing I wish to nevertheless affirm my unshakable devotion to Your Excellency.

Pirandello

To Hon. Senator Morello, Society of Authors Milan
    On leaving Italy for ever I present my resignation as member of this society I retract my repertoire requesting you to give immediate orders so that none of my plays is ever staged by any company in Italian theatres.

Pirandello

To Umberto Fracchia[32] Maddalena 2 Milan
    On leaving Italy for ever I wish all my activity to be suspended forthwith. I therefore suspend publication of my novel in the next number. Please announce same to your readers. I will reimburse you all or part of advanced fee as appropriate.

Pirandello

To Pirandello Via Pietralata 23 Rome
    I leave Italy for ever. I am not coming to say goodbye wishing to spare you grief of separation. You will soon receive my instructions news from Germany. Farewell.

Papa.

    Pirandello was due to leave today and was going straight away to Berlin, where, to show the President and Italians that he was no outlaw he would have immediately given a propaganda lecture on the Alto Adige question before all those important people who gather when Pirandello speaks. But Paradossi, whom I summoned in desperation, has been of enormous help and we have together prevented, or at least postponed, the putting into action of such a plan that would have brought shame on Italy. I say postponed because Pirandello had conceded only on condition that the satisfaction owed him comes in the form of Paradossi assuming from now on the management of the Company: Paradossi, Giordano's colleague, answerable to Razza, Paradossi summoned by Mussolini.

Paradossi has given Pirandello his most ample assurances and has assumed the whole task of managing the business, but so that he can play off the highly organised Milanese gang, he rightly requests to have the order from the President, possibly by one written word, or by being summoned again to Rome. It will be enough if the President invests him with this office (in any case a very correct procedure seeing that the company is financed by the State and so that State may want to have some active participation in it) so that Paradossi, not having his hands tied, can fight and win. Otherwise we are back as we were. There is also the question of the boycott to the repertoire which is beginning to be serious and so it would not be a bad idea if you would draw the President's attention to this fact. Apart from the telegram which I enclose, there is also the fact that Niccodemi[33] has not been able to stage *Six Characters* at the Manzoni (as he promised Pirandello he would) nor has Petrolini[34] put on *Bitter Lemons (Agro di limone)* at the Filodrammatici. Instead of burying his head in the sand, Morello must do his duty.

In any case, my dear Interlandi, there is no time to lose. I know that Pirandello's decision will be as painful to you as it is to me. I have managed to prevent him from putting it into practice - and I will not tell you how much I have suffered during these past days to see Pirandello in such a state. This evening, really impressed by Pirandello's condition, Paradossi has behaved like a true friend... but now it is your turn to complete the miracle and to entreat the President to send a telegram to Paradossi along these lines: "I ask you to undertake in my name the management of Pirandello's company" and it would not be a bad idea to get him to add "referring any obstacle you may find in doing this to me".

Everything now depends on this prompt and decisive action. Tell the President that we have persuaded Pirandello to take the Company to Varese and perhaps to Gallarate and tell him that among all the Fascists there is truly none more disciplined than Luigi Pirandello. After these last heady days, the Company will begin its tour as established by Paradossi and it could easily reach Milan in April, but we need the official appointment of Paradossi.

Pirandello is staying here in Brescia until the 4th. I am leaving for Milan, then I think I shall be coming to Rome where I shall wait for Pirandello who has to come to Rome to speak with Volpi, but all of this only if the official appointment of Paradossi takes place...

(I know, I'm being a real bore)

I do most truly and deeply thank you for all that you have done and for all that you will do for Pirandello and I sent you my warmest greetings.

Guido Salvini.

Letter from Guido Salvini to Pirandello (1926)

Guido Salvini (see Document No 43) had his first major contact with theatre design when he became a member of the Teatro d'Arte. He also assisted in direction and soon gained distinction in both fields, and early in his career was invited to European cities to direct Pirandello's plays in performances staged by local actors. In addition to directing plays, he later also directed opera and ballet and often designed his own sets. He stayed in Pirandello's company until 1927. The document that follows is a draft of a letter to Pirandello - it is not known whether there was a fair copy - from the Teatro d'Arte period. It reveals some of the problems the company faced and provides information about the range of materials owned by the company. The autograph of this letter is in the Salvini collection, Fondo Salvini 1360/448, of the Biblioteca-Museo dell'Attore in Genoa. In translating it we have ignored words and phrases crossed through and translated the corrected version.

Whatever Salvini's reservations, he remained loyal to Pirandello as can be seen in the letters we publish in Section 4 concerning the production of *Tonight We Improvise (Questa sera si recita a soggetto)*. For this production Salvini gathered together a number of the actors and actresses from the original Teatro d'Arte company. Like Pirandello, Salvini was a fervent supporter of the National Theatre Movement and of the "teatro stabile" and took a lively interest in European theatrical trends. It was largely due to him that Max Reinhardt and Jacques Copeau visited Italy in 1932.

Document No. 46: Guido Salvini to Luigi Pirandello, 3.9.1926

Genoa, 3 September, 1926.

Dear Maestro,

If, rather than adopting a procedure new to the annals of theatre, invented specially for me, you had summoned me yesterday evening, I would have replied that I had been very upset to read on the order of the day for 2nd September that you had decided to rehearse a play new to the company without first giving me the necessary information for the same, as has always been done in the past. Indeed, caught unexpectedly like that, what could I have got together for the rehearsal? I could have put out the furniture, I suppose, or the battens, according to the stage directions. But for this we have a stage-manager. I, on the other hand, should have presented you with a properly executed design; but it's logical that one morning cannot and must not be time enough to do this. You had told me nothing and I remembered nothing and assumed that this was a repetition of something that had already happened before when an attempt to get an act of a new play together was made by asking a stage-hand advice on how to adapt the existing set.

Nevertheless, even without a command from you, I set to work yesterday morning straight away. I came up with the definitive design having spurned some other five or six. I stayed in the hotel without even taking lunch in order to get it done. I arrived at the theatre at 3.15 with the completed design certain that the rehearsal of *Cap and Bells* had not yet started. And it was logical that it shouldn't have begun, since, having read on the order of the day, *Six Characters, Dancing Tonight* [by Benjamin Crèmieux], then *Cap and Bells*, I could not have imagined that a rehearsal of six acts could only last four hours - without some indication of a timetable, it's a little difficult to be punctual!

But I am not writing to you to justify myself; nor to bring to your attention that it is not permissable to give notes in public to some one who is invested with directorial functions, be they merely technical, and to criticise him in front of his own staff; nor am I writing to tell you that you should not treat as a stranger or some apprentice some one who has suffered much pain on your behalf, much trouble, and even hunger - in Paris, remember? - for the Teatro d'Arte, and who has been loyal, genuinely disinterested, and who has contributed, if modestly to the success of the Company both with the most severe of critics and the public; some one, furthermore, who as asked for nothing, tell Paradossi, and who has given his all even in the most difficult conditions.

But I am writing to tell you that your words yesterday evening about the order of the day have made me decide that I definitively want to resign from the Company. It is no longer a possible life for me. I have no sense of guilt because I know that I have always done what is humanly possible even in the most poorly equipped theatres and in the most adverse conditions. I know that every show has been provided for with passion and love; and I have in the end the intimate satisfaction of knowing that there is no other *capocomico* in Italy whose stage designs have been praised as much as yours and who has spent so little on the corresponding materials. You have, in fact, sixteen canvas sets, twelve paper ones, in addition to 800 square metres of materials and drapes; and you have not yet spent 40,000 lire. What is that compared to the hundreds of thousands of lire spent by all the other companies? It is easy to criticise, less easy to criticise after you've done the sums - far more difficult.

I have had, then, to make this very painful decision; painful because of the affection I have always felt and will always feel for you, but a final decision and one that is necessary to my dignity. If you have nothing against it, I am ready to go this evening after handing over to Merletti explanatory notes on the position of the spots for each play. If, on the other hand, you would prefer to take some one else on straight away - an electrician for instance, which you will certainly need, or the next stage-manager whom I can instruct play by play - or if you intend to make use of what I've done to get together the new works for the rest of the month, I am at your disposition until then; as indeed I always shall be spiritually, and when circumstances permit, materially too. Awaiting your decision, which I hope will be speedy and which I ask you to communicate to Chellini, please believe me

Devotedly yours,

G.S.

Proposal to Mussolini for an Italian National Theatre (1926)

As Pirandello experienced continuing financial strain he became increasingly anxious to establish a national theatre in Italy which would be state financed. The document that follows was a joint venture with Paolo Giordani. Giordani had established the Società drammatica italiana as a private rival society to the Società degli Autori. Pirandello, who began with the Società degli Autori, later jointed Giordani's enterprise, as he felt that the Società degli Autori was a Milanese clique out to crush Southern writers. He subsequently fell out with Giordani and returned to the Società degli Autori, only later to reconcile himself with Giordani. This joint document is a result of their reconciliation. The document was presented to Mussolini in November, 1926.

Document No. 47: Proposal for an Italian National Theatre, 1926

Italy is the only nation in Europe without State Theatres, and does not even have an equivalent theatre organization through which the lack of State theatres might be considered to be a purely formal question. All that Italy has are travelling companies of players, who are forced to lead the kind of life that is bringing theatre to the point of extinction. In fact, even if they wanted to, these companies would not be able to set up an organization for staging their plays, nor for developing acting skills, nor for the selection of an artistic repertoire that would be suited to modern needs. Moreover, audiences have been aware of these deficiencies for some time, and are steadily abandoning our own theatre, whilst foreigners who go to the theatre are unfavourably impressed.

In such conditions, and in order to repair the artistic, financial and political damage that has been caused, State intervention cannot be restricted to occasional short-term action but much be firmly radical and must create a National State dramatic theatre able to work in three theatres in Rome, Milan and Turin. These theatres would be responsible for the artistic reputation of the Nation in the eyes of other countries, and should provide an example and an encouragement to all other private theatres, enabling actors to train and develop their skills, whilst succeeding in bringing audiences back to the enjoyment of seeing plays.

The plan, which could be brought into effect quickly with Fascist intervention, for the establishment of a National State Dramatic Theatre, involves State ownership of the three theatres in Rome, Milan and Turin, since, in all cases, there would be intervention by industrial interests that would seriously prejudice the success of the artistic undertaking. If three separate companies were to perform in these three theatres, there would automatically be a recurrence of the failure of all the other repertory companies, particularly those set up in Rome and Milan. Therefore the chief innovation of this plan consists precisely in the setting up of a single large company that would play every night to three audiences in Rome, Milan and Turin.

The General Management would be entrusted to one individual, who would be responsible for the artistic development of all three theatres, assisted by three Technical Directors, one for each theatre, and aided also by a select committee which would advise on the artistic programme of each playing year and on the rotation of different work performed in the three different theatres.

Alongside the General Manager, there should be an Administrative Director nominated by the State, assisted by a select Committee. The Managing Committee would comprise the Artistic and Administrative committees under the chairmanship of the General Manager. Each theatre would have a group of no more than 15 permanent technicians, while the central nucleus of the large company would be made up of 20 individuals, men and women, who would be carefully selected for each show and could come together in several short term groupings, in such a way that the Company would always seem to be fresh for its three audiences. The actors' contracts and engagements should be made annually, with no specified roles. In all three theatres there should be equal properties and stage machinery, along the lines of the Marais Theatre in Brussels, and this would constitute a fixed endowment, so that the staging devised in any one of these theatres could be reproduced in the other two without transporting anything but the minimal properties required.

The Management would proceed as follows:

1) The Management Committee should approve the artistic programme for the year, after discussions with the General Manager.

2) The three Technical Directors should investigate the staging requirements of the works together with the General Manager, to whom they should submit playwrights' reports, sketches, the distribution of roles etc.

3) The Management Committee should examine and resolve any problems arising from the fulfilment of the artistic programme, according to the criteria established by the Management, both with regard to the necessary expenditure for staging and for the touring programme of the short-term groups in the three theatres.

4) The three theatres should open on the same day, November 1st, after one month's preparation and close at the end of May without visits from other companies.

5) The first three plays should move to the other two theatres while further plays are in preparation, so that the rehearsal of new plays would not only take place during the run of the previous play, as happens with normal companies, but during the run of all three previous plays.

6) At the end of the season those plays that have been most successful should be taken on tour by three companies from the three theatres around Italy and abroad.

The Repertories of the Teatro d'Arte

The history of the Teatro d'Arte can be usefully divided into three periods: as a repertory art company performing in the Teatro Odescalchi; as an itinerant company; and as a repertory company at the Teatro Argentina in Rome. The first period at the Odescalchi theatre ran from 2nd April to 3rd June 1925, a total of sixty-five days. The second began in June 1925 when the company went to London and Paris and resumed after the summer break in Milan to September of the same year. In addition to playing in Italian cities as far afield as Trieste (November-December, 1926) and Catania (December, 1927), the company toured internationally: to Paris and London in June and July of 1925, to Germany in the autumn of 1925, to Yugoslavia, Austria, Hungary and Czechoslovakia in December 1926 and to the Argentine and Brazil in the summer of 1927. In 1928 they played in various Italian cities. The last performance of the itinerant company and of the Teatro d'Arte was of Ibsen's *The Lady from the Sea* at Viareggio on 15th August 1928. The third phase comprises the second attempt to establish a first class repertory company in Rome, this time at the Teatro Argentina. Pirandello signed an agreement with the agent for this theatre, Vincenzo Morichini, which was to give Pirandello the opportunity to present an uninterrupted three month season in the years 1927-1928, and 1928-9. In fact, the company played at the Argentina from 10 March to 18 May, 1927 and 1 March to 2 April 1928. (The 1927 and 1928 theatrical year was a uniquely long one for it incorporated the change from the traditional theatre year - first day of Lent, Ash Wednesday, to last day of carnival, Shrove Tuesday - to the newly instituted one from 1st September to 31st August.)

In the documents that follow we list the plays performed at the Odescalchi theatre in Rome with dates of performances (Document No. 48); an example of a month of touring (Document No. 49); and the repertory played at the Teatro Argentina (Document No. 50). The information is taken from Alessandro d'Amico and Alessandro Tinterri, *Pirandello capocomico*, Palermo, Sellerio editore, 1987 and shows the range of the Teatro d'Arte's repertoire and the intensity with which theatre companies of the period worked. It is clear from these schedules that Pirandello's company was forced to adopt the itinerant life style which he had expressly wanted to avoid when he set up the company.

Document No. 48: Plays performed at the Odescalchi Theatre

April 1925

---

2   Thursday *The Festival of Our Lord of the Ship (La sagra del Signore della nave)* by Luigi Pirandello; *The Gods of the Mountain* by Alfred Lord Dunsany.

---

3   Friday *The Festival of Our Lord of the Ship (La sagra del Signore della nave)* by Luigi Pirandello; *The Gods of the Mountaini* by Alfred Lord Dunsany.

---

4   Saturday *The Festival of Our Lord of the Ship (La sagra del Signore della nave)* by Luigi Pirandello; *The Gods of the Mountain* by Alfred Lord Dunsany.

---

5   Sunday *The Festival of Our Lord of the Ship (La sagra del Signore della nave)* by Luigi Pirandello; *The Gods of the Mountain* by Alfred Lord Dunsany.

6   Monday *The Festival of Our Lord of the Ship (La sagra del Signore della nave)* by Luigi Pirandello; *The Gods of the Mountain* by Alfred Lord Dunsany.

7   Tuesday *The Festival of Our Lord of the Ship (La sagra del Signore della nave)* by Luigi Pirandello; *The Gods of the Mountain* by Alfred Lord Dunsany.

8   Wednesday *The Festival of Our Lord of the Ship (La sagra del Signore della nave)* by Luigi Pirandello; *The Gods of the Mountain* by Alfred Lord Dunsany.

9   Thursday *The Festival of Our Lord of the Ship (La sagra del Signore della nave)* by Luigi Pirandello; *The Gods of the Mountain* by Alfred Lord Dunsany.

10   Friday   no performance

11   Saturday *The Shoemaker of Messina (Il calzolaio di Messina)* by Alessandro De Stefani.

12   Sunday *The Shoemaker of Messina (Il calzolaio di Messina)* by Alessandro De Stefani.

13   Monday *The Shoemaker of Messina (Il calzolaio di Messina)* by Alessandro De Stefani.

14   Tuesday *The Shoemaker of Messina (Il calzolaio di Messina)* by Alessandro De Stefani.

15   Wednesday *The Shoemaker of Messina (Il calzolaio di Messina)* by Alessandro De Stefani.

16   Thursday *The Companion* by Arthur Schnitzler; *The Poor Sick Man's Hand* (La mano del povero malato) by Luigi Pirandello; *The House in the Garden (La casa nel giardino)* by Guido Sommi Picenardi.

17 Friday *The Companion* by Arthur Schnitzler; *The Poor Sick Man's Hand* (La mano del povero malato) by Luigi Pirandello; *The House in the Garden (La casa nel giardino)* by Guido Sommi Picenardi.

18 Saturday *The Shoemaker of Messina (Il calzolaio di Messina)* by Alessandro De Stefani.

19 Sunday *The Shoemaker of Messina (Il calzolaio di Messina)* by Alessandro De Stefani.

20 Monday   no performance

21 Tuesday *The companion* by Arthur Schnitzler; *The House in the Garden (La casa nel giardino)* by Guido Sommi Picenardi.

22 Wednesday *Our Dea (Nostra Dea)* by Massimo Bontempelli.

23 Thursday *Our Dea (Nostra Dea)* by Massimo Bontempelli.

24 Friday *Our Dea (Nostra Dea)* by Massimo Bontempelli.

25 Saturday *Our Dea (Nostra Dea)* by Massimo Bontempelli.

26 Sunday *Our Dea (Nostra Dea)* by Massimo Bontempelli.

27 Monday *Our Dea* (*Nostra Dea*) by Massimo Bontempelli.

28 Tuesday *The Soldier's Story* by Ferdinand Ramuz with music by Igor Stravinsky; *Our Dea (Nostra Dea)* by Massimo Bontempelli.

29 Wednesday *The Soldier's Story* by Ferdinand Ramuz with music by Igor Stravinsky; *Last story* by Pavel Muratov; *The Gay Death* by Nikolai Evreinov.

30 Thursday *Our Dea (Nostra Dea)* by Massimo Bontempelli.

May

1 Friday *Our Dea (Nostra Dea)* by Massimo Bontempelli.

2 Saturday *Our Dea (Nostra Dea)* by Massimo Bontempelli.

3   Sunday *Our Dea (Nostra Dea)* by Massimo Bontempelli.

---

4   Monday *Our Dea (Nostra Dea)* by Massimo Bontempelli.

---

5   Tuesday *Our Dea (Nostra Dea)* by Massimo Bontempelli.

---

6   Wednesday *Paulette* by Eugenio Giovannetti.

---

7   Thursday *Paulette* by Eugenio Giovannetti.

---

8   Friday *Paulette* by Eugenio Giovannetti.

---

9   Saturday *Paulette* by Eugenio Giovannetti.

---

10 Sunday *Paulette* by Eugenio Giovannetti.

---

11 Monday *Paulette* by Eugenio Giovannetti.

---

12 Tuesday *Paulette* by Eugenio Giovannetti.

---

13 Wednesday *Paulette* by Eugenio Giovannetti.

---

14 Thursday *The Pilgrim* by Charles Vildrac; *The Death of Niobe* by Alberto Savinio; *The Gay Death* by Nikolai Evreinov.

---

15 Friday *Our Dea (Nostra Dea)* by Massimo Bontempelli.

---

16 Saturday *Our Dea (Nostra Dea)* by Massimo Bontempelli.

---

17 Sunday *Our Dea (Nostra Dea)* by Massimo Bontempelli.

---

18 Monday *Six Characters in Search of an Author* by Luigi Pirandello.

---

19 Tuesday *Six Characters in Search of an Author* by Luigi Pirandello.

---

20 Wednesday *Six Characters in Search of an Author* by Luigi Pirandello.

---

21 Thursday *Six Characters in Search of an Author* by Luigi Pirandello.

---

22 Friday *Six Characters in Search of an Author* by Luigi Pirandello.

---

23 Saturday *Six Characters in Search of an Author* by Luigi Pirandello.

24 Sunday *Six Characters in Search of an Author* by Luigi Pirandello.

25 Monday Mary Wigman[35] and her dance company; *Six Characters in Search of an Author* by Luigi Pirandello.

26 Tuesday Mary Wigman and her dance company; *Six Characters in Search of an Author* by Luigi Pirandello.

27 Wednesday Mary Wigman and her dance company

28 Thursday Mary Wigman and her dance company; *Six Characters in Search of an Author* by Luigi Pirandello

29 Friday *The Chief Thing* by Nikolai Evreinov

30 Saturday *The Chief Thing* by Nikolai Evreinov

31 Sunday *The Chief Thing* by Nikolai Evreinov
         The Chief Thing by Nikolai Evreinov

June

1 Monday *The Chief Thing* by Nikolai Evreinov

2 Tuesday *The Chief Thing* by Nikolai Evreinov

3 Wednesday *The Chief Thing* by Nikolai Evreinov

Document No. 49   Extract from the repertory for 1926-7 season, March 1926 (new productions are underlined)

1 Monday *Our Dea (Nostra Dea)* by Massimo Bontempelli at Arena del Sole Theatre, Bologna

2 Tuesday *Right You Are!(If You Think so) (Cosí è (se vi pare))* by Luigi Pirandello at Arena del Sole Theatre, Bologna

3   Wednesday *Right You Are! (If You Think so) (Così è (se vi pare))* by Luigi Pirandello at Arena del Sole Theatre, Bolgona

---

4   Thursday *Clothe the Naked (Vestire gli ignudi)* by Luigi Pirandello at the National Politeama Theatre, Forence

---

5   Friday *Right You Are! (If You Think so) (Così è (se vi pare))* by Luigi Pirandello at National Politeama Theatre, Florence

---

6   Saturday *Six Characters in Search of an Author* by Luigi Pirandello at the National Politeama Theatre, Florence

---

7   Sunday *Six Characters in Search of an Author* by Luigi Pirandello *Right You are! (If You Think so) (Così è (se vi pare))* by Luigi Pirandello at the National Politeama Theatre, Florence)

---

8   Monday *Our Dea (Nostra Dea)* by Massimo Bontempelli at National Politeama Theatre, Florence

---

9   Tuesday *Henry IV (Enrico IV)* by Luigi Pirandello at National Politeana Theatre, Florence

---

10   Wednesday *Clothe the Naked (Vestire gli ignudi)* by Luigi Pirandello at National Politeama Theatre, Florence

---

11   Thursday *Six Characters in Search of an Author* by Luigi Pirandello at National Politeama Theatre, Florence

---

12   Friday *Henry IV (Enrico IV)* by Luigi Pirandello at National Politeama Theatre, Florence

---

13   Saturday *Two in One (Due in una)* by Luigi Pirandello at National Politeama Theatre, Florence

---

14   Sunday *Two in One (Due in una)* by Luigi Pirandello at National Politeama Theatre, Florence
Two in One (Due in una) by Luigi Pirandello at National Politeama Theatre, Florence

---

15   Monday *Two in One (Due in una)* by Luigi Pirandello at National Politeama Theatre, Florence

---

16 Tuesday *Two in One (Due in una)* by Luigi Pirandello at National Politeama Theatre, Florence

17 Wednesday *Two in One (Due in una)* by Luigi Pirandello at National Politeama Theatre, Florence

18 Thursday *The Madmen on the Mountain (I pazzi sulla montagna)* by Alessandro De Stefani at National Politeama Theatre, Florence

19 Friday *The Madmen on the Mountain (I pazzi sulla montagna)* by Alessandro De Stefani at National Politeama Theatre, Florence

20 Saturday *Right You Are!(If You Think so) (Cosí è (se vi pare))* by Luigi Pirandello at National Politeama Theatre, Florence

21 Sunday *Right You Are!(If You Think so) (Cosí è (se vi pare))* by Luigi Pirandello at National Politeama Theatre, Florence
Six Characters in Search of an Author by Luigi Pirandello at the National Politeama Theatre, Florence

22 Monday *Clothe the Naked (Vestire gli ignudi)* by Luigi Pirandello at Teatro Valle, Rome

23 Tuesday *Right You Are!(If You Think so) (Cosí è (se vi pare))* by Luigi Pirandello at Teatro Valle, Rome

24 Wednesday *The Madmen on the Mountain (I pazzi sulla montagna)* by Alessandro De Stefani at Teatro Valle, Rome

25 Thursday *Six Characters in Search of an Author* by Luigi Pirandello at Teatro Valle, Rome
The Madmen on the Mountain (I pazzi sulla montagna) by Alessandro De Stefani at Teatro Valle, Rome

26 Friday *Henry IV (Enrico IV)* by Luigi Pirandello at Teatro Valle, Rome

27 Saturday *Two in One (Due in una)* by Luigi Pirandello at Teatro Valle, Rome

28 Sunday *Two in One (Due in una)* by Luigi Pirandello at Teatro Valle, Rome
Two in One (Due in una) by Luigi Pirandello at Teatro Valle, Rome

29 Monday *The Walk on the Waters (Il cammino sulle acque)* by Orio Vergani at Teatro Valle, Rome

---

30 Tuesday *The Walk on the Waters (Il cammino sulle acque)* by Orio Vergani at Teatro Valle, Rome

---

31 Wednesday *The Volcano (Il vulcano)* by Filippo Tommaso Marinetti at Teatro Valle, Rome

---

Pirandello at the Argentina

The plays Pirandello hoped to present at the Argentina theatre can be considered as his last attempt to establish a repertory worthy of a national theatre. With hopes renewed by the joint project with Giordani (See Document No. 47), the Argentina period was seen at the time as a prelude to the establishment of the National Theatre.

Interviewed for *La Tribuna* 18 January, 1927, Pirandello announced that he wanted to present a season of pre-war Italian plays, set in an historical perspective, in addition to some new plays of his own and by Italian contemporaries. He also intended to present some foreign classics: *La niña boba* of Lopez de Vega, *Life is a Dream* by Calderon, a play by Shakespeare and one by Molière, Chekov's *Three Sisters* (which was to open the season), *Arms and the Man* by Shaw, *A True Man* by Unamuno and new plays by Molnar, Vildrac, Romains and Crémieux. The actual programme presented was rather different from this ambitious proposal.

Document No. 50 Teatro d'Arte at the Argentina Theatre, Rome

March 1927
(new productions are underlined)

10 Thursday *Diana and Tuda (Diana e la Tuda)* by Luigi Pirandello

---

11 Friday *Diana and Tuda (Diana e la Tuda)* by Luigi Pirandello

---

12 Saturday *Diana and Tuda (Diana e la Tuda)* by Luigi Pirandello

---

13 Sunday *Diana and Tuda (Diana e la Tuda)* by Luigi Pirandello
Diana and Tuda (Diana e la Tuda) by Luigi Pirandello

---

14 Monday *But It Isn't Serious (Ma non è una cosa seria)* by Luigi Pirandello

---

15 Tuesday *But It Isn't Serious (Ma non è una cosa seria)* by Luigi Pirandello

16 Wednesday *Diana and Tuda (Diana e la Tuda)* by Luigi Pirandello

17 Thursday *The Romantic Bourgeois* by Jean Blanchon

18 Friday *The Romantic Bourgeois* by Jean Blanchon

19 Saturday *The Romantic Bourgeois* by Jean Blanchon

20 Sunday *Henry IV (Enrico IV)* by Luigi Pirandello
The Romantic Bourgeois by Jean Blanchon

21 Monday *Diana and Tuda (Diana e la Tuda)* by Luigi Pirandello

22 Tuesday *But It Isn't Serious (Ma non è una cosa seria)* by Luigi Pirandello

23 Wednesday *Belinda and the Monster (Bellinda e il mostro)* by Bruno Cicognani

24 Thursday *Belinda and the Monster (Bellinda e il mostro)* by Bruno Cicognani

25 Friday *Belinda and the Monster (Bellinda e il mostro)* by Bruno Cicognani

26 Saturday *Diana and Tuda (Diana e la Tuda)* by Luigi Pirandello

27 Sunday *Right You Are! (If You Think So) (Cosí è (se vi pare))* by Luigi Pirandello
Right You Are! *(If You Think So) Cosí è (se vi pare))* by Luigi Pirandello

28 Monday *Henry IV (Enrico IV)* by Luigi Pirandello

29 Tuesday *Right You Are! (If You Think So) (Cosí è (se vi pare))* by Luigi Pirandello

30 Wednesday *The Romantic Bourgeois* by Jean Blanchon

31   Thursday *The Skin Game* by John Galsworthy

April, 1927

1   Friday *The Skin Game* by John Galsworthy

---

2   Saturday *Diana and Tuda (Diana e la Tuda)* by Luigi Pirandello

---

3   Sunday *But It Isn't Serious (Ma non è una cosa seria)* by Luigi Pirandello
Henry IV (Enrico IV) by Luigi Pirandello

---

4   Monday *Right You Are!(If You Think So) (Cosí è (se vi pare))* by Luigi Pirandello

---

5   Tuesday *Six Characters in Search of an Author* by Luigi Pirandello

---

6   Wednesday *Six Charactes in Search of an Author* by Luigi Pirandello

---

7   Thursday *The Labyrinth* by Solomon Poliakov

---

8   Friday *The Labyrinth* by Solomon Poliakov

---

9   Saturday *The Labyrinth* by Solomon Poliakov

---

10   Sunday *The Pleasures of Respectability (Il piacere dell'onestà)* by Luigi Pirandello
The Labyrinth by Solomon Poliakov

---

11   Monday *Six Characters in Search of an Author* by Luigi Pirandello

---

12   Tuesday *Man, Beast and Virtue (L'uomo, la bestia e la virtù)* by Luigi Pirandello

---

13   Wednesday *The Lady from the Sea* by Henrik Ibsen

---

14   Thursday *The Lady from the Sea* by Henrik Ibsen

---

15   Friday No performance

16   Saturday *Clothe the Naked (Vestire gli ignudi)* by Luigi Pirandello

17   Sunday *Six Characters in Search of an Author* by Luigi Pirandello
The Lady from the Sea by Henrik Ibsen

18   Monday *The Pleasures of Respectability (Il piacere dell'onestà)* by Luigi Pirandello

19   Tuesday *Henry IV (Enrico IV)* by Luigi Pirandello)

20   Wednesday *As Before, Better than Before (Come prima, meglio di prima)* by Luigi Pirandello

21   Thursday *Six Characters in Search of an Author* by Luigi Pirandello

22   Friday *Clothe the Naked (Vestire gli ignudi)* by Luigi Pirandello

23   Saturday *The Labyrinth* by Solomon Poliakov

24   Sunday *As Before, Better than Before (Come prima, meglio di prima)* by Luigi Pirandello
Right You Are!(If You Think So) (Cosí è (se vi pare)) by Luigi Pirandello

25   Monday *The Lady from the Sea* by Henrik Ibsen

26   Tuesday *Henry IV (Enrico IV)* by Luigi Pirandello

27   Wednesday *The Wives' Friend (L'amica delle mogli)* by Luigi Pirandello (preview)

28   Thursday *The Wives' Friend (L'amica delle mogli)* by Luigi Pirandello

29   Friday *The Wives' Friend (L'amica delle mogli)* by Luigi Pirandello

30   Saturday *The Wives' Friend (L'amica delle mogli)* by Luigi Pirandello

May 1927

1   Sunday *The Wives' Friend (L'amica delle mogli)* by Luigi Pirandello

The Wives' Friend (L'amica delle mogli) by Luigi Pirandello

2   Monday *As Before, Better than Before (Come prima, meglio di prima)* by Luigi Pirandello

3   Tuesday *The Wives' Friend (L'amica delle mogli)* by Luigi Pirandello

4   Wednesday *The Wives' Friend (L'amica delle mogli)* by Luigi Pirandello

5   Thursday *The Wives' Friend (L'amica delle mogli)* by Luigi Pirandello

6   Friday *The Wives' Friend (L'amica delle mogli)* by Luigi Pirandello

7   Saturday No performance

8   Sunday *Clothe the Naked (Vestire gli ignudi)* by Luigi Pirandello
The Rules of the Game (Il giuoco delle parti) by Luigi Pirandello

9   Monday *The Life I Gave You (La vita che ti diedi)* by Luigi Pirandello

10 Tuesday *The Wives' Friend (L'amica delle mogli)* by Luigi Pirandello (preview)

11 Wednesday *The Southern Cross (La croce del sud)* by Telesio Interlandi and Corrado Pavolini

12 Thursday *The Southern Cross (La croce del sud)* by Telesio Interlandi and Corrado Pavolini

13 Friday *Henry IV (Enrico IV)* by Luigi Pirandello

14 Saturday *Six Characters in Search of an Author* by Luigi Pirandello

15 Sunday *The Rules of the Game (Il giuoco delle parti)* by Luigi Pirandello
The Life I Gave You (La vita che ti diedi) by Luigi Pirandello

16 Monday *The Wives' Friend (L'amica delle mogli)* by Luigi Pirandello

17 Tuesday *The Pleasures of Respectability (Il piacere dell'onestà)* by Luigi Pirandello

---

18 Wednesday *Two in One (Due in una)* by Luigi Pirandello

---

19 Thursday *The Southern Cross (La croce del sud)* by Telesio Interlandi and Corrado Pavolini

---

20 Friday *Six Characters in Search of an Author* by Luigi Pirandello

---

21 Saturday *The Rules of the Games (Il giuco delle parti)* by Luigi Pirandello

---

22 Sunday *Two in One (Due in una)* by Luigi Pirandello
Right You Are!(If You Think So) (Cosí è (se vi pare)) by Luigi Pirandello

---

March 1928

1 Thursday *Right You Are!(If You Think So) (Cosí è (se vi pare))* by Luigi Pirandello

---

2 Friday No performance (day of national mourning for Armando Diaz)

---

3 Saturday *Other People's Reason (La ragione degli altri)* by Luigi Pirandello

---

4 Sunday *Other People's Reason (La ragione degli altri)* by Luigi Pirandello
Six Characters in Search of an Author by Luigi Pirandello

---

5 Monday *The French Doll* by Yager Schmidt

---

6 Tuesday *Outward Bound* by Sutton Vane

---

7 Wednesday *Outward Bound* by Sutton Vane

---

8 Thursday *Outward Bound* by Sutton Vane

9   Friday *The Vice (La morsa)* and *The Grafting (L'innesto)* by Luigi
    Pirandello

10 Saturday *The Vice (La morsa)* and *The Grafting (L'innesto)* by Luigi
    Pirandello

11 Sunday *The Wives' Friend (L'amica delle mogli)* by Luigi Pirandello
    The French Doll by Yager Schmidt

12 Monday *Other People's Reason (La ragione degli altri)* by Luigi
    Pirandello

13 Tuesday *The Virgins* by Marco Praga

14 Wednesday *The Virgins* by Marco Praga

15 Thursday *The Lady from the Sea* by Henrik Ibsen

16 Friday *A True Man* by Miguel de Unamuno

17 Saturday *A True Man* by Miguel de Unamuno

18 Sunday *The Virgins* by Marco Praga
    Henry IV (Enrico IV) by Luigi Pirandello

19 Monday *Six Characters in Search of an Author* by Luigi Pirandello

20 Tuesday No performance

21 Wednesday No performance

22 Thursday No performance

23 Friday No performance

24 Saturday *The New Colony (La nuova colonia)* by Luigi Pirandello

25 Sunday *The New Colony (La nuova colonia)* by Luigi Pirandello
    The New Colony (La nuova colonia) by Luigi Pirandello

26 Monday *The New Colony (La nuova colonia)* by Luigi Pirandello

27 Tuesday *The New Colony (La nuova colonia)* by Luigi Pirandello

28 Wednesday *The New Colony (La nuova colonia)* by Luigi Pirandello

29 Thursday *The New Colony (La nuova colonia)* by Luigi Pirandello

30 Friday *Henry IV (Enrico IV)* by Luigi Pirandello

31 Saturday *Henry IV (Enrico IV)* by Luigi Pirandello

April 1928

1 Sunday *Henry IV (Enrico IV)* by Luigi Pirandello

2 Monday *The Pleasures of Respectability (Il piacere dell'onestà)* by Luigi Pirandello

Conclusion

Hopes for a national theatre did not materialise and the company's financial predicament worsened considerably. Pirandello accepted an invitation to go to Germany to assist in the making of films from three of his plays and he left for Germany, as he had threatened he would, in the autumn of 1928. As mentioned in the introduction to Documents Nos. 48-50, the Teatro d'Arte gave its last performance in Viareggio on 15th August, 1928.

As a director, Pirandello belongs to an Italian tradition of author/director. It is a tradition that goes back to the Renaissance and which had its major practiner in Carlo Goldoni in the eighteenth century. Amateur theatricals with friends aside, Pirandello had no experience as an actor, and indeed, apart from joining a professional or amateur company, there was little opportunity for such experience in late nineteenth and early twentieth century Italy. (Pirandello once read the part of Baldovino in *The Pleasures of Respectability (Il piacere dell'onestà)* when Lamberto Picasso was taken ill). Nor could he have had any training as a director. Despite the enlightened awareness of a few critics and people of the theatre of the need for a person who was not a member of the cast to direct the acting and have an overall vision of the play, the Italian word for director *(regista)*, according to the philologist Bruno Migliorini, did not figure in the Italian language before 1931. Pirandello was excited by innovatory approaches to theatre in Europe and introduced aspects of them into his company. This consisted of some experienced and accomplished actors, and more who were less experienced. In his work as a director, Pirandello concentrated largely on the elucidation of the text and pacing of the speeches; he encouraged his designers to take their inspiration from the stage directions rather than follow them literally, so as to bring out the ideas of the play through the scenic design rather than present a naturalistic set; and he also encouraged his electrician to provide mood rather than straight lighting.

In his time, Pirandello gained the reputation he had set out to achieve. His company was known for its careful preparation, its excellent acting, and exciting stage designs and lighting. He also enlarged the Italian theatre's repertoire. His ambitions exceeded his practice here but nevertheless he introduced nine foreign plays to the theatre going public and staged fifteen world premières, mainly of contemporary Italian plays. Years after their presentation, these performances with others in the repertoire were remembered with admiration. "I have seen Pirandello achieve miracles" wrote Massimo Bontempelli, "and I am convinced that he is as great a director as he is a writer."[36] However, Pirandello was unable to achieve the revolution of theatrical practices that he saw as stifling the potential for a renewal of Italian theatre. Pirandello man of the theatre was, as Richard Sogliuzzo has called him, "the playwright in the theatre". But in the period when speeches were often cut from a play to enhance the leading actor's presence, delivery was flamboyant and gestural, and stage settings were superficial approximations to naturalism, Pirandello's careful elucidation of the meaning of a play, his stress on accuracy and authenticity, his insistence that actors subordinate themselves to the character they are representing, constituted in itself a radical, if conservative approach.

Notes

1. Gaspare Giudice, *Luigi Pirandello*, Turin: U.T.E.T., 1963, pp.412-51.
2. See Introduction to Document No. 24.
3. As above.
4. As above.
5. Maria Letizia Celli, 1889-1969, actress. She was a much admired Fulvia Gelli in the first production of *As Before, Better than Before (Come prima, meglio di prima)*, March 1920.
6. See Introduction to Document No. 36.
7. See Introduction to Document No. 24.
8. Riccardo Gualino, Massimo Bondi and Senatore Borletti were all major industrialists. Massimo Bondi's business empire in iron and steel collapsed in 1925; he left the country in November of that year and made his way to Norway to avoid extradition.
9. "Teatro degli Italiani" was the name given to a short-lived attempt to launch a national theatre: see Document No. 20.
10. Giovanni Cavicchioli, free-lance writer and dramatist, see Document No. 25.
11. Corrado Pavolini was a poet, dramatist, theatre and cinema critic who also became a theatre director in his forties. One of his plays, *The Southern Cross (La croce del sud)*, written in collaboration with Telesio Interlandi, was presented by the Teatro d'Arte in May, 1927 (see Document No. 50).
12. Elsewhere in his *Luigi Pirandello* manuscript, Marchi clarifies the antithesis between the scenic realism, inherited from the nineteenth century and the synthetic scenography propounded by the avant-garde: "When the Company began to work on the stage I was able to note the dualism of two diametrically opposite concepts of theatre. When Albertini, the technician from La Scala who had set up the electrical system, talked to me as Chief Technician about the effects he wanted to create, we found ourselves on two completely different wavelengths, such that it was impossible to reach an agreement. When I thought about my synthetic designs which had been agreed with Luigi Pirandello, I found myself faced with Boito's *Nero (Nerone)*, which had become the basic text of that time for anyone who wanted to create the open sky with clouds and great fires that we did not see the slightest dramatic need for.

    In the end everything was reduced to an open-air set, where a crowd of some hundred and fifty people were going to raise hell, but where nevertheless it was sufficient to create stylistic harmony through elements proportional to the small size of the dimensions. So that in order to create the walls around a vast imaginary city in the first act, it was sufficient to raise a few white screens that were architecturally designed to mathematical proportions, according to my concept of stage perspective in limited spaces, using a lunar spotlight and a reflector.

    In the following acts the obstacle presented by all the linking points forced us to restrict ourselves to the usual panels that concealed a green giant behind the eastern archway, which could only be shifted by three men, unseen. Now this early, very proper, experiment in staging, through its fairy tale quality, went quite beyond all the realist techniques of the old methods of staging. We had to spotlight images instead of paper and cardboard, or rather the gestures and words of those images."
    [Translation of Alessandro Tinterri's note.]
13. Alfredo Biagini (1886-1952 was born in Rome. He specialised in religious iconography. [Translation of Alessandro Tinterri's note.])

14. Cipriano Efisio Oppo (1891-1952) was born in Rome. His greatest work was for *The Shoemaker from Messina (Il calzolaio di Messina)*, Alessandro De Stefani's new play that was presented at the Teatro Odescalchi for the first time on 11 April, 1925. [Translation of Alessandro Tinterri's note.]

15. Donatello Bianchini, painter and stage designer, was director of Mario Corsi and Co. scenography studies from 1921 to 1927. [Translation of Alessandro Tinterri's note.]

16. "Teatro degli Indipendenti" was directed by Anton Giulio Bragaglia; see Introduction to Section III.

17. Luigi Almirante, 1886-1956, actor and director. He took the part of the Father in the first production of *Six Characters in Search of an Author*, May, 1921.

18. S. Sudeikin, Russian stage designer who broke away from the naturalistic three-dimensional staging. Corrado Alvaro is here referring to Sudeikin's predilection for painted curtains and panels.

19. Pablo Picasso's involvement in theatre design began in 1917 when Cocteau invited him to design the costumes and settings for Diaghilev's ballet *Parade*.

20. Wanda Capodaglio (1890-1980), actor and director.

21. Romano Calò: see Section II, note 9, p.86.

22. Pio Campa, actor and director, Wanda Capodaglio's husband.

23. Egisto Olivieri: see Section II, note, note 8, p.86.

24. Filippo Scelzo, actor particularly respected for his character parts.

25. Enzo Biliotto, comic actor. He joined the Teatro d'Arte for the year 1925-6; his best remembered role was that of Belcredi in *Henry IV*.

26. Guido Salvini: see Introduction to Documents Nos. 43 and 46.

27. Forges Davanzati, writer and journalist, was a founder journalist of the newspaper *Idea Nazionale*.

28. Stefano Landi [Pirandello].

29. Alberto Fassini was an industrialist who developed an empire in artificial silk and viscose.

30. Giovanni Treccani degli Alfieri was a wealthy industrialist and patron who founded the *Enciclopedia italiana* in 1925 and later the *Dizionario biografico degli Italiani*. In 1923 he acquired the Este Bible and bequeathed it to the nation.

31. Beppe Morello was the current President of the Authors' Society (Società degli Autori) which looked after dramatists' interests.

32. Umberto Fracchia was the editor of *La fiera letteraria* to whom Pirandello had submitted the instalments of his novel *One, Nobody and a Thousand (Uno, nessuno e cenotmila)*.

33. Dario Niccodemi (1874-1934), popular dramatist and well-known theatre director. He directed the first production of *Six Characters in Search of an Author* in May, 1921.

34. Ettore Petrolini (1886-1956), famous variety theatre actor who moved into straight theatre in 1920. *Bitter Lemons* is a Roman dialect version of *Sicilian Limes*.

35. Mary Wigman, a pupil of Rudolf Laban, opened a dance school in Dresden in 1920 and later worked with Erwin Piscator.

36. Massimo Bontempelli, "Il teatro degli Undici o Dodici", *Scenario*: Rome, 1933, quoted in Alessandro d'Amico/Alessandro Tinterri, *Pirandello capocomico: La Compagnia del Teatro d'Arte di Roma 1925-1928*, Palermo, Sellerio, 1987.

SECTION IV: THE LATER YEARS AND AFTER, 1929-1967

Introduction

After the collapse of the Teatro d'Arte, Pirandello went abroad, principally to Germany in hopes of reshaping himself a career in the cinema. His movement into voluntary exile marked the end of the period of "Pirandello-mania" that had swept through Europe in the early and mid-Twenties. Little attention was paid to his later plays, which were often heavily criticised by the press, both in Italy and abroad and, even today, several of those plays remain unavailable to English-language readers. The letters from this period reveal a man who felt persecuted and misunderstood, a man with a grievance whose health had also begun to fail. In the letter to Salvini of 2 March 1930 (Document No. 53), Pirandello discusses his relationship with Marta Abba, the actress for whom most of his later plays were written, hinting at some difficulties with her and hinting also at his concern for public opinion of their friendship. Marta Abba was obviously a crucial figure in his life at that time, both as his muse and as his companion and defence against the loneliness that emerges from between the lines of his letters.

In spite of the problems and the decline of popular interest in his work, Pirandello wrote some of his most ambitious and exciting plays in the years between the collapse of the Teatro d'Arte and his death in 1936. In this section we have reproduced documents relating to the two most extraordinary plays, *Tonight We Improvise (Questa sera si recita a soggetto)* and *The Mountain Giants (I giganti della montagna)*. Both rarely performed until recently, - Pirandello never saw the production of *The Mountain Giants* since it did not take place until after his death - they involve complex staging devices, large casts and big playing areas. *Tonight We Improvise* was first performed in Germany at Königsberg and then in Berlin where it received very hostile criticism from audiences and reviewers alike. In the letters to Salvini we can follow Pirandello's sense of enthusiasm before the play was staged, his old determination and almost naive belief in the power of his own work to win over audiences. The letter of 30 March 1930 (Document No. 54), written after he had seen the production at Königsberg, gives a long account of the play, both in terms of plot and staging, and Pirandello offers suggestions to Salvini for the

Italian version.   Interestingly, he notes a point made by Salvini about the "danger of having officers on stage", and recommends the replacement of the military sign system with another less offensive to the fascist authorities. He also adds the cryptic comment for a supporter of the regime that he is depressed "to think we have sunk so low".

In contrast to Pirandello's enthusiastic letter is Herbert Jhering's review of the Berlin opening of *Tonight We Improvise* (Document No. 56).   Jhering damns the play and the production, attacking the incompetence of the actors, the lack of talent of the director, the poverty of the text and the dullness of Pirandello's ideas.   Jhering's opinion of Pirandello's plays is that they are vague, mediocre and uninspiring.   After reviews such as this, it is hardly surprising that Pirandello's morale sank even lower.

The letter of Salvini of 20 April 1930 (Document No. 55) refers to *The Mountain Giants*, which Pirandello left unfinished when he died. The play was first performed in the Boboli Gardens in 1937, directed by Renato Simoni[1] and Giorgio Venturini[2], but then sank into obscurity until it was revived a decade later in the new post-fascist Italy, a society in the process of rebuilding itself and restoring the shattered confidence and buildings of a country ravaged by war, both international and civil, invaded by both German and Allied armies. Mussolini's brand of nationalistic patriotism had been destroyed as surely as the name of Il Duce has been erased from all public places, and in this context there was a need for a redefinition of Italian culture. Into this vacuum came one of Italy's greatest directors, Giorgio Strehler, who has made *The Mountain Giants* very much his own play. He first directed it together with Paolo Grassi in 1947, in the Piccolo Teatro di Milano, and then revived it in November 1967 on the occasion of the Pirandello centenary.

Pirandello's theoretical statements on theatre that date from this period ("Will the Talkies Do Away with Theatre?" 1929 (Document No. 51) and "The Address to the "Volta" Conference on Dramatic Theatre", 1934 (Document No. 58)) are very different in tone from the earlier essays. His basic belief in the theatre as "the highest and most mature expression of art" remains unchanged, but the emphasis in these pieces is on the function of theatre in society, rather than on the vexed question of the role of the writer. Pirandello's years of bitter experience after the collapse of the Teatro d'Arte had left their mark on his work.

Pirandello on the talking film

In this essay Pirandello tackles the controversial and highly relevant question of the relationship between the cinema and the theatre. Until the advent of the talking film in 1927, the question of the cinema being in competition with live theatre had not seriously arisen. Pirandello chose to approach the problem by considering Europe and America as two contrasting societies - the one being too concerned with its own past, the other having no tradition on which to rely. By taking up this attitude, he avoided the pitfall of considering cinema as the theatre's poor relation, and argued for the separate coexistence of both forms. His years of work in cinema had given him an insight into the complex processes of film making.

Document No. 51: Will the Talkies do Away with Theatre? (Se il film parlante abolirà il teatro) 1929.

Anyone who has heard me talk about the experiences of my many travels will know the admiration with which I have talked about America and the great liking I have for Americans.

What interests me above all else about America is the birth of new forms of life. Life, pressured by natural and social needs, looks for and finds these new forms, and to see them being born is an incomparable pleasure to the soul.

In Europe the dead go on making life, crushing the life of the living with the weight of history, tradition and custom. The consistency of old forms obstructs, hinders, cuts off any vital movement.

In America life belongs to the living.

Except that life, though on the one hand it needs perpetual movement, has nevertheless a need to consist in some form or other. These two needs which are opposed to one another do not allow life to have either perpetual movement or perpetual consistency. Consider that if life were to move forever, it would never be consistent, whilst if it were always consistent, it would never move.

Life in Europe suffers from too much consistency in its old forms, and perhaps in America life suffers from too much movement without any lasting, consistent forms.

So that in response to an American gentleman who boasted to me that "We have no past. We are completely future-oriented!" I was able to immediately say "I see, dear sir, that you are in a great hurry to make yourselves a past".

Forms, whilst they remain alive, that is, while vital movement remains within them, are a conquest of the soul. To destroy them in that living state for the pleasure of replacing them with other new forms is a crime, it is the subjugation of an expression of the soul. Certain original, almost natural forms through which the soul expresses itself cannot be subjugated, because life itself virtually expresses itself through these forms; therefore they cannot grow old and be replaced without murdering life in one of its natural expressions.

And one such form is the theatre.

My friend Evreinov[3], author of a play which the Americans too have greatly appreciated, reaches the point of saying in one of his books that all the world is theatre and that not only do all human beings act out the role they have assigned to themselves in life, but that all animals act out roles too, as do plants, in short, as does all of nature.

Perhaps this is going a little too far. But that theatre, before becoming a traditional literary form was a natural expression of life, is completely and utterly undeniable.

And yet, in these days of great universal infatuation for the talking film, I have heard a certain heresy being passed around; that the talkie will do away with theatre, that in two or three years' time there will be no more theatre, that all theatres and music halls will be closed down because everything will be cinema, talking film or musical film.

If this were said by an American, with that ease which is natural to Americans, that cheerful arrogance, even though it might seem to be a heresy (which it is) it would be heard sympathetically because the Americans have a genuine pride in the grandiose.   That pride has the peculiar grace of an elephant, whose beady little eyes laugh as he waves his trunk about playfully, and you are in trouble if you take it seriously.   But when that heresy is repeated, as I have heard it repeated, by a European, then something so huge and beast-like loses any natural grace and merely becomes clumsy and stupid.   The elephant's sharp little devilish eyes do not laugh any longer.   What you find instead are two eyes facing you veiled with tiredness, and great size does not give a sense of the sparkle of pride but rather the dilation of fear, and that menacing, joking power of the trunk changes into the silly wafting of an ass's tail trying to swat flies which represent the irritations and worries of a new undertaking.

Because all those European film magnates really are worried and frightened by this devilish invention of the talking machine, and like old fish who have been waving their tails and fins around in the stagnant waters of a silent marsh for too long a time, they let themselves be hooked, since they are defenceless and all have their mouths left open.

Meanwhile, the theatre, both the classical and the music hall, can stay calm and be certain that it will not be abolished, for one simple reason: that the theatre is not trying to become cinema, it is the cinema which is trying to become theatre, and the greatest success it can aspire to, putting itself even further along the road towards becoming theatre, is to become a photographic, mechanical reproduction of theatre, one which is more or less good and which, like all copies, will simply arouse desires for the original.

The fundamental mistake of the cinema was to set off from the outset on the wrong road, on an unsuitable road, the road of literature (prose or drama).   Along that road the cinema found itself inevitably in a double bind, that is:
1)   in the impossibility of replacing words;
2)   in the impossibility of doing without words.
And with this double defect:
1)   an intrinsic defect, that of not being able to find its own free expression through the word (both expressed and implied);
2)   a defect in literature which, when reduced to a single viewpoint, inevitably sees all its spiritual values diminish, which can only be fully expressed in the most complex medium of expression available, the one which properly belongs to it, that is through words.

Now giving words mechanically to the cinema does not help the fundamental error, because instead of curing the sickness it aggravates it, pushing cinema even more firmly down into literature.   When the word is mechanically imposed onto film, cinema begins inexorably to destroy itself in order to become a mechanical, photographic copy of theatre, because cinema is the silent expression of images and the language of appearances. That copy will necessarily be a bad one, because every illusion of reality will have been lost for the following reasons:

1) because the voice belongs to the living being that uses it, and in film there are no actors' bodies as in the theatre, merely their photographic images moving on the screen;

2) because the images do not speak, they are there to be seen. If they do speak, the living voice is in irreconcilable contrast with their quality as shadows and disturbs one like something unnatural that exposes and denounces the mechanical;

3) because the images in film can be seen moving in those places represented on film: in a house, a yacht, a wood, a mountain, a valley, a street, anywhere other than in the cinema where the film is being shown, of course, while the voice can always be heard in that cinema. The result of this is to create an unpleasant effect of unreality, and attempts have been made to create an even worse remedy for this, by bringing into close-up the images of the speakers, with this dire effect: the scenic frame is lost; the succession of talking images on the screen tires the eyes and removes all effectiveness from the dialogue; finally, there is the clear realisation that the lips of those great foregrounded images are moving emptily because the voices are not coming from those mouths but coming grotesquely out of a machine, with the voice of a machine and not that of a human being, accompanied by the dreadful buzzing and spluttering of the gramophone. When technical skills have succeeded in eliminating the buzz and obtaining a perfect reproduction of the human voice, the main evil will not be cured in the slightest, because it is obvious to all that the images will stay as images, and images cannot talk.

This road to perfection will certainly not lead to the cinema abolishing theatre, if anything it will lead to cinema destroying itself. Theatre will stay as the original, always alive and, like any other living thing, changing from time to time. Cinema, however, will always be the copy it once was, stereotyped and basically still as illogical and unnatural as ever, no matter how hard it tries to move closer to its original so as to replace it.

What is happening to the film may be compared to that absurd misadventure which Aesop tells us about in one of his most famous tales, when the vainglorious peacock is mockingly flattered by the diabolical fox on account of his magnificent tail and the majesty of his regal bearing, and opens his mouth to let his voice be heard, whereupon he makes everyone burst out laughing.

So long as it kept quiet, so long as it was a silent expression of images understandable to all with a few brief written notes that could easily be translated into a range of languages, then the cinema was a sizeable rival or threat to the theatre, especially in recent times, because of its vast international distribution network and the taste it had succeeded in creating in the general public for silent performances. There were various signs that indicated how far the theatre was becoming concerned by the rivalry of the cinema: certain directorial abuses that tried to make theatre become a visual spectacle above all, or as much as possible, some imitation of cinematic techniques that occasional directors used, such as gradually darkening a stage and letting another emerge from the blackout, accompanied by music; the choice of a new repertoire of plays, a lighter, less consistent one, that could be easily manipulated so as to obtain the special effects of sudden changes and other devices specially laid on for visual impact. The great danger for theatre lay precisely in this attempt to resemble the cinema. And now, in contrast, the cinema is trying to become theatre. And so theatre has nothing more to fear. If I cannot see anything in the cinema except a poor reproduction of theatre, and if I have to listen to photographic images of actors speaking in strange voices through a mechanically operated machine, then I prefer to go to the theatre, where at least there are real actors speaking with real voices. A talking film may aspire to replace theatre altogether, but can only obtain the effect of making me regret that I do not have real, living actors before me playing tragedy or comedy and only have their mechanical, photographic reproductions.

So indirectly the talkie has helped the theatre, rather than damaged it, because in using language it has inevitably lost its international quality. All peoples have eyes to see with equally; but every nation has its own language to speak with. There will have to be as many special editions of a film as there are countries which want to show it, though not all will have the market ability to pay the cost of a special edition. The translations of a single edition which were feasible for short stage directions simply are not possible for actors' dialogues, because they cannot possibly speak in all languages. So the international market will be lost. The directors of talking films will not be the same as those of the silent film; they will have to come from the theatre. And actors, if the characters in films have to talk from now on, will not be the same as the actors of the silent cinema (with a few exceptions) who do not have the abilities and are not used to speaking, and who have neither the disposition nor the vocal talent to speak. They will have to be stage actors. And the same applies to the writers who will have to make the characters speak; those writers certainly will not be the librettists of the silent cinema, they will have to be theatre writers. Anything but the end of theatre! In every conceivable way it will be the triumph of theatre!

Meanwhile a grave misfortune has afflicted the cinema. The public was for many years used to silent viewing, and now that the cinema has spoken, albeit badly, grotesquely, repellently, anyone going back to see a silent film experiences a certain disillusionment, a sense of dissatisfaction, an irritation that was not there before. The silence has been broken. It cannot be remade. Now a voice has to be given to the cinema at all costs.

It is quite in vain to persist in burying one's head in the initial error by trying to find that voice in literature. When literature wants the characters born in the minds of its poets to speak, it has theatre. You must not touch theatre. I have tried to show, and I believe that I have indeed shown with irrefutable proof, that if the cinema goes along this road it can only reach a point of self-annihilation. The cinema has to free itself from literature in order to find the true expression of itself, and only then will it have fulfilled its true revolution. Leave narrative to the novel, and the play to the theatre. Literature is not its proper element; its proper element is music. Let it free itself from literature and steep itself in music. But not in the music that accompanies singing, for singing is words and the word even when sung cannot be an image. Just as the image cannot talk, neither can it sing. Leave melodrama to the opera house and jazz to the music hall. I am talking about the music that speaks to everyone without words, the music that is expressed through sounds and of which the cinema can become the visual language. For that is it: pure music and pure vision. The two principal aesthetic senses, sight and hearing, joined in a single pleasure; eyes that see, ears that hear, hearts that feel all the beauty and variety of feelings that are expressed in sound and represented in images evoked by those feelings and that stir the subconscious in all of us, unimagined images that can be as terrible as those of nightmare, as mysterious and changeable as those of dreams, either in dizzying succession or bland and restful, with the very movement of musical rhythm. The name of the true revolution is cinema: the visible language is music, any music, from the popular which expresses genuine feelings, to that of Bach or Scarlatti or Beethoven or Chopin. Just imagine what a wealth of images might be aroused by the whole folklore of music, from an ancient Spanish dance to the Volga Boat song of the Russians, or the *Pastorale*, or the *Eroica* of the *Nocturnes* or one of the *valses brillantes*.

If literature so far has been a stormy sea over which the cinema has steered with difficulty, then tomorrow, once the twin Herculean pillars of narrative and the play have been passed, the cinema will burst out freely into the ocean of music, where, at full sail it will finally be able to discover itself and reach the fortunate havens of the miraculous.

Questa sera si recita a soggetto

The period Pirandello spent in Berlin from late 1928 to the end of 1930 was a particularly productive one.[4] A man now in his early sixties, he seemed to take on a new lease of life. Never before a great frequenter of cafés, he was now to be seen in dance halls, cabaret clubs and variety theatre. For a period of time, a table was kept for him every evening at the Romanisches Café which was visited by celebrities from various walks of life: Einstein, Georg Kaiser (whose works Pirandello admired), his fellow Sicilian dramatist, Rosso di San Secondo, the actor, Emil Jannings and Max Schmeling, the boxer, were all to be seen here. With his fluent German learnt while he was a student in Bonn, Pirandello was able to converse with cabaret and variety artistes and, according to the writer Pietro Solari, reporting in *L'Italia letteraria*, of 3 November, 1929, seemed particularly interested in the psychology of transvestite performers. Something of this fascination comes through in his play *As You Desire Me (Come tu mi vuoi)* which belongs to this period. It is *Tonight We Improvise (Questa sera si recita a soggetto)*, however, which owes most to this German environment. The critique this play offers of the role of the director owes its genesis to debates taking place in Berlin about the function of the *regisseur*;[5] and something of the excitement of the multi-media show was inspired by Pirandello's ambivalent admiration for the disciplined variety of German stagecraft. Writing in *L'Italia letteraria* of 14 April, 1929, Corrado Alvaro reports Pirandello's views: "I admire German theatre for its discipline and for the perfect means which it has at its disposal. The director here can achieve any amount of technical miracles. German actors are the most disciplined and meticulous in the world. They don't act, they live with the appearances of a minutely observed reality. They lack, perhaps, the actor in the Italian sense of the word, the inspired improviser among a crowd of mediocre walk-ons. Here, they are all perfect, from the first to the last. You can often go to a theatre and see a great actor who has only a very small part. But how important this all is for the balance and efficacy of the production [....] But the possibility of obtaining any effect, technique carried to its maximum perfection will end up by killing theatre. Sometimes these *regisseurs* just take an outline of a play which allows them to bring on stage all manner of things never before seen there and make a show out of them. Dance, acrobatics, circus horses, quick scene changes effected by powerful and perfect stage machines, are becoming so many means of corrupting theatre itself. I intend to react to this tendency with my new play." And this he did. Something of Pirandello's ambivalence in this play can seen in its dedication. The German edition of the play was dedicated to Max Reinhardt; but it was precisely Max Reinhardt whom the Berlin audiences were convinced was being satirised in the character of the director Hinkfuss. And it was at least in part this identification which triggered the poor reception the play received in Berlin.

Document No. 52: Letter from Pirandello to Salvini, 4.4.1929

Berlin W10 4/IV/29
Hotel Herkuleshaus
Friedrich-Wilhelmstrasse 13

Dear Salvini,
    The ever increasing recognition that your work is gaining brings me greater satisfaction than any good that could come to me (if indeed any now can come to me). And I thank you for the affection that you have always shown and continue to show towards me.
    I have delayed replying to you expecting each day to be able to send you a copy of my play *Tonight We Improvise*. But unfortunately, the copyist, whom with great difficulty I have managed to find in this foreign country, has not kept a promise to finish it. I will have the first four copies tomorrow perhaps, or the day after, and one of these will certainly be for you. There is a great interest in the play here. Pallenberg[6] himself has come to ask me to keep the main part for him. I don't know yet whether it will be staged by Reinhardt[7] or Hartung[8]. It will be a magnificent test for a director, a test of self denial as well, because, as perhaps you know, the play comes out against the excesses of stage direction. I tell you the following, not to boast but just to add news that could be useful to you. In addition to others, a Russian translator has turned up, the writer Marianoff, representative here in Berlin of Lunaciarski (I don't know whether that's the way to spell his name)[9], someone well thought of in Moscow, to do the translation of the play. So there will be a Russian translation too. But I know that many of my works have been translated into Russian, although no one has given me any indication which ones.

You will see the work. In the event that it seems unsuitable, for reasons that you will be better able to judge than I can, I leave it to you to choose another.

Affectionately yours,

Luigi Pirandello

Document No. 53: Letter from Pirandello to Salvini, 2.3.1930

Berlin W.10 2.III.1930
Herkuleshaus
Friedrich-Wilhelmstrasse 13

My dear Salvini,

Thank you for your affectionate letter. With my sudden departure I was sorry not to have been able to say goodbye to you and to keep the appointment with Ricci[10] and Silvani; but my departure having been established for the morning of Wednesday, I had hoped all day Tuesday to see you, either at the hotel or in the theatre; but you did not turn up. After the theatre I went to eat; I got back to the hotel about 2 a.m.: too late to 'phone. I left in the morning at half-past eight, accompanied to the station by Marta, who despite my opposition and her great tiredness, insisted on getting up early to show me her great affection and devotion. I was also accompanied by Nulli. Mario Pelosini also came to greet me in the train, just as it was about to leave. You will understand, my dear Salvini, why I am telling you all of this. I know that you are like a son to me, as affectionate as you are discreet; and I know that, if in order to hurt the *signorina* in some way, the rumour was spread of some disagreement between us, you would deny the rumour and say that there was no longer any disagreement between Marta and myself, and that if ever there had been one, it was not with her but with her relatives; and you would say that Marta has behaved towards me like the affectionate, devoted daughter that she has always been. Because of all the affection I feel for this dear person (and you know its nature) I could not bear the least harm to come to her on account of it. I will stay far away - and more lonely than ever. I only hope that God will give me the strength to resist. And so from a distance, I will follow and assist Marta as long as she wants me to and as long as she feels the need for my help.

On Tuesday I shall leave for Königsberg and on Wednesday I shall attend the performance of *Tonight We Improvise*[11] which continues to be performed with extraordinary success. I am sending you the first two pages of *Chiarivari* which has some opinions about it from the German press. When you have looked at them, would you please pass them to Enrico Piceni of the Mondadori Publishing House (via Maddalena 1) so he can use them. Dr. Martin, director of the Volksbuhne, currently one of the leading theatres in Berlin, will come to Königsberg with me to see the performance, because Felix Bloch-Erben, seeing no possibility at present of a Reinhardt production, would like to give it to Martin. The performance at Frankfurt will take place at the end of the month.

I have not yet received the letter from Gino Rocca.[12] Tell him that if he goes to Rome to speak with Bottai, to get in touch first with Interlandi who has a copy of all my correspondence with the *Società degli Autori* and a copy of my paper. Bottai[13] must be told of this. I shall return from Könisberg on Thursday, and I will stay in Berlin until the 10th, then I shall leave again for Paris to see the production of *The Life I Gave You* which will take place on the 13th and get in touch again with Pitoëff about *Ce soir on improvise*[14]. I will let you have my Paris address as soon as I arrive.

Please give my greetings to your brother Celso and to all my friends. Always affectionately, my dear Salvini,

Luigi Pirandello.

Document No. 54: Letter from Pirandello to Salvini, 30.3.1930

Berlin W.10 30.III.1930
Herkuleshaus
Friedrich-Wilhelmstrasse 13

My dear Salvini,
I have received your letter of 27th from Florence and hasten to reply.

As you will know, I have been to see the production at Königsberg. Admirable. The play is completely alive, wonderfully alive, it never falters for a moment, and the audience would like to have a hundred eyes and ears, so enchanted are they from beginning to end. Wonder is the play's natural climate, which means that the sudden movements from the comic to the tragic seem natural; the audience receives everything with a child-like joy, responding with laughter and tears at one and the same time.

Some cuts in Hinkfuss's speech will have to be made, but very careful cuts, bearing in mind the new and essential things he has to say.

The régisseur Hans Carl Muller[15] has given a magnificent and marvellously colourful emphasis both to the religious procession and to the Cabaret scene, which exploded immediately afterwards in strident contrast and to extraordinary effect. After the introduction scene, done in front of the closed curtain, you begin to hear the bells, the sound of the organ and the singing of the congregation in the church. Then at the back of the auditorium the bagpipes and the steel whistles begin. Then your attention is cleverly turned to a priest who comes out of the church on stage: he is in all his regalia, three-cornered hat, surplice and stole, and preceded by four altar boys, the first two with censers, the other two with lighted candles, and followed by four little virgins carrying the heavenly canopy. They move slowly from the church and approach the footlights where they pause, waiting for the "holy family", followed by the procession, to cross the whole hall singing and accompanied by bagpipes and steel whistles which bring up the rear. They take the "holy family" from underneath the canopy and go into the church. The procession is long and of superb visual effect. The transparency device of the cabaret wall is superb: a sudden rush of sounds, lights and colours. Lights of various colours and tones, dark and lugubrious on the Chanteuse's side, garish on the dancers' side. The dancers are very lively and vivacious and intersperse the Chanteuse's powerful song with shrieks of joy and bursts of laughter, slapping their thighs and clicking their fingers in an orchestration of marvellous dissonance. Meanwhile the jazz reaches its peak. The scene with these effects goes on for quite a while. Just at the right moment, when the horns have been put on Sampognetta's head, attention is drawn to the role of one of the customers who holds back the Chanteuse, when she moves forward to tear those horns from Sampognetta's head. This customer becomes very violent, slaps the Chanteuse, knocking her to the ground. Clearly he is her lover, the one who will later knife Sampognetta. So while some of the customers take Sampognetta out of the Cabaret, others inside lift the Chanteuse up off the ground and the transparent effect ends on this double scene of Sampognetta going out and the Chanteuse getting up, achieving the double effect marvellously, so that it seems to people in the audience that they are leaving the Cabaret together with Sampognetta and the others who take him out.

With no less success, Muller has arranged it so that the scene in the theatre takes place not just in one box but in two, opposite one another, and in such a way that no section of the audience is disadvantaged. All those young men with their girls and their unspeakable mother are placed in two boxes, some in one, the rest in another opposite. The mother speaks from one, the daughters from the other.

In the meantime, the Cabaret is cleverly transformed into an opera scene, with a few synthetic, parodying elements. The transparent wall returns, while the audience, no longer thinking about it, turns its attention to the two illuminated boxes and to what is happening there, and tries to work out what's what. At this point, a prima donna and a baritone can be seen towards the back of the stage through the curtain which has been closed so as to show only the transparent wall: they are singing badly to the accompaniment of a gramophone, amplified by a radio, the finale of the first act of an Italian opera. The effect is irresistible. It seems a work of real magic - that quite outstrips Fregoli.[15] In the twinkling of an eye, everything is changed: we are really in a provincial opera theatre, both a caricature and a parody, with singers strutting around in their velvet and feathers - to a gramophone instead of an orchestra.

And immediately after this, another surprise and new idea. After lowering the curtain on the scandal that takes place in the theatre on account of Signora Ignazia, the auditorium is lit at Dr. Hinkfuss's command. He has now climbed back on to the stage. But the audience doesn't go out of the auditorium, although the doors that lead to the corridors have been opened by the ushers. People do not go out because, while Dr. Hinkfuss goes on speaking on stage, they can see through the open doors the couples of the young men with the La Croce girls taking a walk, and they can also see that Signora Ignazia has remained in the box with two of the officers. When Dr. Hinkfuss has finished his speech, he has the curtain opened again, and then the miracle happens: the whole theatre becomes a stage!   On the stage itself, Dr. Hinkfuss gets the technicians and stage hands to strike the set; in the meantime, down in the illuminated auditorium, a young lad comes in, in his braided cap, with his box slung over his shoulders, selling chocolates, sweets and newspapers. Nenè and Totina see him and drag the two young men, Pomarici and Sarelli, from the corridor near the prompter's box to buy some of those chocolates; and the first little scene takes place there.   Then these four go off and come to stop right underneath the box where the girls' mother has remained, and meanwhile Dorina and Nardi come in from another entrance at the back of the auditorium, chattering to each other and they call out to the others and join their group.   And when their little scene is over, they go back and out into the corridor; but before they have done this, Verri and Mommina come into the auditorium to do their part, leaning up against the rail of the first row of the stalls.   The audience does not know where to look first, as things are happening everywhere.   The last of these little scenes, the one between Signora Ignazia and the two officers takes place in the box.   During all of this, up on the stage Dr. Hinkfuss has had the stage hands strike the set of the church and the cabaret and has started assembling the airfield.   He tries it out.   In a twinkling of an eye he has it dismantled and orders the curtain to be lowered to give the La Croce family time to get back home.   As if speaking in confidence to the audience, he says the "real" interval is about to begin and disappears behind the curtain.

As you can see, my dear Salvini, everything takes place in the auditorium in front of the audience, who really enjoy themselves.

It does not seem to me right at all to put the interval after Sampognetta's death, as you would like to do, because the actors' revolt and their refusal to carry on with the show would naturally happen during that interval and not afterwards.   Hinkfuss must know nothing of the actors' decision after the failed effect of Sampognetta's death; he must believe that with his speech to the audience he is putting everything right. The revolt must take him by surprise, while he is dragging out his speech, expecting someone to indicate to him at any moment that the women are dressed in black.   It must appear obvious that he is expecting such a sign from little movements and gestures of impatience that the actor can easily put in, until he draws up the edge of the curtain and expresses his impatience clearly.

With reference to the talking film, I have told you what you can do by describing what has been done here at Königsberg; you can solve every difficulty the same way.

You must bring in Dr. Hinkfuss at the end.   The tragic effect must be gained with Mommina's death and the survival of her husband, mother and sisters.   It is natural for Dr. Hinkfuss to break the effect immediately by expressing his satisfaction.   That tragic final scene must not be an end in itself.   It is necessary to reach the conclusion of this whole experiment with improvisation.   And the conclusion must be that the theatre must be reintegrated into its three elements: dramatist, director, actors.   I have thought of adding a few lines to make the meaning clearer.   When Verri leans over Mommina as she lies on the ground and says to her, more or less "Get up, signorina, haven't you realised that it must end with a joke?",

Mommina, pulled up by her arms, lies inert as if she were really dead, fainting and exhausted: she has lived, not acted. The actors cannot do this every evening. At an enormous cost of effort and energy, they can do it for one evening. The actors must have a part to play. And so the dramatist is needed to provide it for them. This is what is really expressed, but perhaps in too condensed a way, implicit rather than clearly stated. I do not have a text with me to add the three or four extra lines. I am waiting for Mondadori to send me some printed copies. I shall try them out for the moment and you can then add them to your printed text. They should go something like this:

VERRI: Get up, Signorina, haven't you realised yet that we have to finish with a joke? (He tries to drag her up by the arms; Mommina resists; she lies there inert, exhausted; then leaning over with the others), Oh, my God, signorina, what's the matter?

DORINA: Does she really feel ill?

SIGNORA IGNAZIA: Is it her heart?

COMIC ACTOR: Oh, go on. She hasn't just been acting - she's lived the part. We can make these great efforts for just one evening, but you don't want us to die doing this, do you?

VERRI: Come along, signorina, gently does it. Let me help you ... a chair ... smelling salts ...

COMIC ACTOR: (to Hinkfuss) We need an author, a dramatist, to give us parts to act ... etc. etc. as in the text.

The sketch you have made for the rooms in the La Croce house agrees with the stage directions; except that the dining room is on the left and the drawing room on the right. It would be better to make the walls solid as in the photographs I am sending you.

As to the danger of having officers on stage, make them into young Belgian mining engineers, answerable to a Belgian society, which has taken over a mine in Sicily. Ricco Verri can figure as an apprentice with this group. Imagine it as a school for these engineers, a school of practical experience, for which they can have a kind of uniform, blue or khaki jackets and white trousers, leather Bavarian caps, or something similar, provided it is colourful. In this case, Dr. Hinkfuss can set up a mine instead of an airfield, with some Gill ovens, with the Belgian engineering school in the background.

As to the Ave Maria, what can I say? It depresses me to think we have sunk so low.

I think I have replied to all your questions. I look forward to hearing your news and send you my warmest greetings.

Yours

Luigi Pirandello.

Document No. 55: Letter from Pirandello to Salvini, 20.4.1930

Berlin W.10 20.IV.1930
Herkuleshaus
Friedrich-Wilhelmstrasse 13

My dear Salvini,

    I am typing this letter to you in bed on Easter Sunday. I have been confined to bed for some days, threatened by pneumonia which I have miraculously managed to escape, or shall we say because of a very violent reaction to some very rough massage treatment ordered by a doctor and performed by a nurse with hands of iron, which has taken the skin off my chest and shoulders. Some trace of the harm still remains; four or five finger prints over the left ribs underneath the shoulder blade and under the armpit, which hurt a lot if I press them, and because of which I must keep myself well looked after.

    But on to other matters. (I have always attached very little importance, as you well know, to my body's ailments.) So: *Tonight We Improvise* went better than we dared hope.[16] I am really very pleased about that, as much for you as for me. More, my dear Salvini, for you, considering the courage you had in attempting it after those rogues in Milan had decreed that only a madman could have written such a work and only a madman could have tried to stage it. I am sure they told you with self-satisfied certainty that you were heading for a mighty flop. I like to imagine what they are feeling now, after the news of your triumph. And after the resounding failure of their fine undertakings, they must be biting their nails with rage for having had the work in their hands for seven months and then thrown away a play that could have more than put them back on their feet. But let us not say any more about them. I have read the good reviews by Bertuetti and also the one by F. and B. of *La Stampa* who was so against me when I did *Lazarus* (I do not even know who he is). He says it is over wordy in only one place, the final scene, the one I think is best. But if the performance really turns out to be too long, make some further cuts, boldly but carefully, my dear Salvini. You must make the work perfect, taking into consideration the restrictions of the stage, the capabilities of your actors and the tolerance of the audience.

    If the proprietors and managers of the theatres were not all such villains, they should give you a triumphal tour and the opportunity to come into your own in a long series of repeat performances in Milan and Rome, so that you could make a lot of money, which you must really need in order to maintain such a large company and to recoup on expenses. I have written to Nulli asking him to do his utmost for you in this respect and to help to in every way he can. You must strike while the iron is hot. And to bring the play to the awareness of the public, you need a great publicity programme, everywhere, as the Americans do. So said those gentlemen of *Za Bum*,[17] but with them the public drank lees and dregs; you will give them good wine, clear, bubbling and abundant. Keep me informed of how things go.

    As to the two things you ask me, my dear Salvini, I cannot say yes for certain. *The Mountain Giants* will certainly be for you (and into whose hands could I give it with greater trust?) As to the other request, I can only make the promise that if it is possible, you will have your wish. Next Tuesday the rehearsals of *Tonight We Improvise* are starting at the Lessing Theatre under the direction of Hartung. The work will have its opening night some time during the middle of May. Ill as I am, I will not be able to be present at the first rehearsals; but I must be there for the last ones. I could come for two or three days at the most and I will tell you that, weak as I am, it makes me nervous to think of facing such a long journey, there and back, without having time to rest a little in between. And then, for so many other reasons, to set foot again in Italy... But I do not want to give a categorical no straight away. Let us see.

Please greet and thank on my behalf all your fine actors.
Yours very affectionately,

Luigi Pirandello

Document No. 56:   The Pirandello Scandal: Jhering's review of Tonight We Improvise (1930)

The scandal that took place on Saturday in the Lessing Theatre at the opening of Pirandello's *Tonight We Improvise* was the worst that Berlin has experienced in recent years. Fighting over a play? A discussion between opposing intellectual viewpoints? There was no battle, no discussion, merely self-defence against a duststorm of boredom.

The fashion for Pirandello was never genuine in Germany. *Right You Are - if You Think So* was a partial success in Königratzer Street. Even *Six Characters in Search of an Author*, despite Reinhardt's excellent direction and a distinguished cast, did not mark the start of any public following after the initial impact. Pirandello's plays show the boundary line between seeming and being, between acted and lived reality. And for whom does that have meaning today? As insights they are mediocre. As plays they are vague. The latest *Tonight We Improvise* is once again about the problem of the theatre, the problem of the actor, what is a play, what is improvisation, what is role-playing, what is the private quality of the actors? This latest play was quite stunningly uninteresting in its own right, even though it might have been good. However, it is uninspiring, devoid of wit, endless, dust blowing, dust and more dust.

So why was it brought into repertory in the Berlin Festival week? Who is responsible for this decision? There was no new German play that might have given the author the chance to learn something even if it failed, just a Pirandello, whose literary development has now come to an end. And, furthermore, in the performance of this play, not once was any attempt at a rescue undertaken. Where lightness, wit and inspired direction might have been helpful, there was the grimmest clumsiness, the gloomiest seriousness. And furthermore, that seriousness was badly performed. The audience were never able to adjust their hearing properly. One actor mumbled, another declaimed loudly. The characters always played wrongly. Wrongly in terms of the meaning of the show (if such a thing can be said at all). Wrongly for the stalls, wrongly for the stage, wrongly for the acoustics. Herr Anderson was playing Othello. Elizabeth Lennarts should be praised for her bravery in seeing it through to the end. Before this she had managed to conceal the fact that she was an actress. There are some remaining: Hedwig Wangel and Lupu Pick. Lupu Pick was the only one who managed to play with slight sincerity and slight humour between seeming and reality.

It was Herr Hartung who, in the midst of the storm of public protest, shouted back: *You bunch have no respect.* His direction showed no respect. No respect for Berlin that still has some right to a performance. No respect for the audience who still have the right to be able to hear even the most barren of texts. Herr Hartung is a grossly over-rated director, who had some good fortune with performances in Berlin when he played himself as if he were an actor: *Das grosse ABC* (The Great ABC), *Ton in des Töpfers Hand* (Clay in the Potter's Hand) and, as basic material, *Krankenheit der Jugend* (The Sickness of Youth). Herr Hartung is an Epigon of Expressionism, and has never found the way to move beyond the fixed stare and the forced Prestissimo to a freer, inspired, self-comprehending style of speech. He cheated in an arty way with his shrieking and now he is cheating with overcaution. The disaster was unbearable. It should be answerable.

The Mountain Giants

We have translated Strehler's notes on the play (Document No. 57), notes which show the extent of his involvement with Pirandello's text. Strehler sees the play as a parable about the theatre, with a universal message that applies to all times and contexts. The Giants, he suggests, are ourselves, a manifestation of everything that is most insensitive in mankind. They are the personifications of philistinism, and through philistinism, of inhumanity and intolerance. Strehler removes the play from the context of fascism and re-examines the ideological bases in order to produce a version that is very much part of the new Italy. It is entirely consistent with this belief in man's search for goodness that a director who is determinedly of the left should have been able to re-integrate the work of a disillusioned man of the right into society and into the history of the Italian theatre.

Document No. 57:   Giorgio Strehler's Production Notes for *The Mountain Giants*

I want this to be a magical, fantastic spectacle that is also true and terribly human, where so many of Pirandello's themes, from the bourgeois theme and the theme of the theatre's own dramas right up to the theme of popular dialectics are somehow summarised. I do not feel that one can explain an interpretation, one can only offer it. All that can be done is to recount the images through fragments, a gesture, a shout, to point out a sound, a movement, a colour, a plan. In this case we had no final scene, for Pirandello had not written one and we only know it through the account of his son, Stefano.

This missing final scene is the most crucial point about *The Mountain Giants* for me, and is weighted with reponsibility for myself as interpreter. Imagine a vast play in which all the characters of Pirandello's theatre are found with all their words and gestures and, in a corner, the characters from *The Giants,* the actors with Ilse, the Count, all of them, in short, who cannot fulfil their story by a single word more because Pirandello never managed to write it. What a silence! They can only cry out their passion to a certain point and not beyond, because beyond that writer's final word there is nothing but imaginary movements and gestures in an action that has been denied sound. There are faces and mouths opened in a scream that will never be heard. Ilse's death, when she is killed by the Giants who cannot understand her, happens in total silence. In front of the lights of a bare ramp, lit with acetylene lamps that flicker blue and yellow, the funeral procession must become both heart-rending and tender at the same time, with the actors who have taken up the body of their dead sister showing in their faces where the make-up has run, long dark streaks descending from their eyes, running down their cheeks. In the darkness of the empty stage only one lamp remains lit when all the others are put out, and it pulsates like a planet in the shadows without ever going out.

The opening. An iron curtain, hermetically closed: An unadorned curtain: force, structure, pitiless matter (shadows and stone). It rises slowly, to the sound of faint music, glides close by the wide, wooden benches on the stage and reveals a light decor in faded green that rises up through silvery grass brushed with evening light until the whole has a sense of magic that is both transparent and mysterious at the same time. Everything seems clear as if suspended in the void, it is air, it is evening: the sweet violet colour of an Italian evening, deep and tender, inspired by the lightly drawn themes and tones of Italian painting, both metaphysical and real.

The curtain quivers in a breeze, trembles like a live thing with short shudders, or else it fixes itself in total immobility: a shade of colour, a wall or an imagined house, a simple cloth that becomes house or theatre.

The phantom house. The theatre house. The curtain house. The giants: a performance before, behind and around a curtain. The simplicity of a cloth stretched and quivering in the evening air. The mysterious hiding places, the shelters of childhood.

Interplay of light with the lamp lit under the blankets, transparencies, shadows. The theatre, the carnival, the game of Chinese shadows where you make a swan with your hand, the magic lantern in the silence of a room full of shadows.

The curtain opens and closes again, hides and reveals the stage. It becomes a shapeless heap on the floor.

The game of the folded curtain like the sheets that women fold after ironing.

"The arsenal of apparitions": the mystery of the theatre itself. It is a place where things make themselves, where everything is possible. It is the vessel that contains all the "tools" of theatre - actors, mimes, puppets moved by hands, jumping jacks, string puppets, dolls, make-up, illusions, sets, costumes, screens, machines, objects, spotlights, tricks, games, sound and light effects that animate and create life, in all its different forms in spectacle, in performance: commercial theatre or variety theatre, cinema, mime, musical theatre.

"The understage" - laborious, obscure, massive symbol of theatre work, a heavy, monstruous machinery that can give birth to anything, mysterious and cruel in its arid immensity. It represents the cold matter from which, with a lot of effort and through taking a lot of risks, the life-blood of art is drawn. "Theatre-machinery". It is the reverse of the airy lightness of the empty "stage". From the emptiness of the opening to the creation of life given to poetry and the incarnation of the character through interpretation. It is the unfathomable, hermetic mystery of the closed curtain that releases warmth, tenderness, fantasy, apparitions, "theatre-poetry" the moment it opens. It is the "back cloth" for the story of the changeling.

Two flaps of canvas stitched together with an opening like a curtain-wound that, at some other time, served as a little back cloth.

It is pinkish grey in colour, faded by countless showers of rain and countless days of sunshine. It is poor and old, with the odd tear carefully sewn up but still visible, like the rents in sails. It is unfolded and suspended on a rope with aerobatic skill, following an automatic ritual process that is nevertheless not without unconscious love. It barely touches the ground, sags slightly in the middle without disarranging the folds. It is an actual reproduction to scale of the great curtain that represents the Villa known as "Bad-Luck House". Where there is therefore an examination of the staging according to the structure of the play, in the sense of a progressive structural and visual purity that follows the gradual shifts in Pirandello's language; from the first to the last words: "I'm afraid...I'm afraid" to the gestural significance of the "final performance", acted in mime right up to the ultimate tragic silence. *The Giants* is perhaps the only great play about theatre, a play that shows the problems of making theatre in different forms and sums up the very life of the theatre itself.

Theatricality; Different groups of players; Different theatre designs

The Villa is the possible design for a theatre, it is agnostic, it has itself as its own end, it is a stranger to reality. It is a global theatre to which everything else comes, one that was never created for an audience but which is pure game. (Think about the childlike innocence of theatre, of children's "theatre-play" which is perhaps the only serious theatre, that habit then forgets, and dismisses, rather than the daily professional practice that interferes with fantasy and the capacity for inventiveness). The Villa is seen as an existing theatre on which a strange crowd of human beings converge, all of whom were rejected by society or distanced after being rejected, all for different reasons, through different processes, according to circumstances determined in a certain way or to decisions that were taken. This is not the world of madness or of death (the phantom world) but it is the kingdom of poetry (theatre-poetry), of innocence, of a purity which offers the positive-negative enchantment of non-commitment.

In the staging there has therefore been a rejection of plastic values in favour of a desperate but pleasant fluidity, inspired by a metaphysical painting of the kind by Carrà, Rosai, Sironi that becomes a king of peasant national-popular reality and an insular mystery, on the fringe of reality and unreality ... As a result the inhabitants of the Villa must appear as realists, that is potentially popular but also "exceptional", as rarities, as invented characters.

Another theatre group: The Company of Actors who sum up and destroy the different aspects of "theatricality". The actors must seem to be real, identifiable, plausible in the way in which they belong to the petit-bourgeois world, clearly able to be located in a precise professional category (as a member of the minor aristocracy so far as the Count is concerned). They have different origins: islanders, from central Europe, with slight cadences and dialect inflections. They show signs of professional decay, but should not therefore become masks of actors or portray schematised roles. They are theatre people, all united in decay, in suffering and in the pathetic that always characterises an actor who has reached the end of the road. Their ravaged make-up is a symbol of everything monstrous and ugly in the theatre, the obscenity of its anti-nature aspect, but also of its terrifying character, its mystery, its deep game that consists in disguising someone as another person, of being others with pain, the voluptuousness of not being able to be anything but others. They speak the typical slightly rhetorical language of actors; their tone is painfully yet artificially enthusiastic. Their sorry entrance at the start of the play suggests the rite of congratulations from a box at the end of the show. They smile with despair in their eyes but they make gestures of pleasure, blowing kisses with their fingertips, waving, flaunting a show of great satisfaction and basking in their skill as actors. Faced with them, a sober curiosity that borders on indifference. The actors are carrying a weight of tension, a selfishness barely concealed under the ancient ritual. The meeting between the two groups must seem to be unimaginable. The actors are carrying a weight of tension and despair, their daily mourning which clashes with the detachment, the clarity and the tenderness of the inhabitants of the Villa.

The game of refraction in Pirandello's theatre exists and must be clearly shown on both the poetic and dialectical level. The play opens with a theatrical incident: the inhabitants of the Villa play at being "phantoms", therefore they create a primitive elementary theatre.

Then the actors, the "stage artistes" appear one after the other on a raised playing space that emphasises their theatrical nature and they act for the inhabitants of the Villa. Ilse's "cart" becomes, through imagination, a small secondary "stage" for the representation of poetic theatre. The audience in the theatre see the inhabitants of the Villa in the same way, as they become the audience for the actors, who, in turn, watch Ilse. This relationship develops further as a "formal triplication" in the mimed action of the finale: theatrically for others, poetry offered for rejection, for indifference in the relationship between actors-public/society-giants. And the performance is interrupted again when the private drama of the actors is played out amongst themselves, the story of a poet who died for love, the travels of Ilse and the Count ...

The whole thing has been almost excessively Pirandellian: distorting sentences and body movement, mingling speed and effort, destroying truth that has been exhibited shamelessly to view in the midst of a collective public, for that collective public to view. This is the essential "tripling". "Men" who, being "actors" behave as actors, play the part of actors in real life (incarnations of Ilse as woman-actress-mother). There is a glaring contrast with the abstract worlds of the inhabitants of the Villa. "Actors" who, being such, act and play roles (the story of the changeling). They are beings who give body to other theatrical situations by tearing each other apart - this is "theatre life". By disguising themselves. Fired by the discovery of fantastic props, they succumb to the enchantment of disguise, unconsciously projecting onto the costumes that they put on all the reality that they ardently desire for themselves, pure love, unrecognised dramatic submission. They are not aware that they love the theatre precisely because they do love it.

The demystifying process of "disguise" as a poetic projection of the self can thus be explained.

Theatre carnival: they "imagine themselves" in the place of the characters who are being interpreted, victims of that somnambulistic theatre fever that both damns them and conditions them. The actor's physical doubling remains "attached" to his role against his will, as the theatrical projection of consciousness, an "oneiric theatre".

In the two different theatre worlds proposed by the play, that of the inhabitants of the Villa and that of the Countess' company, the eternal theme of theatre-poetry is embodied, the dialectical relationship between text and performance. On the one hand there is ideal thought, pure spirituality bursting out of the imagination of the poet (the puppets, Cotrone) pure theatre; and on the other hand, there is the performance as an essential phase that determines the theatre work (theatre exists in so far as it is created) as reason, the choice of a "genre". The performance, therefore, involves commitment on the part of the actor who is necessarily conditioned by uncertainty, by risk taking, by mistakes of evaluation and interpretation (either by exaggerating or by not going far enough) and remains nevertheless bound to a concrete reality of means, things, peoples and audience. "Performed theatre" (Ilse's company).

In addition to showing dialectically the opposition of two concepts of theatre, Pirandello schematizes the "various modes" of "making theatre", of being on a stage through the characters of Ilse, Cromo and Cotrone. "Ilse" represents missionary commitment, martyrdom, an object lesson in purity. Detached from all contingencies, she is dedicated to the values of the work that she is presenting against the audience (which nevertheless always exists) and is constantly on a stage that she will only leave when she dies. This is "committed theatre".

"Cromo" might represent, as one of his many components, the "honourable" job that is undertaken each day, professional consciousness in humble, pitiable, thankless work which makes all critical judgement an abstraction but which presupposes deep, unconscious love. Theatre as "job".

Cotrone: he summarises all types of theatre, beginning with an act of faith in the possibilities of poetry. He invites you to believe in play, like children, in all the tricks of the trade without asking questions and looking for definitions ... He is "theatre as inventiveness". And perhaps he is also a reflection of Pirandello's speculative image, which is classical in its absolute clarity of the oppositions between form and substance, appearance and truth, magic and reality. Although he has refused to take part in the struggle and has voluntarily gone to live in the Villa, he seems to belong to a company of actors, and so marks the boundary line, the point of dramatic cut-off between the two worlds.

The unwritten conclusion of *The Giants* probably offers the possibility of enabling a work that is in many ways dated and inexorably bound up with certain typical styles of a particular moment in Italian literary history to become something that can still belong to our own time. The series of unresolved questions at the end of the play, even after the unfolding of such a lengthy story, transmits a sense of adventure directly into our own lives. In fact, the world of the giants is not behind us. The giants are still among us, in us, around us, with their temptations and their prevarications, caught in the trap of the system, weighed down by daily life. The history of the imagination, the theatre poetry of the poor actors who are tenderly and blindly and, let us be frank, outside the course of history, bound to their art as their sole salvation, is not over yet. The anarchical, fantastic solution of the Inhabitants of the Villa is wrong, just as to other eyes the unequal, almost maniacal struggle of Ilse and the players is wrong, as they stubbornly, through self-sacrifice try to change the world through poetry. Equally wrong and monstruous - in the unconscious innocence of brutality - is the incomprehension, the evasion, the collapse into instinct on the part of the Giants (who are obtuse, anonymous slaves of other even more inaccessible giants) which suffocates and repudiates poetry as action.

How can the contemporary public grasp reciprocity of defeat, the different degrees and different states of the various modes of existence beyond the unwritten, in silence? "The Giants always win. The Giants are always defeated." This could be the formula that encapsulates the ideological core of the play and that offers coherent a solution to the unfinished work. Ilse rejects the absolute, rejects non-being, in order to fight her battle among men and Giants ... and the Giants kill her. This is not a conscious rejection, that is both positive and responsible; on the contrary it is icy indifference, the absence of feeling that kills poetry along with Ilse. The theatrical relationship of Ilse-theatre/giants-audience reflects the relationship between poetry/society.

We are the Giants, lying in wait in the life of every day, each time that we reject poetry, and, through poetry, reject mankind. This is the meaning and reason for the choice of a text that throws new light on the historical context in which we operate. Ours is a society that is increasingly allowing itself to be conditioned by its own structures, a society that is daily becoming more and more insensitive and resistant to pressures of art and that seems almost to want to make itself incapable of creating poetry, understanding poetry or loving poetry.

The Volta Conference

The Volta conferences were so called because they were funded from the Alessandro Volta Foundation. The 1934 conference on theatre, held in October in Rome, sponsored by the Italian Royal Academy, was the fourth of these gatherings. It was an auspicious occasion, designed to promote Italy as a centre of European theatre and drama, to which major theatrical practitioners, writers and academics were invited. Not all guests were able to attend, however, and among the list of absentees are to be found André Antoine, James Barrie, Paul Claudel, Noel Coward, Gerhart Hauptmann, Allardyce Nicoll, Max Reinhardt and Bernard Shaw. Pirandello was the president of the conference, the futurist leader Filippo Tommaso Marinetti its secretary. The conferencees discussed the following topics during ten sessions: the relationship of theatre to cinema, radio, opera and sport; theatre architecture and stage design; theatre and popular morals; and the relationship between theatre and state.

    Pirandello's position as president in the year he won the Nobel Prize for Literature is evidence of his status as a grand old man of Italian Theatre after his return from exile in 1933. His address is a fitting statement on his theatre career, coming as it did shortly before his death in 1936, for in it he progresses beyond the more limited concerns of his earlier years, where the emphasis was on the role of the writer. He still sees the play as the focal point of theatre, but argues here for the great social heritage of theatre itself, comprising both play and performance. Pirandello's address is an appeal to a generation, to an age in which the importance of theatre has diminished resulting in "closed theatres every evening". Pirandello calls for new plays and for new purpose-built theatres, aided by State financing. A decade after the founding of his Teatro d'Arte, after the period of exile and declining popularity, Pirandello is still able to express optimism in the enduring nature of theatre itself.

Document No. 58: Address to the Volta Conference on Dramatic Theatre (Discorso al Convego "Volta" sul teatro drammatico) 1934

Your Excellencies, Ladies and Gentlemen,

    Having been invited, due to the trust placed in me by my colleagues, to chair this Volta Conference dedicated to the theatre, I have the honour to welcome you here most warmly on my own behalf and on theirs.

    It is indeed a great pleasure for the Royal Academy of Italy to see as its guests, and as guests of Rome, that city whose immortal spirit urges it to welcome every aspect of life's expression, the most illustrious theatre people of all nations: writers and directors, critics and scholars of those most complex artistic and technical problems offered by the stage. And I thank you all most sincerely for having accepted our invitation to participate in this Conference and for having worked so hard and so brilliantly in producing your papers and contributions that we have heard and are still about to hear, for the way in which you have brought your gifts of comradeship and intellect to us all.

There are a great many, perhaps even too many, international theatre conferences. This shows us that either very little can be achieved with such conferences or else there is a deep need of mutual understanding, of much assistance, in solving problems, and that the theatre should perhaps be compared to a patient who needs to be constantly helped and sustained with medical advice. Though I should, of course, add that all the doctors who have come here with advice to offer have come to give the patient hope for life rather than death, since they are all quite certain that the patient cannot die.

The theatre cannot die.

It is a form of life itself and we are all actors in it. If theatres were abandoned and left to rot, then theatre would continue in life, it could not be suppressed, and the very nature of things would always be spectacle. It is therefore quite absurd to talk about the death of the theatre at a time like this, so full of contrasts and therefore so rich in dramatic material, in such a ferment of passions and vertiginous events that change the face of whole nations, a vortex of incident and unstable situations where there is a continual need to emphasise some kind of new certainty in the midst of this tempestuous whirlpool of doubts.

It is true that life can either be lived or written about and that when it is being lived it is very difficult to put oneself in the right conditions for art, since one is right in the middle of all the action and the passion. Art requires one to start with the moment and go beyond it in order to consider that moment and to give it a universal meaning and an eternal value. What this means, of course, is that the drama of our lives will not be so much the theatre of today but will be the theatre of tomorrow. Art can anticipate life, can predict it, but to invalidate the life of today and to categorise it under *specia aeternitatis* is both rare and difficult today, though it will be easier tomorrow. Of course everything can be material for art and the artist reflects the life of his time, nor indeed could he do otherwise, since he is himself a product of a civilisation and of the moral life of his own time. However, to do it deliberately, that is with the intention of making it a practical, voluntary act of the moment, even though this may be for the best of ends is extraneous to art, is to make politics, not art. Of course, this is not to say that at certain moments in the life of a nation, art should not take on this role, as has happened many times, and became the tool of a noble civil or political act, that is, to diminish its own quality as art in order to remain an historical document, if not an artistic monument to the history of a nation's civilisation. But at times this is not desirable or necessary or pertinent, and beyond any interested passion art needs to be considered in terms of how its nature alone can assist fictions and inventions. Real, true documents can be of infinitely more value, together with facts, persuasive, eloquent testimonies through which art, by sacrificing and annihilating itself would come to serve as an inadequate tool, since the mystery of every artistic birth is the same mystery as any natural birth and not a thing that can be made, just something that has to come to life naturally. Nor should it come to life through an author's whim, freely and outside all laws, as those who do not understand often falsely suppose, but should adhere to its own unalterable vital laws, in such a way that it is free from any taint of expediency because it wills itself to be and has not other aims than those pure ones within itself. If such is not the case, then it will no longer be a work of art and is therefore to be condemned, not only in the name of all things to which wrong has been done, but above all in the name of art itself.

Now we must bear in mind the fact that this Conference has its own particular character, its own culture, which sets it apart from the usual type of Conference. It is in fact described as a Conference and not as a congress: a conference of select scholars invited with the specific aim of discussing a carefully chosen subject, one which excites us all but with that selfless excitement which characterises serious study. And it is in that frame of mind, without any polemical intentions on my part, that I have begun to discuss the relationship between art and politics, setting the discussion in terms that we can all relate to in the abstract, in order to reach a conclusion which, since art is the kingdom of selfless feeling, sees any assistance deemed important and timely as having to be equally outside motives of self-interest.

But I should not, nor indeed do I wish in any way to cause concern to the minds of those who have gathered together here to tackle the subjects of this Conference with my particular quibbles. What I can do is to express the hope that these discussions and debates will lead to a clear and detailed account of the present conditions of the theatre in relation to other types of performance, and to equally clear and detailed suggestions as to how we may improve those conditions. And so, if it is true that the theatre cannot die, it is no less true that it has to be defended, or rather, to be put into a position of being able to defend itself. And to defend itself against its rivals, regardless of whether these other performances have help in the form of State subsidies and grants, from public bodies, such as the opera has, or whether they happen to be in fashion, like the athletics shows for which new stadiums are always being built these days, or whether they are novelty shows which have the advantage of being mechanically reproduced and so easily distributed and can be repeated several times a day in great purpose-built halls or projected by a small machine in private houses that are thus turned into theatres, without the need for any special building.

In other times people were drawn to performances on the occasion of major feasts and great religious festivals. Now that no longer happens, and people go on a daily basis, drawn by habit that has become a need, which is a sign of a developing civilisation. It does still happen that in the summer months or in Spring people are drawn to extraordinary performances in the open air, in ancient amphitheatres, for annual or biennial celebrations in certain cities, in piazzas or other designated places. But magnificent though these may be, they do not solve the problem of the theatre and with time every nation that seeks to be considered civilised has had to deal with a problem of civilisation: closed theatres every evening. I leave it to you to decide whether the so-called theatre of the masses can solve this problem, or whether this concept does not derive from the opposite viewpoint, that is for celebratory performances and grandiose one-off shows, like the athletics which draw such huge crowds, yes, there is indeed a vast public, but all these performances are extraordinary and cannot, nor could ever be mounted on a daily basis.

So far only the cinema has succeeded in satisfying this daily hunger for performances that is now so widespread. If we want the prose theatre to solve it, especially in the conditions in which it now finds itself vis-à-vis the cinema, then we must consider whether the time has not come to take the steps taken by some other countries and to limit evening showings of films to one a night and at a fixed time. In this way the prose theatre would not so much be placed in the position of having an advantage, but would at least be competing on equal terms. The public would have to choose between types of performance, and the cinema would not have the advantage of being able to reproduce mechanically the same show, since until the cinema can find its own artistic expression, as everyone hopes it will, multiple showings are detrimental to the theatre. But we should also plan to build new theatres, just as new stadiums are being built for sporting events, since in the theatre we are still breathing the musty air of old places that are no longer suited to modern needs, not only the needs of art but also, and principally, the needs of custom and economics.

In all its manifestations, new life is fleeing from the old categories, both those of class and those of acquired privilege, and so the theatres which were built in times when those distinctions were keenly felt now give the impression of being anachronistic places from which we almost instinctively seek to distance ourselves.

It is to be hoped that out of the proposals and discussions held at this Conference the most efficacious and practical way of attracting people back to the theatre will be in the building of new playing spaces, and perhaps in this way the question of the hoped-for mass theatre will also be solved in spirit. What is needed are purpose-built halls, capable of holding enough people to more than cover the costs of performances whilst keeping the prices level with those of the cinema, and with seating arranged in such a way that there are no other visible distinctions than the obvious one of greater or lesser distance from the stage; stages with new equipment, with all the technical apparatus needed to transform every performance into a spectacle, more suited and no less attractive than those to which the cinema has now accustomed people to see.

Stage designers have a huge open field here for their ideas and plans. And it is to be hoped that the question which has been debated for so long will be finally resolved, that is whether the theatre is there to offer a performance in which the play, the writer's creation is only one of the many elements controlled by the director, together with the sets, the lighting, the acting, or whether, on the contrary, all these elements, together with the unifying work of the director, responsible for the performance, alone should not be put to the task of giving life to the play so that it can be understood by everyone, for without it nobody would have any reason to be there, night after night. By giving life, I mean the life that is inviolable, because it is coherent in every way that the work of art claims for itself, and therefore it is not up to the director to alter it nor to manipulate it in any way.

The play is what remains even though it exists in time in the fleeting performances given in theatres. And amongst all the types of performance that can enter into the life of a nation for a time, the theatre is the one which contains and mirrors most intimately all moral values: the theatre is what remains. Giving voice to feelings and thoughts which are all too obvious in the lively play of the passions represented and that, through the very nature of this art form need to be put in clear, precise terms, the theatre presents human actions as they truly are for honest public judgement, in all their eternal, clear reality created by the mind of the writer as an example and a warning to the confusion of daily life. That free, human justice effectively reawakens the consciousness of the judges themselves and reminds them of a higher, more demanding moral life. Every period of human history has handed down its theatre to us, living through different nations, and that theatre has always been a sign of a great moment in the life of those nations. It is a sacred, monumental heritage and one which all States, both great and small, have felt the need to accommodate with specific places of performance. Nor is it a museum of motionless statues, but a place in which the most worthy plays can continue forever to come to life, whilst new works that just happen to have been created can live outside all those adverse and precarious conditions of the present.

In this Conference for the first time there will be detailed and exact information on all the resources that various European states have agreed or tried to agree to give in order to ensure the fate of their national theatres. I am sure that the representatives of various state organisations will want to offer reciprocal congratulations on the information supplied by the conference papers, and in this way the sum of other experiences may be useful to those nations where a State theatre has not yet emerged, together with information on programmes, examination of those programmes, the processes whereby exchanges are set up between different national theatres, the hopes of improving legislation for national theatres, all of which are discussed in many of the papers.

And while we apply ourselves with the calm minds of scholars to the discussion of the subjects proposed and examine in detail technical and practical questions, we must not lose sight of the goal that our work may serve to keep alive, the belief in and to determine the future of what the Greeks held to be the highest and most mature expression of art: the Theatre.

Notes

1. Renato Simoni; see Section I, note 15, p.52.

2. Giorgio Venturini, theatre director and dramatist.   He is best known for his production of Vecchi's *Amfiparnaso* in 1938.

3. Nikolai Nikolavic Evreinov (1879-1953) dramatist, theatre and cinema director, theorist and historian of theatre whose ideas have much in common with Pirandello's.

4. See Michele Cometa, *Il teatro di Pirandello in Germania,* Palermo; Novecento, 1988, pp. 287-311.

5. See Graziella Corsinovi, "*Questa sera si recita a soggetto*:   il testo.   Tra progettazione vitalistica e partitura musicale", in Roberto Alonge, Franca Angelini, Umberto Artioli, Graziella Corsinovi, Lucio Lugnani, Paolo Puppa *et al., Testo e messa in scena in Pirandello*, Rome, La Nuova Italia Scientifica, 1986, pp. 105-32.

6. Max Pallenberg (1874-1934) was an Austrian theatre and cinema actor of extraordinary range and competence, often referred to in his time as the greatest German actor.

7. Max Reinhardt (1873-1943) began his career in the theatre as an actor and became one of the dominant directors of his period. In 1929 he was no longer working full-time in Berlin, having left the city in 1920, and only returned there as a guest director. See also Section II, Document No. 16.

8. Gustav Hartung became the Director of the Renaissance Theatre in Berlin in 1927.

9. Anatoli Vassilievitch Lunatcharsky (1875-1933), politician, dramatist, theatre critic and essayist and screen writer.

10. Renzo Ricci, actor, was the juvenile lead in Virgilio Talli's company in 1922; he later performed in the long-lasting production of *The Trial of Mary Dugan (Processo di Mary Dugan)* presented by the Za Bum company (see note 17).

11. The first night of *Heute Abend wird aus dem Stegreif gespielt*, translated by Harry Kahn took place at the Neues Schauspielhaus, 25 January 1930.

12. Gino Rocca, dramatist and drama critic of the Milanese newspaper *Il popolo d'Italia*.

13. Giuseppe Bottai (1895-1959), fascist politician, man of letters and journalist. In 1927 he was nominated minister for the fascist corporations.

14. George Pitoëff took the part of Hinkfuss in his own production of *Tonight We Improvise*, the first night of which took place on 17th January, 1934 in the Théâtre des Mathurins, Paris.

15. Leopoldo Fregoli, a very popular quick-change artist, whose name has since become a term in Italian indicating *volte-face* or some one who changes their views very quickly.

16. The Italian première of the play took place in the Teatro di Torino, Turin, 14 April 1930.

17. *Za Bum Spettacoli (Za Bum Shows)* was the name given to a number of *ad hoc* companies in the twenties and thirties, managed and directed by Mario Mattoli and Luciano Ramo. *Spettacoli Za Bum* were reviews, light comedies, musicals and were very popular, not least because of the excellence of the performers. *Spettacoli Za Bum* was the first theatrical organization in Italy to use the *ad hoc* system, that is to say, the actors were contracted separately for each show.

CONCLUSION

As the twentieth century enters its last decade, interest in Pirandello's work appears once again to be increasing, with the publication of new studies of his career in the theatre[1]; and the ending of the fifty year copyright period in 1986 has opened the way for more translations and productions of his plays.[2] But above all, there seem to be signs of a re-evaluation of his work, that has its place in the more widespread process of re-evaluation and reassessment of European cultural history in the light of the tremendous changes still underway that have altered the map of Europe. Significantly, perhaps, there have been a number of productions of Pirandello's works throughout Eastern Europe, particularly of those plays which tackle the highly relevant issues of relativity of perception and relativity of truth.[3] The plays that were written during and shortly after the holocaust of the First World War that devastated Europe east and west, can be given a new reading in the post-Berlin wall era, as problems of defining national and individual identity are very definitely placed back on the agenda.

The fortunes of Pirandello, from the moment when he first appeared as a major figure on the world stage, with the arrival of his Six Characters, have varied considerably. After a period of being lionised and travelling the world as a celebrity, the euphoria fell away, and with the collapse of his Teatro d'arte project (see Documents Nos. 42-44 above) Pirandello's disillusionment was compounded by the decline in popularity of his plays both in Italy and elsewhere. *Diana and Tuda*, his first new play to be performed after the collapse, premiered in German, at the Schauspielhaus, Zurich, in 1926, well before the first Italian production, and this was to become a pattern, as Pirandello's popularity at home remained low. *Lazarus* (entitled *Though One Rose*) opened in English, at the Theatre Royal, Huddersfield, in 1929, *Tonight We Improvise* opened in the Neues Schauspielhaus, Königsberg in 1930, *A Dream, But Perhaps It Isn't*, opened in the National Theatre, Lisbon, in 1931, *When One is Somebody* opened in the Teatro Odeon, Bueños Aires in 1933, *The Changeling* opened in the Landtheater, Braunschweig in 1934, *You Don't Know How* opened in the National Theatre, Prague, in 1934. Despite being awarded the Nobel prize for Literature in 1934, Pirandello's popularity remained at a low ebb, and the number of productions of his plays, in Italy and elsewhere declined rapidly through the late 1930s and 1940s.

Towards the end of the 1950s, interest in Pirandello's work began to revive somewhat, and the closeness of much of his thinking to Existentialist theory and to the dramatists of the Theatre of the Absurd became apparent. The Pirandello of the 1920s had been the pioneer, the experimental playwright who tried and failed to change the course of Italian theatre practice, but the Pirandello who returned to prominence in the 1950s and 1960s was perceived more as a philosopher than a man of the theatre. Tilgher's analysis of Pirandello's ideas became a key text in this period, being translated into several languages, and critics stressed the intellectual quality of Pirandello's humour, the cerebral nature of his writing. However, despite a steady stream of revivals of his plays at home and abroad, attention focussed primarily on those plays which came closest to the mood and techniques of Absurdist drama, on the conundrum plays of his early period, (e.g. *Liolà, Man, Beast and Virtue, Right You Are)*, the plays depicting individuals trapped in hopeless situations, forced to wear masks and play out roles *(The Rules of the Game, Clothe the Naked, Henry IV)* and the first play of his theatre in the theatre trilogy, *Six Characters in Search of an Author.* Revivals of plays such as these suited audiences finding excitement in pieces by such diverse writers as Sartre, Beckett, Ionesco or Pinter, but Pirandello's later work was almost completely ignored. Giorgio Strehler (see Document No. 57 above) saw in Pirandello's unfinished play, *The Mountain Giants*, a work of great importance, and his various productions of this work, beginning with his 1947 version, represent his attempts to understand the text that he describes as "the only truly great play about theatre",[4] but Strehler's high opinion of Pirandello's later output was not widely shared.

The centenary celebrations of the birth of Pirandello in 1967 brought more publications and further productions, but his work remained outside the mainstream, though his name continued to be listed alongside the names of other seminal dramatists such as Brecht, Chekhov and Strindberg. A new generation of playwrights and directors expressed gratitude to one or all of these three figures, recognizing their influence both in terms of theatre practice (e.g. dramatic structural technique, the deconstruction of traditional stage-audience relationships) and in terms of material (e.g. sexual politics, analysis of class consciousness, the dilemma of the private individual in the public arena), but Pirandello remained conspicuously absent. Apart from *Six Characters* and *Henry IV*, and one or two of the early plays, his work remained largely unknown outside Italy and unperformed at home. The story of his move into theatre practice as a director and as a teacher with a vision of what the Italian theatre might become, was still untold. Pirandello had a great reputation, but few people in 1968 could have named more than half a dozen plays and even fewer knew anything of Pirandello other than details of his life as a writer.

That picture has changed radically over the past twenty years, and this present book is indicative of some of the changes that have occurred. The fiftieth anniversary of Pirandello's death in 1986 was a very different event from the centenary birthday celebrations in 1967, because a new phase in the reassessment of Pirandello's work had already begun. The later plays, written after his voluntary exile from Italy, that had been marginalized for so long, started to make a come-back. The "myths" with their strange unreal settings, their large casts and their pessimistic vision of a world in chaos were once again being presented on European stages. As spectacle theatre came back into favour, so some directors looked for works such as *The Mountain Giants* or *Tonight We Improvise*[5] in preference to the more intimate fourth wall pieces of Pirandello's early career.

Moreover, the subject matter of the later plays that had been of scant interest in the high period of Alternative Theatre and the more overtly politicized theatre of the late 60s and early 70s, found its place in a time when many of the assumptions of the middle years of the century had begun to break down. In Italy, the historic compromise of 1977 led to a rethinking of the role of the Left, a process that continued in parallel to another significant shift in European values, a move towards increased nationalism and the rise of the new Right. If Brecht's ideas of alienation, continuing work begun by Stanislavsky, laid down parameters for a theatre of social protest in an age when the struggle against fascism dominated the lives of millions, those ideas seemed curiously out of place in a Europe intent on rethinking its history and rethinking its identity, whereas Pirandello's unreal mythic landscapes strike a new chord. It is no accident that revivals of *The Mountain Giants* went on throughout the 1980s, that a play ignored for so long should suddenly come sharply into prominence, dealing as it does with the question of the role of the artist in a philistine world. Nor is it an accident that so many of the later plays, written expressly for Marta Abba and dealing with themes of sexual role-playing and female power should appeal to an age that has witnessed the rebirth of feminism. Susan Sontag's productions of *Finding Oneself* and *As You Desire Me* are representative of the process of rereading works once regarded as minor plays in the Pirandello canon.[6]

The discovery that Pirandello wrote good parts for women, indeed that he wrote purposely for one woman in particular, reflects another element of the re-evaluation of Pirandello that is currently underway. Far from being the "Author", sitting alone at a desk writing works that actors would then betray, as he claimed in his essay *Actors, Illustrators and Translators*, written in 1908 before he had had the chance to work in the theatre himself (see Document No. 2 above), Pirandello had become a man of the theatre, a manager, director and teacher who had a definite programme for changing and extending the range of the Italian theatre of his day. It is ironic, in the best Pirandellian sense of the word, that he should have been remembered for so long by the image of the playwright he created in that early essay, rather than for the passionate plea on behalf of the theatre that he makes in his *Address to the Volta Conference*, not long before his death (see Document No. 58 above). In that Address, Pirandello argued that "theatre is what remains", making a case for the moral values of theatre across time:

> Every period of human history has handed down its theatre to us, living through different nations, and that theatre has always been a sign of a great moment in the life of those nations.

Pirandello came to love the theatre, despite the misgivings he expressed when he was establishing his reputation as a novelist and short story writer. He came to love the theatre as he came to know it, and in that process he moved away from the position he once held, from a belief in the supreme power of the writer. Theatre, he came to recognize, is a complex medium, and the writer's creation only "one of many elements" that give it life. In this collection of documents we have sought to trace the development of Pirandello's ideas, showing how far he had moved by the end of his life from the views he held thirty five years previously, because in considering a career as long and varied as that of Pirandello, it is important to recognize some of the transitions, to acknowledge that everyone has the right to change their own mind. Pirandello's changed views affected his writing, and the essays change in tone and content, as do his plays. There is as great a gap between the 1899 essay, *Spoken Action* (see Document No. 1 above) and the *Address to the Volta Conference* as there is between a naturalistic piece like *Other People's Reason* (1915) and *The Mountain Giants*. The focus has shifted from the individual with a private pain to the individual in the maelstrom of public life.

Admitting to an obsession with *The Mountain Giants*, Strehler tries to explain why this should be so: the message of the play, he argues, is that the artist, whether writer or actor, is compelled to speak out, even though whatever he or she is trying to convey may never be understood. It is this compulsion that drives Ilse to her death, and Strehler maintains that after such a statement, there could be nothing more for Pirandello to say. That Pirandello never finished *The Mountain Giants*, leaving only notes for a third act, adds to the fascination Strehler feels for the play, and in this age of post-modernism, when meaning is constructed differently by each individual, rather than seen as a concrete entity waiting to be deciphered, an unfinished statement about the impossibility of communicative art chimes in with the times.

The 1920s saw Pirandello, the experimental playwright in tune with fashionable ideas of relativity; the 1950s saw Pirandello as an early existentialist, a brilliant mind in a closed room. Now the 1990s have another Pirandello, the writer-turned-impresario, who wrote in a precise context, and whose struggle to identify a role for himself as artist in a rapidly changing world can be easily understood by artists and members of the public struggling to understand where they are in the changing world they too inhabit today. The more we discover about Pirandello's work in the theatre and cinema of his day (and new discoveries are continually being made about Pirandello's multifaceted career in the theatre, including unpublished screenplays and libretti for musicals)[7], the more significant his place in twentieth century theatre history becomes. This present collection of documents is part of the ongoing process of reassessment of Pirandello as man of the theatre. We hope that it will encourage others to go further, so that the full story of Luigi Pirandello, who was so much more than just the writer of a couple of well-known classic plays, will come to light.

Notes

1. Important recent studies include A. Richard Sogliuzzo, *Luigi Pirandello. Director: The Playwright in the Theatre*, Metuchen, N.J. and London, The Scarecrow Press, 1982; Michele Cometa, *Il teatro di Pirandello in Germania*, Palermo, Novecento, 1986; Alessandro d'Amico and Alessandro Tinterri, *Pirandello capocomico, la compagnia del Teatro d'Arte di Roma 1925-1928*, Palermo, Sellerio, 1987; Jennifer Stone, *Pirandello's Naked Prompt, The Structure of Repetition in Modernism*, Ravenna, Longo, 1989; Felicity Firth, *Pirandello in Performance*, Theatre in Focus, Cambridge and Alexandria, VA, Chadwick-Healey, 1990; John Louis DiGaetani, *A Companion to Pirandello Studies*, New York, Westport (Connecticut) and London, 1991.

2. See, in particular, Pirandello, *Collected Plays* (ed. Robert Rietty) London and New York, John Calder and Riverrun Press, 2 vols., 1987, 1988; Luigi Pirandello, *Tonight We Improvise and Leonora Addio!* (transl. J. Douglas Campbell and Leonard G. Sbrocchi), *Biblioteca di Quaderni d'Italianistica*, 3, Canadian Society for Italian Studies, 1987; Luigi Pirandello, *The Mountain Giants* (transl. Felicity Firth), *The Yearbook of the British Pirandello Society*, 10, 1990.

3. The most important of these are the two productions by the Russian director Anatoli Vasiliev: *Six Characters in Search of an Author* (Moscow, 1987) presented at The Academy, Brixton, July, 1989; and *Tonight We Improvise*, 1991.

4. Giorgio Strehler, "Un cri qui ne retenit pas", *Théâtre en Europe, Pirandello*, 10, April 1986, pp. 53-57.

5. Important productions are *Tonight We Improvise* directed by Julian Beck at The Living Theatre, New York, which opened 6 November, 1959; and Mario Missiroli's *The Mountain Giants* at Turin's Teatro stabile in 1979 (see Felicity Firth, *Pirandello in Performance*, 1990, pp. 62-66; 90-97; and Andrea Bisicchia, "Giorgio Strehler's Production of *I giganti della montagna* in the context of its performance history", *The Yearbook of the Society for Pirandello Studies* [formerly *The British Pirandello Society*] 11, 1991, pp. 1-19. See also the adapted small-stage version of *I giganti della montagne*, entitled *Non c'è tempo*, Abraxa Teatro, Rome, 3 June 1991.

6. See Jennifer Stone, "Beyond Desire: A Critique of Susan Sontag's Production of Pirandello's *Come tu mi vuoi*", *The Yearbook of the British Pirandello Society*, 1, 1981, pp. 35-47.

7. Francesco Callari, *Pirandello e il cinema con una raccolta completa degli scritti teorici creativi*, Venice, Marsilio, 1991.

APPENDIX I

Some Translations into English of Plays by Pirandello

Sicilian Limes in *Plays of the Italian Theatre*, Boston, John W. Luce and Company, 1921, tr. Isaac Goldberg.

Three Plays, London, Dent, 1922. Contains *Six Characters in Search of an Author,* tr. Edward Storer, *"Henry IV",* tr. Edward Storer, *Right You Are! (If You Think So),* tr. Arthur Livingston.

Each in His Own Way and Two other Plays, London, Dent, 1923. Contains *Each in His Own Way, The Pleasure of Honesty, Naked,* tr. Arthur Livingston.

One Act Plays, ed. Arthur Livingston, New York, Dutton, 1928. Contains *The Imbecile* tr. Blanche Valentine Mitchell, *The Judgement of Court (La patente)* tr. Elisabeth Abbot, *Our Lord of the Ship* tr. Blanche Valentine Mitchell, *The Doctor's Duty* tr. Blanche Valentine Mitchell, *Chee-Chee* tr. Elisabeth Abbott, *The Man with the Flower in his Mouth* tr. Arthur Livingston, *At the Gate* tr. Blanche Valentine Mitchell, *The Vise* tr. Elisabeth Abbott, *The House and the Column (L'altro figlio)* tr. Elisabeth Abbott, *Sicilian Limes* tr. Elisabeth Abbott, *The Jar* tr. Arthur Livingston.

As You Desire Me, New York, Dutton, 1931, tr. Samuel Putnam.

Tonight We Improvise, New York, Dutton, 1932, tr. Samuel Putnam.

Diana and Tuda, tr. Marta Abba, London, Samuel French, 1950.

Naked Masks, ed. Eric Bentley, New York, Dutton, 1952. Contains *Liolà* tr. Eric Bentley and G. Guerrieri, *It Is So! (If You Think So)* tr. Arthur Livingston, *Henry IV* tr. Edward Storer, *Six Characters in Search of an Author* (including the Preface) tr. Edward Storer, *Each in His Own Way* tr. Arthur Livingston, the Premise to the Theatre Trilogy, tr. Eric Bentley.

Lazarus. Publication of the Dante Alighieri Society, Sydney, 1952, tr. Phyllis H. Raymond.

Six Characters in Search of an Author (1925 text), London, Heinemann, 1954, tr. Frederick May.

Right You Are: Cosí è (se vi pare), a stage version with an introduction and notes by Eric Bentley, Columbia University Press, 1954.

As You Desire Me, in *20 Best European Plays on the American Stage,* New York, Crown Publishers, 1957, tr. Marta Abba.

The Mountain Giants and Other Plays, New York, Crown Publishers, 1958. Contains *The Mountain Giants, The New Colony, When Someone is Somebody* tr. Marta Abba.

The Rules of the Game tr. Robert Rietty, *The Life I Gave You* tr. Frederick May, *Lazarus* tr. Frederick May, ed. E. Martin Brown, Harmondsworth, Penguin Books, 1959.

A Dream (but perhaps it isn't), in *Stand,* Vol.5, no.3, tr. Frederick May.

The Man With The Flower In His Mouth, Leeds, The Pirandello Society, 1959, tr. Frederick May.

The Man with the Flower in His Mouth in *One Act Short Plays for the Modern Theatre,* ed. Samuel Moon, London, Evergreen Books Ltd., 1961 tr. Eric Bentley.

To Clothe the Naked and *Two Other Plays,* New York, Dutton, 1962. Contains *To Clothe the Naked, The Rules of the Game, The Pleasures of Honesty,* tr. William Murray.

Right You Are! (If You Think So) tr. Frederick May, *All for the Best* tr. Henry Reed, *Henry IV* tr. Frederick May, ed. E. Martin Browne, Harmondsworth, Penguin Books, 1962.

The Emperor (Henry IV), in *The Genius of the Italian Theatre,* ed. Eric Bentley, New York, Mentor, 1964, tr. Eric Bentley.

One-Act Plays, Garden City, New York, Doubleday, Anchor, 1964, tr. William Murray.

Henry IV, London, Methuen, 1978, tr. Julian Mitchell.

Six Characters in Search of an Author (1925 text), London, Methuen, 1979, tr. John Linstrum.

Three Plays, intr. John Linstrum, London, Methuen, 1985. Contains *The Rules of the Game* tr. Robert Rietty and Noel Cregeen. *Henry IV* tr. Julian Mitchell, *Six Characters in Search of an Author* tr. John Linstrum.

Collected Plays, vol. 1, ed. Robert Rietty, London, John Calder, 1987. Contains *Henry IV* tr. Robert Rietty and John Wardle, *The Man With The Flower In His Mouth* tr. Gigi Gatti and Terry Doyle, *Right You Are (If You Think So)* tr. Bruce Penman, *Lazarus* tr. Frederick May.

Tonight We Improvise and *Leonora, Addio!*, Ottawa, Canadian Society for Italian Studies, 1987, tr. J. Douglas Campbell and Leonard Sbrocchi.

Collected Plays, vol. 2, ed. Robert Rietty, London and New York, John Calder and Riverrun Press, 1988. Contains *Six Characters in Search of an Autho*r tr. Felicity Firth (includes Pirandello's Preface to the play), *All for the Best* tr. Henry Reed, *Clothe the Naked* tr. Diane Cilento.

Man, Beast and Virtue tr. Charles Wood, Bath, Absolute Press, 1989.

The Mountain Giants tr. Felicity Firth, *The Yearbook of the British Pirandello Society*, 10, 1990.

Pirandello's Major plays tr. Eric Bentley, Evanston, Illinois, Northwestern University Press, 1991. Contains *Right You Are, Six Characters in Search of an Author, Emperor Henry, The Man with the Flower in His Mouth.*

APPENDIX II

First productions of Pirandello's plays

La Morsa (The Vice), Rome, Teatro Metastasio, "Teatro minimo" Company, directed by Nino Martoglio, 9 December, 1910.

Lumie di Sicilia (Sicilian Limes), Rome, Teatro Metastasio, "Teatro minimo" Company, directed by Nino Martoglio, 9 December, 1910.

Il Dovere del Medico (*The Doctor's Duty*), Rome, Sala Umberto I, "Teatro per tutti" Company, directed by Lucio D'Ambra and Achille Vitti, 20 June, 1913.

Se non cosí [*La ragione degli altri*] (*Other People's Reason*), Milan, Teatro Manzoni, Milan Repertory Company, directed by Marco Praga with Irma Gramatica in the leading role, 19 April, 1915.

Cecè, Rome, Teatro Orfeo, "Teatro a sezioni" Company, with Ignazio Mascalchi and Arturo Falconi, 14 December, 1915.

Pensaci, Giacomino! (*Think it over, Giacomino!*), Rome, Teatro Nazionale, Angelo Musco's Company (in Sicilian dialect), 10 July, 1916.

Liolà, Rome, Teatro Argentina, Angelo Musco's Company (in Sicilian dialect). 4 November, 1916.
Rome, Teatro Orfeo, Company directed by Ignazio Mascalchi, 12 November, 1929 (Italian language version)
Milan, Teatro Nuovo, Tofano-Rissone-De-Sica Company (revised Italian language version, following the Mondadori edition of 1937, Vol. VIII of "Tutto il teatro"), 8 June, 1942.

Cosí è (se vi pare) (*Right You Are! (If You Think So)*), Milan, Teatro Olimpia, Virgilio Talli's Company, 18 June, 1917.

Il berretto a sonagli (*Cap and Bells*), Rome, Teatro Nazionale, Angelo Musco's Company (in Sicilian dialect with the title *'A Birritta cu' i ciancianeddi*), 27 June, 1917.

La giara (*The Jar*), Rome, Teatro Nazionale, Angelo Musco's Company (in Sicilian dialect with the title *'A Giarra*), 9 July, 1917.

Il piacere dell'onestà (*The Pleasure of Honesty*), Turin, Teatro Carignano, Ruggero Ruggeri's Company, 27 November, 1917.

Ma non è una cosa seria (*But It's Not Serious*), Leghorn, Teatro Rossini, Emma Gramatica's Company, 22 November, 1918.

Il giuoco delle parti (*The Rules of the Game*), Rome, Teatro Quirino, Ruggero Ruggeri's Company (Vera Vergani in the leading role), 6 December, 1918.

L'innesto (*The Grafting*), Milan, Teatro Manzoni, Virgilio Talli's Company, 29 January, 1919.

La patente (*The Licence*), Rome, Teatro Argentina, "Teatro Mediterraneo" Company, directed by Nino Martoglio (in Sicilian dialect, with the title *'A Patenti*) 19 February, 1919.

L'uomo, la bestia e la virtù (*Man, Beast and Virtue*), Milan, Teatro Olimpia, Antonio Gandusio's Company, 2 May, 1919.

Tutto per bene (*All for the Best*), Rome, Teatro Quirino, Ruggero Ruggeri's Company, 2 March, 1920.

Come prima, meglio di prima (*As Before, Better than Before*), Venice, Teatro Goldoni, Ferrero-Celli-Paoli Company, 24 March, 1920.

La Signora Morli, una e due (*Signora Morli, One and Two*), Rome, Teatro Argentina, Emma Gramatica's Company, 12 November, 1920.
Florence, Politeama Nazionale, Pirandello's Company (with Marta Abba) with the title: *Due in una* (*Two Women in One*) 14 March, 1926.

Sei personaggi in cerca d'autore (*Six Characters in Search of an Author*), Rome, Teatro Valle, Niccodemi Company (with Vera Vergani and Luigi Almirante), 10 May, 1921.

Enrico IV (*Henry IV*), Milan, Teatro Manzoni, Ruggero Ruggeri's Company, 24 February, 1922.

All'uscita (*At the Exit*), Rome, Teatro Argentina, Lamberto Picasso's Company, 29 September, 1922.

L'imbecille (*The Imbecile*), Rome, Teatro Quirino, Alfredo Sainati's Company, 10 October, 1922.

Vestire gli ignudi (*Clothe the Naked*), Rome, Teatro Quirino, Maria Melato-Annibale Betrone Company, 14 November, 1922.

L'uomo dal fiore in bocca (*The Man with the Flower in his Mouth*), Rome, Teatro degli Indipendenti, "Indipendenti" Company, directed by Anton Giulio Bragaglia, 21 February, 1923.

La vita che ti diedi (*The Life I Gave You*), Rome, Teatro Quirino, Alda Borelli's Company, 12 October, 1923.

L'altro figlio (*The Other Son*), Rome, Teatro Nazionale, Raffaello and Garibalda Niccoli Company (in Tuscan dialect, version by Ferdinando Paolieri) 23 November, 1923.

Ciascuno a suo modo (*Each in his Own Way*), Milan, Teatro dei Filodrammatici, Niccodemi Company (with Vera Vergani and Luigi Cimara) 22 May, 1924.

Sagra del Signore della nave (*The Festival of Our Lord of the Ship*), Rome, Teatro Odescalchi, Teatro d'Arte Company, directed by Luigi Pirandello, 4 April, 1925.

Diana e la Tuda (*Diana and Tuda*), Zurich, Schauspielhaus, (in German version by Hans Feist), 20 November, 1926.
Milan, Teatro Eden, Pirandello's Company (with Marta Abba) 14 January, 1927.

L'amica delle mogli (*The Wives' Friend*), Rome, Teatro Argentina, Pirandello's Company (with Marta Abba), 28 April, 1927.

Bellavita (Eng. title unchanged), Milan, Teatro Eden, Almirante-Rissone-Tofano Company, 27 May, 1927.

Scamandro (Eng. title unchanged), Florence, Teatro dell'Accademia dei Fidenti, presented by the Gruppo Academico, with music by Fernando Liuzzi, 19 February, 1928.

La nuova colonia (*The New Colony*), Rome, Teatro Argentina, Pirandello's Company (with Marta Abba and Lamberto Picasso) 24 March, 1928.

O di uno o di nessuno (*Either Somebody's or Nobody's*), Turin, Teatro di Torino, Almirante-Rossone Tofano Company, 4 November, 1929.

Lazzaro (*Lazarus*), Huddersfield Theatre Royal (English version by C.K. Scott-Moncrieff, entitled "Though One Rose"), 9 July, 1929
Turin, Teatro di Torino, Marta Abba's Company, 7 December, 1929.

Come tu mi vuoi (*As You Desire Me*), Milan, Teatro dei Filodrammatici, Marta Abba's Company, 18 February, 1930.

Questa sera si recita a soggetto (*Tonight We Improvise*), Königsberg, Neues Schauspielhaus (German version by Harry Kahn, entitled "Heute Abend wird aus dem Stegreif gespielt"), 25 January, 1930.
Turin, Teatro di Torino, specially formed company directed by Guido Salvini, 14 April, 1930.

Trovarsi (*Finding Oneself*), Naples, Teatro dei Fiorentini, Marta Abba's Company, 4 November, 1932.

Quando si è qualcuno (*When One is Somebody*), Buenos Aires, Teatro Odeon (Spanish version by Homero Guglielmini, entitled "Cuando si es alguien"), 20 September, 1933.
San Remo, Teatro del Casino Municipale, Marta Abba's Company, 7 November, 1933.

La favola del figlio cambiato (*The Changeling*), Braunschweig, Landtheater (German version by Hans Redlich, entitled "Die Legende von vertauschten Sohn"), 13 January, 1934.
Rome, Teatro Reale dell'Opera, music by Gian Francesco Malipiero, with Florica Christoforeanu and Alessio De Paolis, conducted by Gino Marinuzzi, 24 March, 1934.
Bari, Teatro Piccinni, "Piccolo Teatro della Città di Bari", straight textual version without music, 27 June, 1949.

Non si sa come (*You Don't Know How*), Prague, National Theatre (Czech version by Venceslas Jirina, entitled "Clovek ani nevi jak"), 19 December, 1934.
Rome, Teatro Argentina, Ruggero Ruggeri's Company, 13 December, 1935.

Sogno (ma forse no) (*A Dream (But perhaps it isn't)*), Lisbon, National Theatre (Portuguese version by Abreu Beirao, entitled "Sonho (ma talvez nao)"), 22 September, 1931.
Broadcast on radio, Ente Italiano Audizioni Radiofoniche, 11 January, 1936.
Genoa, Giardino d'Italia, Student Group from the University of Genoa, 10 December, 1937.

I giganti della montagna (*The Mountain Giants*), Florence, Boboli Garden Company directed by Renato Simoni (with Andreina Pagnani and Memo Benassi), 5 June, 1937.

Sgombero (*Clearing*) Taormina, Palazzo Corvaia, "Teatro Ciellepi" directed by Giovanni Cutrufelli (with Paola Borboni) 2 February, 1951.
(*Sgombero* is one of the unpublished stories collected by Manlio Lo Vecchio-Musti in the last volume "Omnibus" of *Novelle per un anno*. It was able to be staged since it basically consists of a monologue with extended stage directions, which suggests that it might originally have been conceived as a play rather than as a story).

Pari (*Equals*), Radio broadcast, Radio Italiana, Third programme, 15 March, 1965.

REFERENCES AND SELECT BIBLIOGRAPHY

Alberti, A.C. (1974) *Il teatro nel fascismo*. Rome: Bulzoni.

AA. VV. (1967) *Atti del congresso internazionale di studi pirandelliani*. Perugia: Le Monnier.

AA. VV. (1986) *Testo e messinscena in Pirandello*. Rome: La Nuova Italia Scientifica.

Barker, C. and Bassnett, S. (1985) Locating Pirandello in the European Theatre Context. *The Yearbook of the British Pirandello Society*, 5, 1-19.

Bassnett-McGuire, S. (1983) *Luigi Pirandello*. London: Macmillan.

Bassnett, S. Pirandello's Debut as Director: the Opening of the Teatro d'Arte. *New Theatre Quarterly*, Vol. III, No. 12, 349-352.

Bassnett, S. (1989) *File on Pirandello*. London: Methuen.

Bentley, E. (1986) *The Pirandello Commentaries*. Evanston, Illinois: Northwestern University Press.

Bisicchia, A. (1991) Giorgio Strehler's Production of *I giganti della montagna* in the context of its performance history. *The Yearbook of the Society for Pirandello Studies [formerly The Yearbook of the British Pirandello Society]*. 11, 1-19.

Bradbury, D. and Cozzi, E. (1991) On Directing *The Mountain Giants*. *The Yearbook of the Society for Pirandello Studies [formerly The Yearbook of the British Pirandello Society]*, 11, 26-31.

Bragaglia, L. (1969) *Interpreti pirandelliani*. Rome: Trevi.

Büdel, O. (1966) *Pirandello*. Cambridge: Bowes and Bowes.

Buonanno, G. (1990) *I giganti delle montagne*, dalla dissoluzione del Teatro d'Arte alla rappresentazione del Maggio fiorentino. *Il castello di Elsinore*, III, 8, 71-107.

Callari, F. (1991) *Pirandello e il cinema con una raccolta completa degli scritti teorici creativi*. Venice: Marsilio.

Cambon, G. ed. (1967) *Pirandello. A Collection of Critical Essays*. New Jersey, N.J.: Englewood Cliffs.

Cometa, M. (1986) *Il teatro di Pirandello in Germania*. Palermo: Novecento.

Corrigan, B. (1972) Pirandello as a Director. *Theatre Research,* XII, 2, 155-163.

D'Amico, A. and Tinterri, A. (1987) *Pirandello capocomico.* Palermo: Sellerio.

De Castris, A.L. (1962) *Storia di Pirandello.* Bari: Laterza.

DiGaetani, J.L. ed. (1991) *A Companion to Pirandello Studies.* New York, Westport, London: Greenwood Press.

Esslin, M. (1969) *Reflections.* Garden City, New York: Doubleday.

Firth, F. (1990) *Pirandello in Performance.* Cambridge and Alexandria, VA: Chadwyck-Healey.

Fitzpatrick, F. (1985) Strategies of Antithesis: The Opening of *Sei personaggi in cerca d'autore. The Yearbook of the British Pirandello Society,* 5, 20-42.

Gordon, J.B. (1972) *Sei personaggi in cerca d'autore.* Myth, Ritual and Pirandello's Anti-Symbolist Theatre. *Forum Italicum,* VI, 3, 333-55.

Gramsci, A. (1954) *Letteratura e vita nazionale.* Turin: Einaudi.

Giudice, G. (1963) *Luigi Pirandello,* Turin, U.T.E.T. [Tr. (1975) as *Pirandello: A Biography,* Oxford, Oxford Univerity Press. This is an abridged version.]

Lepschy, A.L. (1981) Notes on the figure of the Actor in Pirandello. *The Yearbook of the British Pirandello Society,* 1, 1-18.

Lorch, J. (1982) The 1925 text of *Sei personaggi in cerca d'autore* and Pitoëff's Production of 1923, *The Yearbook of the Pirandello Society,* 2, 32-47.

Lorch, J. (1987) Theories of Theatre in two plays by Pirandello. In *Pirandello poetica e presenza,* edited by Franco Musarra, pp. 191-200. Rome and Leuven: Bulzoni and Leuven University Press.

Lorch, J. (1991) The Rise of the "Mattatore" in Late Nineteenth-Century Italian Theatre. In *Writers and Performers in Italian Drama from Dante to Pirandello,* edited by J.R. Dashwood and J.E. Everson, pp. 115-128. Lewiston, New York; Queenston, Ontario; Lampeter, Wales: The Edwen Mellen Press.

Lucas, F.L. (1963) *The Drama of Chekhov, Synge, Yeats and Pirandello.* London: Cassell.

May, F. (1964) Three Major Symbols in Four Plays by Pirandello. *Modern Drama,* VI, 4, 378-96.

McLintock, L. (1951) *The Age of Pirandello,* Bloomington: Indiana Press.

Moestrup, J. (1972) *The Structural Pattern of Pirandello's Work.* Odense: Odense University Press.

Palombi, C. (1986) *Il gergo del teatro: l'attore italiano di tradizione.* Rome: Bulzoni.

Pearson, T. (1991) The Modern Theatre Trilogies of Pirandello and Evreinov. *The Yearbook of the Society for Pirandello Studies* [formerly *the Yearbook of the British Pirandello Society*], 11, 67-83.

Pitoëff, G. (1949) *Notre théâtre.* Paris: Messages.

Possenti, P. (1987) *I teatri del primo novecento.* Rimini: Orsa maggiore.

Ragusa, O. (1978) Pirandello's "Teatro d'Arte" and a new look at his fascism. *Italica,* 1978, 236-53.

Ragusa, O. (1980) *Luigi Pirandello, an approach to his theatre.* Edinburgh: Edinburgh University Press.

Reale Accademia d'Italia, Fondazione Alessandro Volta (1935) *Convegno di lettere: il testo drammatico*. Rome: Reale Accademic d'Italia.

Salvini, T. (1895) *Ricordi, aneddoti ed impressioni*. Milan: Fratelli Dumolard.

Serao, M. (1896) Carlo Gozzi e la fiaba. In AA.VV., *La vita italiana nel Settecento, conferenze tenute a Firenze nel 1895*. Milan: Treves.

Sogliuzzo, A.R. (1982) *Luigi Pirandello, The Playwright in the Theatre*. Metuchen, N.J. and London: The Scarecrow Press.

Starkie, W. (1965) *Luigi Pirandello, 1897-1936*. Berkeley and Los Angeles: University of California Press.

Stone, J. (1980) Mirror Image/Collage: Reality, Representation and Revolution in Pirandello, in *1936, The Sociology of Literature*, edited by F. Barker et al., pp. 47-71. University of Essex.

Stone, J. (1981) Beyond Desire: A Critique of Susan Sontag's Production of Pirandello's *Come tu mi vuoi*. *The Yearbook of the British Pirandello Society, 1, 35-47*.

Stone, J. (1989) *Pirandello's Naked Prompt*. Ravenna: Longo.

Tamberlani, C. (1982) *Pirandello nel "teatro che c'era"*, Rome: Bulzoni.

Tinterri, A. (1983) Two flights of Steps and a Stage Direction: Pirandello's Staging of *Six Characters in Search of An Author* in 1925. *The Yearbook of the British Pirandello Society* 3, 33-37.

Tinterri, A. (1986) Pirandello regista and *The Gods of the Mountain* of Lord Dunsany. *The Yearbook of the British Pirandello Society* 6, 36-39.

Tinterri, A. (1987) *The Gods of the Mountain* at the Odescalchi Theatre. *New Theatre Quarterly*, Vol. III, No. 12, 352-358.

Tinterri, A. and Jansen, S. (1990) Questa sera si recita a soggetto: da Könisberg a Torino. *Rivista di studi pirandelliani*, VIII, 41-94.

Vicentini, C. (1983) La trilogia pirandelliana del teatro nel teatro e le proposte della teatralità futurista. *The Yearbook of the British Pirandello Society*, 3, 15-32.

Vicentini, C. (1984) Pirandello and the Problems of Theatre as an Impossible Art. *The Yearbook of the British Pirandello Society*, 4, 1-20.

Vicentini, C. (1987) Concepts of Acting in Pirandello's Dramaturgy. *The Yearbook of the British Pirandello Society*, 7, 45-57.

Vittorini, D. (1935) *The Drama of Luigi Pirandello*, Philadelphia: University of Pennsylvania Press.

INDEX

(The Index covers pp. 1-183; it excludes the Preface, Appendices and Bibliography).